D1712995

A
BRIEF AUTUMN'S
PASSAGE

A BRIEF AUTUMN'S PASSAGE

A Season of Bird Dogs
and
Upland Dreams

written and illustrated by
Steven Mulak

DOWN EAST BOOKS
ROCKPORT, MAINE

Jacket design by Phil Schirmer
Text design by Janet Patterson

Printed at Versa Press Inc., East Peoria, Illinois

5   4   3   2   1

ISBN 0-89272-598-2

Library of Congress Control Number: 2003107966

Countrysport Press
P.O. Box 679
Camden, ME 04843

For book orders or catalog information, call 1-800-685-7962, or visit
www.countrysportpress.com

Countrysport Press is a division of Down East Enterprise, publishers of
Shooting Sportsman magazine, which can be visited at www.shootingsportsman.com

Dedication

"... So you settle down
And the children come
And you find the place
That you come from;
Your wandering is done.
And all your dreams
Of open spaces
You find in
Your children's faces,
One by one ..."

Harry Chapin
"Story of a Life"

This book is dedicated to the two women I most admire, Jennifer and Sharon Mulak, my daughters. There are many stories in my life, but bringing up two baby girls to become successful, caring young women has been the one that's dwarfed everything else.

Table of Contents

Preface: Is There a Trick to It?

WHEN MY WIFE and I took the new puppy Hanna for a walk, we also had five-year-old Sophie along. The puppy liked to chase Sophie, and Sophie, for her part, seemed to enjoy being chased.

Our meanderings took us through a line of trees and into a park beyond. Two girls were using the playground equipment, and had the family's toy poodle with them for company. All those tiny dogs seem to be overly nervous, and this one was no exception. He started yipping and scrambling as soon as he saw us. The two girls chased after him, trying to run him down, but the poodle dodged their efforts and continued the noisy barrage.

I scooped up my puppy, then turned to Sophie in the distance and called her to a stop with a loud "Hut!" All of my dogs will stop when told, but Sophie was something of a circus performer when it came to obeying commands. I'd say "Hut" and the dust would rise where she skidded to halt. It was one of the amazing things she did.

When the girls saw what had happened, they began shouting "Hut! Hut!" as they chased the yipping poodle. It was a funny scene. After a fruitless minute or two they gave up.

When they looked my way I told them, "It's only a magic word if the dog believes that it is."

Maybe that should be a motto, written down somewhere.

9

CHAPTER ONE

Well Below the Horizon

Day One: September's Song

"Warm September brings the fruit,
Sportsmen then begin to shoot."

Old Nursery Rhyme

THERE IS AN ALMOST hypnotic quality in driving through the alternating stripes of light and shadow that spill through the trees bordering the back road. At the bottom of the hill I slow and find a familiar place where I can ease the truck off the right-of-way without putting its tires into the ditch. I glance at my watch and take note of the time, because opening day in Vermont is about to begin.

The puppy will get her turn tomorrow. She has been chewing the seat belts in the truck for the past month, but she'll have to wait another day. Today I have Stella with me: *Old Miss Belle*. It wasn't so many years ago that she was *Young Stella*. She looks out the side window of the truck as I get out, and her tail thumps against the truck seat. She knows.

With the gun under my arm, I feel through the outsides of my pockets for the things I know are there—keys, knife, wallet. After a glance up and down the empty back road, I wave Stella out of the truck, put on her bell, and start her beeper collar. Then we head into a small field that borders the cover called Vermont Electric.

We've hardly gotten started when the bell goes silent and the beeper signals. Although it can sound like a gravel truck backing up, I've used the beeper collar for the past several seasons. I set it up so that it only sounds when the dog is on point. After twenty years in the engine room of a tanker my hearing is no great shakes, and searching for a bell that has stopped making noise is like looking for something that has suddenly gone transparent. Thus, the gravel truck.

Stella is standing in a little puddle of sunlight, pointing with one front leg crossed over the other. A march in front of her flushes a woodcock. When the gun comes up it catches on a

13

sapling, and in the moment it takes to pull free the bird vanishes into the glowing yellow foliage overhead. Then a second wood-cock twitters up, and I track the bird until it too disappears into the trees.

"I'd have had that second one, Stella."

I make believe I'm talking to the dog rather than just bab-bling out loud. It's still September, and only grouse are legal game today. Pointing woodcock without me shooting is nothing new for my bird dogs, but I always wonder what they must think when birds are taken one day and then "thrown back" on another.

No matter what the calendar may have already had to say about the equinox, the clear haze-free sky marks this as the REAL first day of autumn. The trees are still fully leafed and mostly green, and I can hardly see the sky overhead. Explain, then, the carpet of fallen leaves? Several dozen come down with a shake of a thin maple. I scan the dense foliage again, knowing it won't be long until autumn's passage clears my vision.

Leaf color—*The Color* in New England lingo—will be early this year. We've had a wet summer, but just why the leaves turn early—or late—is one of those guesses that's subject to argument. Certain sumacs and road-side maples under stress began to put on their autumn war paint back in the middle of August, but that sort of thing is always more a preview of what's to come than the beginning of the change. But now the birches are turning to their distinctive clear yellow, the leaves on the very ends of the swamp maples are reddening up, and in the distance the ash trees are turning a dull but indisputable purple. The Color is starting.

When Stella looks back I direct her uphill. We cut into the pine woods, intending to come out through some scattered apple trees that border a little clearing. Every cover has a sweet spot, and those apples are it. There's just a handful of trees—hardly an orchard—but this is a poor year for wild apples and the few trees that managed to bear fruit can be grouse magnets. And one tree on the edge of that clearing ALWAYS has apples.

But my approach cannot be quiet, and there is the briefest rumble of grouse wings in the foliage ahead. I stand for a moment, straining my ears for a direction, but hear only Stella's bell—the bird must have short-hopped into a tree. I approach the apple grove cautiously, but there is another rumble, more continuous this time, and I know I've flunked the first grouse-test of the fall semester. When I exhale I realize I've been holding my breath.

In that moment another grouse rockets up off to my left. Although the gun comes up cleanly, I'm not quick enough and the shot passes behind the bird.

No matter how much shooting you do ahead of time, nothing can prepare you for the jackrabbit quickness of the season's first grouse flush. There had been two birds, and now I'm acutely aware that there might be three. I stand quietly for a half-minute until Stella comes in, panting. That seems to diffuse the possibility of another grouse in the immediate vicinity.

Firing the gun shouldn't hurt, but that last shot did. Beneath my vest I feel where the metal clip of my brand-new suspenders has been sitting in the hollow of my shoulder exactly where the butt plate nestles when I mount the gun. I make an adjustment and a mental note to have Susan cut some slack out of the elastic so that the clip will make up lower. It seems that no matter how thoroughly I prepare, opening day manages to find a few over-looked deficiencies.

For that matter, the Chief Inquisitor who lives inside me asks, *why wasn't the accused alert for the possibility of a second bird, particularly this early in the season?*

I plead stupidity, Your Honor.

It's a long time between seasons. I forget how to do some of this stuff. It'll take a few outings to get back in step.

15

New England bird season seems to consist of three parts: the
early going when the foliage is still up; then November, with all
the wonderful things that that single word can infer; then hunting in the snow. Although I like to dream about a heaven where
it's always the beginning of November and the hunting never
ends, there is something about the inevitable wax and wane of
the seasons that gives meaning to it all—a meaning that a continuous November could never have. I know for sure that it all
slips by too fast, and it seems I've no sooner hit my midseason
stride than Susan is making up her Thanksgiving grocery list and
I begin to feel a panic that comes of seeing yet another autumn
slipping away.

Hey, take it easy. It's not even October yet. Go slow. Enjoy.

There's a place a bit farther down the road where, a few
years back, one of my setters and I had a "discussion" about her
penchant for chasing wild turkeys. Old Amy is retired now and
her turkey-chasing days are over, but I still call the cover the
Turkey Ranch. When I drive up, the signs go unnoticed until
I'm at the spot where I pull off the road. The place isn't legally
posted—there is no name or date on the signs—but what's lacking in quality is more than compensated for in quantity: NO
TRESPASSING is proclaimed every thirty or forty feet. That takes
some of the starch from my outlook. There'll be no hunting the
Turkey Ranch today.

On the drive back to town I go by an old homestead where
a fellow is tinkering with a garden tractor in his driveway. There's
a rack of antlers over the open garage door. I pull over and go
through the amenities of how the weather's been and how early
The Color is. Then I cut to the chase.

"About a half-mile back on the left there are a bunch of
brand-new posted signs. I've hunted birds in there for years. You
wouldn't happen to know who I could talk to about getting back
in there, would you?" I'm hoping that I'm talking to the landowner, but he grimaces.

"Some folks from Massachusetts bought that piece last year. They're only up here two or three times a summer, but they've got some funny ideas." He pronounces idea with an *r* at the end.

I admit to being a visitor myself from the land of funny ideas, but I'd like a chance to talk to those fellow out-of-staters. I won't, though. Most absentee landowners are all but anonymous and nearly impossible to locate without a great expenditure of time and effort. I know, because I've often tried it, and rarely had success.

Each year I seem to lose a few more coverts to posting. Much is written about loss of habitat and increasingly restrictive legislation, but the greatest problem faced by outdoorsmen today is posted land. In the Northeast there is more than enough open land for everyone, but so much of it is behind NO TRESPASSING signs that we're all being squeezed. And not just hunters, but anyone who does anything out-of-doors.

In this litigious time when the legal community regularly gives landowners a hundred reasons to post their land, it would seem that the Fish and Wildlife folks might come up with a few good reasons for landowners to keep their property open. The lines of NO TRESPASSING signs that define New England's road-sides are a graphic symptom of that failure. In many places the signs have been up since the Eisenhower administration—no date, no name, just an anonymous KEEP OUT across the years from an absentee landowner. The signs remain, since the guy who pays taxes on the property has never been given any incentive to take them down. Some western states offer tax rebates on land with public access, and New York has a cooperative state–landowner program that seems to be working. Creative leadership is what's needed in Fish and Wildlife Departments—and what seems to be lacking.

As I drive off, Old Stella snoozes behind the seat. At eleven years old, she's certainly not an all-day hunter any longer, even on a cool morning such as this. My plan had been to make a charge at the Turkey Ranch, then go into town for lunch. But that's out now, so I mull over my options. Most of my spots close by are primarily woodcock coverts—not that there couldn't be a grouse in them, but Stella has just a few hours of hunting in her and I'd rather spend them where the odds are favorable.

I'll drive north of town and, after stopping to check at the owner's farmhouse, give the Isaac Newton cover a try. The place has grouse, though it runs to brushy undergrowth and spruce that seems more like Canadian flora than what's usually found in central New England.

Ten years ago, on the day I first hunted the cover's steep hillside, there was a single beat-up apple on the ground along the brook at the bottom of the hill. Apples and grouse go together like rock-and-roll, so I looked around for the tree that produced the apple. There wasn't one that I could see, and any of the several explanations I came up with about how the apple got there would have made the *National Inquirer*. A quarter-hour and several zigzags later I was halfway up the hillside and passed beneath an apple tree. I picked up a windfall and took a bite, then tossed it aside. Even with the bite out of it, the apple was semi-round and rolled all the way down the hill to the spot below where the other apple had been fifteen minutes before. In my mind, the headline read, *Nincompoop Finally Discovers Gravity*. Isaac Newton had nothing to worry about.

Stella and I continue up the hill, but the thick brush slows me down, and after a short while I find I'm not hunting so much as struggling in the heavy cover. This early in the season with the leaves still on, fighting the thick stuff soon strips your internal gears. In my eagerness to find a grouse I've made a poor decision, and after twenty minutes it's time to turn back.

At the truck I twice fill a plastic bowl with water and watch as Stella laps it up. A half-day is all I expected out of her, and she's only got another half-hour or so before her gas needle hits E. She's old, of course, but no matter what I do in the way of

conditioning, nothing seems to prepare my dogs adequately—
regardless of their age—for a full day afield. Dog writers like to
talk about hard-charging all-day bird dogs having *heart.* Super-
man doesn't exist in the real world, and there are no super dogs,
either. Heart is made up of *conditioning* and *youth,* and both Stella
and her owner are short of both commodities.

I've never hunted the hillside across the road, mostly because
there are two houses at the top and the rest of the cover looked
like so much open pasture and brushy woods when I first came
here. But lately ash trees have sprung up in the fields, and the
shadows are dappled with pools of sunlight. I've been meaning
to scout the place, and from my seat on the tailgate it suddenly
seems like a good idea.

As soon as I enter the cover, I am reminded that looks can
be deceiving: habitat that appeared promising when viewed from
the road turns out to be made up of separated pockets of ash and
poplar (New Englanders call them "popple") without the understory that grouse require. Stella finds a single woodcock in the
twenty-five minutes it takes to work the hillside to the bottom.
Before we break out and start back up the road, I send her into
the thick stuff along a little stream, more to get a drink than out
of any hope of finding a bird.

Once she's into the hemlocks Stella's bell goes silent. I've
forgotten to activate her beeper collar, and now I'm no longer
sure where she is. I whistle, then whistle again, but hear nothing
when I strain to catch the sound of her bell. My first setter,
Hazel, used to move her head when I whistled, even if she was
on point, and her bell would ding and let me know where she
was. Stella wouldn't move even if she could hear me. Her problem is that she is too staunch on point. Believe me, I've made a
study of problems, and being too staunch is a good one for a bird
dog to have. But that doesn't do me any good right now.

I hate pussyfooting, but that's what I'm doing as I search for
the dog. I stop for a moment and whistle softly, then, when I
start again a grouse erupts close behind me. The bird is heading

19

for a hemlock-framed patch of blue sky, and I quickly snap off a shot just as he disappears. A moment later I hear the grouse falling through the branches, then there is a quiet thump as he hits the ground.

"Stella!" I yell, and hear her bell somewhere. I call for her again, sounding like Stanley Kowalski in *Streetcar Named Desire,* and push my way through the thick stuff toward where the bird fell. Now Stella is behind me. Under the evergreens I cannot stand upright. When I turn and tell her to fetch, she is already holding the grouse.

She must have been pointing, and because I didn't know where she was I inadvertently flushed her bird. At least, that's the interpretation that will go into my journal. I hope Stella is equally charitable when she tells her own version to the dogs back in the kennel.

I have her carry the first grouse of the year to a sunny open-ing where I can sit on a fallen tree trunk and tell her how lucky I am to have a dog like her.

It's now just a little after 2 PM. With a bird in the cooler, a half-day of hunting seems like enough. There was a time—not so many years ago, to be sure—when opening day was all about hard charging. If I was still that young athlete there are several more covers that could occupy my time until dark. But I'm pooped, and hunting tired can be a lot like work. Of the many things bird shooting is, it should NEVER be anything but fun.

Quitting early isn't something I'm quite used to, and getting home before dark will be a change. I'll stop at a farm stand on the way home and pick up the Macoun apples Susan asked for. It'll be fun to see the new puppy's reaction when I ask her to fetch a grouse wing that actually smells like a grouse. She has been retrieving wings left over from last year's birds, which can't smell like much of anything except dog spit any longer.

For a formerly young man on the far side of the half-century mark, each grouse season is something to be savored, and best eased into.

It feels good to ease into this one.

Day Two: Just Potential

> *"No great deed, private or public,*
> *has ever been undertaken in a bliss*
> *of certainty."*
>
> Leon Wieseltier
> In the *New Republic*

DRIVING ALONG THE North River, I note that the leaves are still on the summer side of autumn. But beneath the summer-green trees the woodbine has already turned its characteristic deep crimson.

I'm going to hunt the Vermont towns immediately across the border. The puppy is with me and I don't really have much in the way of expectations, so maybe "hunt" in that last sentence should be changed to "visit."

Along the back roads heading north, some of the dairy farms resemble the pastoral scenes in landscapes by the painter John Constable. There's a winery where they make wine from everything except grapes. A little farther along is a farm where the corn has been harvested and pigs are permitted to roam the cut cornfield. A sow is surrounded by a dozen piglets. Their pink flesh seems so unnaturally naked that it's easy to imagine them asking, "Hey, Ma, can we run around bare-ass today?"

I drive across the river and by the Ice Farm. I have hunting permission from the landowner, and I've found birds in this cover in the past, but I no longer want to do what must be done to hunt there. The place is all juniper-choked hillside, so just walking upright is a struggle. It's so steep that there are no apples under the apple trees. The birds know how to survive and always flush higher up than wherever I happen to be. It must be what chukar hunting is like. I'm not sure if I was ever young enough to hunt the Ice Farm. I glance back at it in the rearview mirror and keep going.

This will be the puppy's first outing under the gun. She has been yard trained, and through September we've spent a daily hour or two in the woods near home. Not only does she know nothing about wild birds, but she doesn't even suspect very much. But today it's time to jump in with all four feet.

This is Hanna, born on Washington's Birthday and just seven months old. She sits behind the seat of my stretch-cab truck and whacks her face against the rear window each time a roadside bird takes flight. I'm unsure if I should be pleased by her eagerness or distressed by her idiocy.

There was a time when woodcock opened before grouse, but not lately. The powers that be have determined that the woodcock population is in trouble, although not from hunting, they assure us. Nevertheless, the season has been shortened and the bag limits reduced. In years past I've found plenty of woodcock in late September and early October, indicating that there's a part of the population that migrates early. They're safe from me now, since the season doesn't open anywhere in America before October 6.

There are still a few days to go until the sixth, so supposedly I'm hunting grouse, and although I scratched one down on opening day, the possibility of actually getting a shot is low. The leaves are still thick, and the puppy won't be of any help. The right mind-set might be to look upon this early grouse hunting as an extension of the puppy's training period. The gun is all but superfluous.

Rocky Brook is a wonderfully productive area that runs behind some farms that border the main road. The huntable part of the cover is long and, in some places, fairly narrow.

I pull off the road into the driveway of a ruined house trailer. I've been parking here for years, and am vaguely relieved to see that nothing has changed since last season. There are no KEEP OUT warnings, no surveyor's stakes, no signs of life. Good.

When I bring Hanna out of the truck, I immediately put her through her paces: "Heel," "Hut," "Come," "Heel," "Go ahead,"

"Hut," "Heel." It's become something of a one-minute drill that the dogs get put through whenever I let them out of the truck. Even experienced gun dogs need to practice that routine for the same reason infielders throw the ball around before each inning: not to learn anything—hell, they know how to throw and catch—but to remind their brains and their arms and their gloves what they're there for. At a time when she's most excited, it's important to give Hanna a short obedience refresher course as a reminder of what I expect of her. That's what warm-ups are all about.

We move into the cover.

The puppy is obviously having a good time, but what she's doing is not to be mistaken for hunting. She knows the command "In front," and as long as there's nothing distracting her she complies; that is, she stays out in front of my progress through the cover. But as often as not there's a chipmunk or a mouse off to the side that grabs her interest, and the command has to be repeated. She knows from experience that ignoring me has its consequences, but inevitably what she's fooling with scampers out of hiding and gives her the chipmunk equivalent of the finger at exactly the wrong time. So now I've given her a command that I'm certain she's heard, yet she's chosen to ignore me in favor of the chipmunk. Something has to be done: I chase after her and drag her back by the ear.

Bird dogs and bird-dog training are all about emotions, so it's important not to become angry with the puppy. At least, that's what I tell myself. She's learning, after all. But with branches snapping back at me and spiderwebs in my face, my patience quickly wears thin, and after the fifth repetition I need a break. I put her at heel for five minutes, and when I release her again she's not quite so wound up.

The most important bird you'll ever shoot for a puppy is the very first one, but since woodcock won't be legal game for another few days, that'll have to wait. We're passing through a stand of alders that I refer to in my journals as the Woodcock Flats. There on the ground immediately in front of me are two white puddles of woodcock crap. I whistle to Hanna and call her in, intent on getting her a noseful of fresh scent. As she makes her way to me she runs into the very woodcock that made the puddles. The bird bounces up from under her chin and twitters away through the leafy tops of the alders. I point the gun overhead and shoot to make some noise. Hanna stares after the bird for a moment, then becomes a runaway vacuum cleaner focused on scooping up all the scent left behind by the woodcock in its wanderings on the fallen leaves.

I put the gun aside and take hold of her collar and lead her to the spot where the bird took off. There's something called *standing the dog up,* which amounts to holding the dog's head and tail as if she were on point. I wait until she has stopped squirming, then tell her to "Hut" while I push on her rear end. Although they are contradictory commands—a verbal "Hut" and a physical "Go ahead"—in response, a small, predictable miracle happens. Hanna points.

I step away from her, and she softens and looks back at me.

"Go ahead," I tell her, and she returns to her vacuum cleaner imitation. How can I not grin?

We flush two more woodcock in the alders, and the stand-up lesson is repeated each time. She knows how to point a pheasant wing dangled from a fly rod, and she knows what to do when I stand her up and handle her. Field training amounts to translating those lessons learned in the make-believe situation of the backyard into something that makes sense to the puppy out here in the reality of the grouse woods. I remind myself of the Chinese proverb that says a journey of a thousand miles begins with a single step. It'll take a bunch of mishandled birds before the puppy starts to make the connection between scent and point, so each bumped bird should be a learning opportunity. I try to make sure each is.

The cover narrows, squeezed by pastureland on one side and a spruce woods on the other. Working along the brook valley, the puppy bumps a grouse that heads back and to my left—not a long chance, but one made difficult because of the still-thick foliage. I snap off a shot and look hard for results but see only falling leaves. A moment later the grouse is gentleman enough to show himself to me as he flies on, unhit.

As I'm reloading, the puppy comes in. Her wild-eyed look says she REALLY likes the smell of grouse. She previously encountered woodcock at home during September, and I've worked her on a few released quail, but as far as I know this is her first scent of a live grouse.

I know where he is. At least, that's what I tell myself. We make an about-face and start back in pursuit of the bird. But we pass without incident through the grove of hemlocks where I suspected the bird had retreated, and then I have some trouble getting Hanna to stay in front after she discovers a red squirrel.

I'm trying to get the puppy to behave when the bird flushes from my right, heading steeply uphill. The chance was long to begin with, and by the time I refocus my attention and get the gun up, the bird is well into the treetops and gone. No shot is possible. I put the safety back on.

If the leaves were down I might have been able to get a better line on him. But it seems he's flown out of the valley and is somewhere up on the flat above the steep hillside.

On our way out of the valley Hanna and I pass through a stand of pines. Poison ivy covers the ground and climbs on the lower branches of the trees. Its leaves are turning to a pale autumn yellow. People who can't recognize the stuff seem to think it's some sort of mysterious exotic plant, but in truth poison ivy might be the most common ground cover in the Northeast. It's everywhere. Unfortunately, there's enough difference between varieties so that none of the identification keys are positive: leaf size and shape are variable; the leaves are not always dark and not always shiny. Sometimes it has a reddish spot at the joining of leaflets, but sometimes not. "Leaves of three, let it be," says the adage, but there are literally dozens of plants in the woods that present their leaves in groups of three, everything from wild strawberry to jack-in-the-pulpit. Most problem prevention is a commonsense matter of avoiding contact between bare skin and broken, sappy leaves.

Up on the narrow flat, tucked into the woods at the edge of a pasture, is an overgrown orchard that hasn't produced an apple crop in years. Many of the old trees have fallen over and re-rooted, and the ground is given over to blackberry thickets. The grouse is in one of the apple trees, but waits until I've passed before he flies. I turn toward the sound of the flush, but the bird is shielded from my view and the gun relaxes. Then the bird flashes across a little opening where I might have had a shot and is gone.

"Let me have that one again," I say out loud, but that's a strategy that only works on the skeet range. In the woods, the Guy With The Button gives you just one chance.

I sit with the dog for a minute, catching my breath and gathering my thoughts. Puppy Hanna will get more than her share of experience over the next three months. If the grouse numbers are even just average, she'll see between 150 and 200 birds. I hadn't planned on rushing her into action, but all that went out the window when Sophie died during the summer.

If, like me, you're more than a weekend bird hunter, you know you can't get away with just one working bird dog. At least I can't. Since gun dogs only last ten years or so, there has to be a master plan in place to assure having at least two trained dogs available season after season. It's a matter of logistics.

One version of that plan—the one I follow—is to put five years between puppies. That way, when the new puppy arrives you've got a fully trained five- or six-year-old dog in his prime and another ten- or eleven-year-old dog heading into his last season. Since it will take at least a year to get the puppy up to speed, the plan has the new dog coming on line as the old dog fades out. And at the same time, you've got the mainline dog to enjoy. That's the plan, anyway.

Filling in the blanks in my version of that master plan, Stella is the old dog and puppy Hanna is the new kid on the block. Sophie would have been the five-year-old dog in her prime if she had lived.

But the best-laid plans of mice and men and bird hunters have a tendency to go asunder. Sophie began losing her coat a month before her fifth birthday. That was in March. During the summer she lost her appetite and began running a fever, and at the end of an agonizing two weeks of treating her for diseases she didn't have she was finally diagnosed with liver cancer. She had been a fifty-six-pound setter when she was healthy. On the day I put her down she weighed fifty-four pounds, but she had been reduced to skin and bones. That tumor inside her must have been a monster.

Although she had come from field-champion stock, in truth Sophie wasn't anything out of the ordinary as a finder of birds. But she trained easily and was a pleasure to hunt with, and if I was ever angry with her I honestly can't remember when. On the day I scratched her ears for the last time, I said out loud that I wished she had been a barker or a hardhead or a runaway or something else equally bad so that at least a small part of me could be glad she was gone.

But she is gone, and I'm not at all glad.

Without Sophie, the prospects for the coming season were—and still are—in the poor-to-grim category. I'm left with an eleven-year-old deaf dog and a seven-month-old puppy that has never pointed a wild bird. Under ordinary circumstances, gun training the puppy and hunting the old dog would be dalliances I'd fool with two or three days each week, and I'd hunt for keeps with the mainline dog on the other days.

My bird season might not amount to much without Sophie, but one thing is certain: puppy Hanna is going to get one hell of an education.

After Rocky Brook, we stop at the Corn Patch. I've never taken a grouse here, but the place has always looked good. It's one long edge, really a series of broken-down apple trees between an open field and a spruce woods with a little brook thrown in for good measure. There are barberry clumps along the rocky run of the brook and thornberry roses along the edge of the pasture. Here and there the bordering spruces crowd right out to the edge of the field. At the end of the rocky run we'll make a loop in some side cover, but mostly it's a one-way trip, and we'll come out walking on the same ground we covered on the way in. It'll take about a half-hour or so.

Occasionally, when I name a covert I have to scratch pretty hard to come up with something that fits. There's no extensive patch of corn here at the Corn Patch, just someone's garden by the side of the road. When I take a good look at it now I find that this year the absent gardeners elected not to grow sweet corn at all. They've probably had enough of the constant battle with deer and raccoons, the one that every country gardener fights.

There's a lot of horizontal in the rays of the late-afternoon sun as we cross a little wire fence and start down toward the stream. Hanna seems to have as much energy as she did when we started five hours ago. It would be nice to be puppy-age again. Instead, I'm nearly seven and a half in dog years.

There are ash trees along the stream, some of them huge and towering. One has been recently blown down and has fallen diagonally across the brook. At one end its shallow root system has lifted a disk of soil and rocks like some huge opened umbrella laid aside to dry after a rain. At the other end, its now-dead branches have invaded and occupied a grove of young hemlocks. I navigate around the roots of the deadfall as Hanna passes easily under the tree trunk and investigates the far end. Grouse begin taking wing, the sound of one flush merging with the next like a string of Chinese firecrackers going off. I scramble back toward the brook, but see only moving branches and shadows in the hemlock grove. There's another multiple eruption mixed with the sound of Hanna's bell. I haven't actually seen a bird, but there must have been a half-dozen, maybe more. Family groups sometimes remain together into the early season, so this was likely a hen with her nearly grown chicks.

The puppy comes back with an expression that says, "There were some wild birds up ahead, but I scared them all away, and it's okay now."

There's a part of me that wants to kick her in the rear end, but the other part, the one with all the patience, brings her over to the hemlocks and stands her up. I'm trying to give her the idea that these grouse-things ought to be pointed. She can't be expected to point anything for a while, but she has to be shown.

I train puppies according to *The Shotgun Method*. Rather than a progression, everything is applied at once—in one shot. The whole theory is based on the single idea that you should never permit your dog to do anything you will later have to teach him not to do.

I'm pretty sure I'm not the first to think of *The Shotgun Method,* although you won't find it touted in many dog-training books because it's not for everyone. Even when explained simply, it comes off sounding like a lot of work. And, in reality, it is—but only for a little while. After that, you have a puppy who hunts and retrieves and is a pleasure to be with, and all in his first season.

There are two truths behind *The Shotgun Method:* The first is that dogs learn from us whether we think we are teaching them or not. The second is based on the first, and is that an untrained older dog really IS trained—but good ol' Sparkey has learned to

30

do things we don't necessarily agree with. We call those things he learned *bad habits,* and it's those bad habits that drive us crazy. Since happiness, essentially, is pretty much not being unhappy, *The Shotgun Method* stresses not permitting the dog to learn bad habits in the first place.

So it follows that if I'm going to want Hanna to point birds rather than run them up, then I must at least make an attempt to show her how she should have pointed every bird she flushes. I'm not pretending that Hanna or any other puppy is going to instantly learn to do it right, but it's important that she be shown what I expect.

An aside about puppies: in the field, the unvarnished truth is that they're all a pain in the neck—they only vary by degree. If you're loyal to *The Shotgun Method,* you're going to have your hands full for a while. Puppies are fast cars with lousy brakes and a driver who doesn't even have a learner's permit, let alone a legitimate driver's license. Puppies are interested in taking corners on two wheels, and you're out there trying to teach the doggy equivalent of parallel parking.

But a wonderful reality is that in most instances, you're asking the dog to do something he wants to do anyway. All you really need to do is show the puppy what you want, scratch his ears and tell him he's a good boy when he does it right, and let him know you're mad as hell when he doesn't. And be patient.

In most cases that's all it takes. Really.

We work beneath the Corn Patch cover's dark spruces, searching for the scattered grouse family. Two birds flush unseen while I'm struggling in the thick stuff, and the one I find won't fly from his perch. He sits there gawking at me, an obviously young bird sporting a half-grown tail. Shooting sitting grouse isn't for me, even though in this case it might equate to mercy killing. When I throw a stick at the bird, he departs to rejoin his brood and hopefully learn a thing or two about wariness in the next few weeks.

On the way back out Hanna finds where the birds were feeding in the barberries near the grove of young hemlocks. Again I stand her up and go through the motions of having her remain firm while I toss my hat in the air and make a noise like a flushing grouse.

We've got some ground to cover together first, but one of these days she'll point a grouse. That fact is a certainty in her future and mine, but right now it's still out there ahead of us, well below the horizon.

Day Five: That Lovely Autumn Serenade

*"There is a harmony
In autumn, and a luster in its sky."*
Percy Bysshe Shelley

WOODCOCK SEASON opens today in Vermont. During the past week the puppy and I have made a couple of additional training/ gunning trips up here, outings that were long on training and short on gunning. Today I'm going to spend an overnight in Vermont and hunt tomorrow as well. Both Stella and Hanna will make the trip, with one dog staying in the truck while the other hunts. I've squeezed a dog crate behind the seat of my stretch-cab truck. Using both dogs alternately is a refreshing habit I started in past puppy-training years. Hunting an hour or two with the old dog can offset the insanity that hunting with a puppy can sometimes bring on.

On Interstate 91, I drive north past Brattleboro and then Springfield and lose my FM station before the music has finished. I've got to pass through southern Vermont to get to where I'm headed, and driving past places where I know birds are waiting for me is tormenting. I try to be careful about not overhunting, and even though none of my coverts are truly private, I don't visit the same place more than twice in a month.

That said, going through towns where I have coverts is no less painful.

Off the main highway it seems every other house and farm and vacant property is for sale. The state of Vermont could save a lot of money by taking down all the signs and replacing them with a single notice at the border: it might read, THE ENTIRE STATE IS FOR SALE.

For that matter, they could do the same thing with the MAPLE SYRUP SOLD HERE signs. Every house in Vermont has maple syrup for sale. Even if they don't have a sign outside, just knock on any door in the state and they'll sell you some.

It's nearly a two-hour drive and a half-tank of gas to the first stop in the shadow of Mount Ascutney. Today it looks just as Maxfield Parrish painted it—maybe bluer. I ease off the road where somebody once had a sign advertising goats for sale; thus my journal entry will read "Started at the Goat Farm at 9:45."

Hanna gets put through her obedience drill at the edge of the road, then we start in, hoping for some woodcock in an alder run that borders a swamp. It soon becomes apparent that the place has changed—beavers have flooded much of the lowland, and the pointed chewed-off stumps are like so many bungee sticks left over from the Vietnam War. We work to the far side of the swamp where scruffy gray birch borders a snowmobile trail that winds up a hill. I try to keep the puppy in front of me to work one side of the trail up and the other back down again.

Hanna is wound up. There's a school of thought that says I should have taken her someplace where she could run off her excess energy for twenty minutes or so, but that's a theory I have trouble subscribing to. Woodcock cover quite often begins at the door of the truck.

Off to my left I notice a woodcock flying by, heading down the snowmobile trail with Hanna in hot pursuit. I holler "Hut," but of course she doesn't stop. After a rundown, she gets dragged back uphill by her check cord. She's not happy.

At seven and a half months, the puppy can't yet be faulted for chasing, but I'm sure she heard my command to stop. If we're ever going to make any headway with field training she's got to stop when she's told. Oh, she'll do it when nothing else is going on, but right now it's more than she can handle when birds are flying and excitement is high. We arrive at the spot where she was when I hollered. I stand her up, repeating "Hut" the whole time. I leave her there and walk up the trail, and each time she starts to move I yell "Hut" again. Dog training is demonstration and then enforcement, and right now we're having a factory-authorized sale on that enforcement thing.

I've written that nobody can teach a dog anything of any use without the command "Whoa," but I don't say "Whoa." Instead, I follow writer George Bird Evans's lead and use the command "Hold," which comes out as the staccato "Hut." Most trainers use "Whoa," but it's always sounded too much like "No" and "Go" to my ears, and, I would imagine, to the dog's as well.

We find the first woodcock's wingman in the birches on the other side of the trail. Hanna seems to be working scent but she's surprised when the bird flushes. I pause a half-second until it tops the bushes, then shoot and see the bird fall somewhere ahead.

When it comes to retrieving, it's never wise to assume the dog has seen a bird fall. Standing around hollering "Fetch," even to an experienced dog, often creates problems rather than results. I adopt a different strategy: I walk the puppy to the spot where I marked the bird down, using her check cord as a leash to keep her close.

"Dead bird here," I tell Hanna. "Find dead."

We've been through this drill before, but always with a pheasant wing. This is her first time with a warm bird. She wants to wander off, but I keep her immediately in front of me where the bird fell.

"Dead bird. Find dead." I keep pointing to the ground.

Finally, I spot the woodcock lying ten feet away. I want Hanna to find it, and lead her there. She sniffs at the bird without much interest and keeps going. She gets brought back and has another chance to pick up the woodcock, but she hasn't made the connection yet.

She has been force-trained to retrieve. I sit her down and hold the bird in front of her and say, "Fetch." She automatically reaches for the bird, but acts like a little kid forced to take his cod liver oil—she's sure she's being abused. When she moves her head, the bird falls out of her mouth. She gives me the world's most pathetic look.

One of the great things about the whole force-training routine is that there are a number of remedial lessons that the dog can be put through in the field. I sit Hanna down and hold out my hat. "Fetch," I say. She takes the hat, and brings it to me when I back up and command her to "Fetch" again. Now I drop the hat and repeat the drill. Finally, I substitute the woodcock, and this time she takes the bird and brings it to me. I toss the bird a few feet and tell her to "Fetch." She does.

Is it possible that progress is being made? It's a beginning.

About the only time I shoot nonpointed woodcock is in situations like this, when I'm training a puppy and need to help her make the mental connection between the birds she's discovering and the reason we're hunting.

Some men won't shoot a bird their dog hasn't pointed in the belief it would teach the dog that he doesn't have to point. I won't say they're wrong, but thinking a puppy is going to learn to point ONLY by ignoring birds he hasn't pointed doesn't stand up to reason. It's akin to thinking you're going to teach a little boy table manners by ignoring him when he picks up mashed potatoes with his hands. He's got to be shown what you want him to do, and that applies both to boys and to puppies.

There certainly comes a time in Sparkey's development when he knows full well how to work and pin a bird, but hasn't yet mastered his own eagerness and he busts a bird that could have been pointed. Then I'd agree—don't shoot. If you killed the bird and the dog retrieved it, you'd be rewarding him for doing something wrong when he knows better. But it takes judgment on your part.

As an advocate of *The Shotgun Method* I've become an evangelist for judgment rather than hard-and-fast rules. Sometimes not shooting a nonpointed bird means passing a chance to pump up a puppy and show him that this-right-here is what we're after—that's what I'm doing with Hanna today. Not shooting might also mean passing a chance to reward a puppy for hunting well and doing everything right except that little bit at the very end. It might mean passing a chance to have the dog make a retrieve, and it certainly means passing a chance to stand the puppy up and show him how you want him to point with the bird replaced in its original position, as I'm also doing with Hanna.

Again, I want to emphasize the importance of judgment. I don't want to be misquoted as the guy who advocates shooting birds the dog hasn't pointed. But in training you've got to come to grips with the dual concepts of demonstration and enforcement, and realize that enforcement involves something ACTIVE on the part of the trainer. Not shooting a bird is a PASSIVE act that might send a message, but then again it might not.

Shooting or not shooting is hardly the main issue. If the dog busts a bird, it's what you actively do afterward that matters. Physically handle him. Stand him up back where he should have pointed. Walk in front of him and don't let him move. Throw your hat in the air and make a noise like a flushing bird. Fire your gun. Tell him he's done just right.

Show Sparkey what you want, then make him do it. Demonstrate, then enforce.

When you become addicted to this bird-dog business, whether or not you've shot the bird won't matter a whole hell of a lot.

That's just my opinion. I could be wrong.

The morning warms up a bit, but it remains comfortably cool, the sort of clear October day when the sky seems to have been washed clean of a summer's worth of haze.

The day before yesterday I tried hunting in Vermont, but it turned out to be a hot summer day. Back in August we had a cool spell, and people said that it felt like October. Wednesday was one of the days that the August cool spell displaced—it was early August all over again, hot and humid, a day that certainly didn't belong in October. If I had made an early start, I might have had a couple of hours of good hunting, but I didn't and I didn't. In the heat I first tried the puppy and then Stella, but I've never seen any bird dog do anything worthwhile while his tongue was lolling out the side of his mouth. There's nothing like hot weather and no birds to take it out of you.

So for a change the old guy used his head: I drove into town and started a painting. I worked up the road and the shadows, but left the trees sketchy in anticipation of the coming autumn color.

I'll use Stella at the Kangaroo Ranch. Bordering an over-grown orchard is a twelve-foot wire fence that looks as if it were designed to keep kangaroos out, or maybe in. In Vermont, deer damage can cause farmers to go to extremes.

Old Stella is well past her prime. She did okay on opening day of grouse season, but it would be easy to let her overwork herself. I have to be careful because although she tires, she doesn't show it; she just slows her pace and keeps going. Some old dogs never make that adjustment. They run like a puppy and quickly wear themselves out.

We'll look for grouse in the scattering of apple trees that rim the bottom of a mountain, then follow the lowlands back along the edge of the cover. Stella will understand if I don't shoot any woodcock she might point. I'm going to save the birds I'm permitted for the puppy. I start the beeper collar and we head across the road and into the cover.

Although there is a dog whistle tucked into my shirt pocket, I seldom use it. Instead, I whistle. It's nothing loud and strident, just a little signal to the dogs that might be mistaken for a bird's song. After years of whistling, it's tough to adjust to the fact that Stella is nearly deaf and doesn't hear me. I keep whistling at her and can't stop myself.

For that matter, my own hearing is going. The old guy I used to laugh at—the one driving down the interstate with his turn signal still on—lately, that's me. There was a time not too many years ago when I could always hear the dog's bell. At times it even seemed too loud. Now that particular range of my hearing is diminished. Sometimes I can hear the dog panting, but not the bell. Writing that, I don't expect anyone with "20/20" ears to believe it, but you older guys understand. The beeper collar has became a necessity, and now I don't even hear that signal very well on windy days or when the dog gets out beyond eighty yards or so.

In the cover there's a rumble of wings ahead of us, and then Stella points. It's easy to conclude that the bird has gone, but I approach in the hope that the departed grouse had a partner or two that Stella has now located. Of course there are none, and Stella softens and moves ahead.

Pointing a grouse this early in the season must be akin to shooting a gun with a hair trigger: after a layoff of months, even an experienced bird dog might need to regain the right touch needed to do it.

Stella wants to go up the side of the mountain after the grouse, but I've been there once before and I'm not going there again. There are boulders strewn all along the slope and no flat spots in between where I might walk upright. So I wait for Stella to come back down, then we start along the scalloped margin at the base of the hill.

An old dog is not at all visual. When Stella could hear, she'd only look for me when I'd audibly signal her. Now that she's deaf there is no reason for her to ever look back. But she knows good cover and her manner of covering the ground was always more back and forth than straight ahead. Those traits serve her well in her old age. As with every other good-dog-become-old, hunting behind Stella takes patience. Much of the time I'm following her lead rather than directing her where I want to go.

Ahead, under an apple tree at the edge of a little ravine, she's not quite pointing as she waits for me. Among the rocks is a dead doe, incompletely eaten and partially covered with leaves. It takes a long moment for me to realize what I'm seeing, and then I can feel what little hair I have left standing on end.

A few times in the past I've stumbled across deer that poachers have shot, but this one has been chewed on. Black bear don't normally kill deer, but they'll take a cripple if they can, then cover what they can't eat and return to it later. I glance around for sign, but the leaf fall is well under way and if there are bear tracks nearby they're covered with swamp maple leaves. Suddenly the shotgun I'm carrying seems pretty puny, and I feel like a fellow after Bengal tigers with a .22-caliber pistol. I have the puppy's check cord in my game bag, and I snap it on Stella's collar and keep her at close heel. I don't want to find out if bears or whatever it was defend their kills. There are supposedly mountain lions in the Green Mountains, although I've never seen one.

When we've put some distance between the deer kill and us, I release Stella and we work our way back to the road along the margin where wet meets dry. I expect to find a woodcock or two in the swamp edge on the way back, but today those birds are vacationing elsewhere.

We're almost out, and up ahead I can glimpse the truck through a break in the trees where a little brooklet parallels the road. When Stella casts by again I intend to put her at heel for the walk out.

I'm still poring over the image of the half-eaten doe when a grouse blasts out of a thin pine tree. The shot is an exact replica of a skeet shot from high-house two, with the overhead bird quartering left-to-right, more away than across. I don't have time to act, only react, and on this occasion my reactions are good and the bird folds. His forward momentum carries him into the opening where the little brook flows, and he comes down among the rocks and pine needles. Stella saw the bird fall and goes directly into the brook to make the retrieve. In apposition to the half-grown birds at the Corn Patch, this one is a large adult cock grouse with a full tail that will measure fourteen and one-half inches. Later, I'll staple the fan to the carrier beam in the cellar as a souvenir of the shot, but I'll never look at it without also seeing the partially hidden deer kill. It is not something easily forgotten.

We drive on. In Vermont there's a state law that prohibits outdoor advertising, so the wonderful vistas are uncluttered by billboards. Instead, the state puts up little inconspicuous green roadside signs that advise travelers that Joe's Eatery is a half-mile ahead on the left. I guess the thinking is that if you're looking to eat at Joe's, they'll tell you where it is and you'll find it. But because of the advertising ban, Joe's isn't in an ad war with Bob's Greasy Spoon down the road. And, best of all, the rest of us don't suffer the fallout from that battle.

After two uneventful stops and a break for lunch (Joe's? Bob's? I flipped a coin), we arrive at Bellknap where I'll end the day with Hanna. You have to wade a river or walk some railroad tracks to get into the cover, and even then there's a factory that hides the place from view. I always park in the employees' lot—nobody seems to care—and walk the tracks with the dog at heel, then cross a vacant field and a little brook to get into the cover by the back way.

The field is all clusters of New England asters, with bees still in attendance even on this cool day. At this time of year wild asters seem to fill every roadside and sunny vacant plot. Like all wildflowers, they're just weeds that nobody really notices until they blossom. Their hues range from the familiar pale lilac to a less common deep vibrant violet that's the color of a grape Popsicle. Under the heading of one-man's-weed-is-another-man's-flower, New England asters may be the only local weed that people routinely take into their gardens, although recently something that looks a lot like joe-pye weed has been appearing in flower beds.

The Bellknap cover is on a bend in the river, a low flat grown almost exclusively to popple. Years ago someone cut a series of drainage ditches through the place, and even though the ditches are now overgrown with aspens, they seem to serve as boundaries between one part of the cover and the next. It can be a woodcock hot spot. There have been times when the birds were so thick you could take them with a tennis racket. That's an exaggeration, of course, but when you're in a flight of woodcock they can be like land mines, and at times I've had to avoid walking anyplace the dog hadn't first covered. My first setter, Hazel, had a twenty-point day in here years ago.

Beyond the field Hanna crosses the little brook, then waits as I balance my way across on a few exposed rocks that serve as stepping-stones. I'm still in midstream when a grouse flushes. I see little more than a shadow, but I've got a line on where the bird headed.

Once on the other side I ponder my options. Should I go after the shadowy grouse, or work the pup on the flats where there ought to be woodcock? Before I can decide, Hanna sticks her nose into a ditch off to the right and a second grouse comes barreling out low and fast. The bird crosses close in front of me, right-to-left. My first shot passes well behind it, but then the opportunity turns into a near straightaway and the tight barrel finds the mark.

As I've done earlier, I lead Hanna to the spot where the bird fell, and when I tell her to "Find dead," I keep her close with the check cord. The dead grouse is in some hip-high weeds, and

Hanna sniffs at the bird but doesn't quite know what to make of it. I help her out and put the bird in her mouth, and have her carry it to me while I back up. Then we repeat the process and she carries the grouse around while she walks at heel. *It'll take some time,* I tell myself.

We never relocate the shadowy first grouse. On the flats the puppy finds and bumps two woodcock, but they're of the *no-chance* variety and there's little I can do other than call her to a stop when the birds flush. We go through the this-is-how–I–want–you–to-point routine.

Sometimes woodcock appear to be dodging on purpose, flying a fairly straight course but flip-flopping to either side. It's a tactic with its own name: *woodcocking.* At other times, particularly when crossing an opening, they will fly as deliberately as a goose and become a fairly easy mark.

We're on the way out, and I'm a little disappointed that we haven't found more than just two woodcock for the puppy to work when I nearly step on one. This bird gives me the sky-rocket routine. He rears his head back and somehow propels himself straight up toward the overhead opening in the aspen canopy. The shot isn't difficult, and when the bird falls back he nearly strikes Hanna on the way down.

Without being told, she pounces on the bird and brings him to me with her head high, then sits on command to deliver just as she has done a thousand times before in the backyard with a pheasant wing.

If I spend a little too much time telling her what a good dog she is, it's only because that lovely autumn serenade is playing in the background. I never get tired of it even though I know the melody by heart. It never changes, but it has never been lovelier.

Interlude: Wood Smoke

SPENDING THE NIGHT in Vermont makes sense if I expect to hunt the next day, particularly when I'm three hours away from my own driveway. But even Vermont's economy motels double their rates during the foliage season. In October, you don't get much change back from your one-hundred-dollar bill. So at the end of the day I'm on my way to spend the night at a friend's house.

The first time I navigated through town to Bruce's place, Leon Redbone was playing on the car stereo. Now, as I turn up the winding gravel back road, he automatically starts to sing again in my head: . . . *I don't stay out late, Don't care to go, I'm home about eight, Just me an' my radio; Ain't misbehavin', Savin' my love for you.*

Mr. Redbone is my kind of singer. I like Willie Nelson for the same reason: not only can you sing along with him, you can actually sound better than he does.

Bruce is waiting in the driveway. I can smell the wood smoke from his outdoor grill.

"Let's see that meat, boy," is his greeting when he sticks his head in the truck window. Earlier, on the phone, I had told his wife that there were two grouse in my cooler. Bruce is a skeet shooter and a deer hunter and has been known to shoot a pheasant or two, but he leaves the grouse hunting to those of us with bird dogs. I show him the birds, then let the dogs out to run around his yard and visit.

Mrs. Bruce is making Hanna's acquaintance. "Where's that big one with the black ears?" she asks. "How come you left her at home?"

Ouch. I haven't told them about Sophie, and I have to relive the summer's heartache all over again. And, of course, there's Hanna's first retrieve to be recounted, and the story of the bear-killed doe.

Before whiskey and the catching-up that we have to do, I open the birds and make note of the contents of their crops for my hunting journal. The hen from Bellknap has a standard assortment of ground greens, fern tips, and barberries. But the cock bird from the Kangaroo Ranch was feeding on some strange seeds that neither Bruce nor I can identify. They seem to be envelopes of tissue-paper-like stuff about the size of a fingernail, and they have a small seed inside. If I didn't know better, I'd say they looked like dried-up salvia from my flower border.

Then I cut a fillet from each side of the breasts. What comes off looks like the skinless, boneless chicken cutlets that you buy at the meat counter, except that these might contain a pellet or two of No. 8 shot at no extra charge. I've already field dressed the birds in the woods, and they've spent the past two hours in a cooler in the back of the truck. The fillets cut much more cleanly when the meat has been chilled.

In game cooking, it becomes important to identify your expectations. Are you looking for an exquisite gourmet meal or just supper? Me, I'm of the supper persuasion. All the poetic chatter surrounding the ruffed grouse sidetracks some folks—he's the king of game birds, after all. Rather than enjoying the bird for the outstanding poultry that he is, some men insist on making a sacrament out of him. When all the ritual is past, you're left with the fact that grouse are pretty good to eat. (I wish the same could be said for woodcock, but that's another story.)

When properly handled postmortem in the field, grouse have a delicate, nutty flavor, and good recipes celebrate those qualities. Recipes that treat the bird like *wild game* and call for the use of bacon strips or salami or some other strongly flavored additive fail to acknowledge the bird's subtleties. Those are bad recipes.

I wrote a grouse-hunting book a few years back and called it *Wings of Thunder*. When it came out, at least half of the comments and mail I received had to do with the cooking chapter titled "The Other Side of the Coin: The Bird on the Table." Complementing the indoor recipes listed in that chapter is a marinade-and-outdoor-grilling method for grouse fillets that I'm using tonight at Bruce's place. Italian dressing makes an ideal marinade, and there are a bunch of commercial thirty-minute marinades that treat the bird well without adding fat, salt, or huge flavors to what is arguably the healthiest piece of meat you can eat.

Here's how it's done. Fillets have a bone side and a membrane side. With a very sharp knife lightly score the membrane side with a crosshatch of cuts so that the marinade can get in. Splash the fillets on both sides and let them sit in a covered dish in the refrigerator while you take off your boots and have a VO—maybe two.

When your host announces that the grill is hot, put your drink down and get to it. Sear the fillets on each side for a minute or two directly over the fire, then move them to the far end to finish cooking with the grill lid down. Things vary, but it should take about ten minutes or so on a typical outdoor grill.

The recipe is simple, but here's the one crucial part. When the fillets are cooking, watch 'em like a hawk—a hungry hawk at that. There's no fat on grouse fillets, so two minutes too long will result in overly dry birds. You've got to pay attention. And remember, too, that the fillets will keep cooking once you take them off the fire, so waiting until they're done all the way through is a mistake.

Tonight's marinade is Dijon & Honey, and the birds come from the grill still sizzling and smelling like something far too good for ordinary people. Along with the grouse, I've brought wine—a good German Riesling—and a fresh loaf of crusty bread from a storefront bakery in Crows' Corners. We toast the birds and Hanna's first retrieve and Sophie's memory and the generosity of my hosts, and after the first bite Bruce rhetorically asks how things could be any better.

I'm supposed to be the wise guy with all the smart-ass answers, but for once all I can do is agree with Bruce's opinion that fresh grouse done on an outdoor grill couldn't be any better.

Day Six: West of the Greens

*"The days come and go, and they
say nothing. And if we do not use
the gifts they bring, they are carried
as silently away."*

Ralph Waldo Emerson

THERE'S A WIDE SPOT in the gravel road above the Thistle
Paddock where I always park. There are a couple of clumps of
thistles right next to the road, and as far as I know they're the
only ones in the place. The goldfinches have found
them and have been working at the seed heads.
The disturbed floss seems to erupt from the
bracts, and the breeze carries off a few fluffs
even as I watch.

The Thistle Paddock is mostly a hillside
orchard, long since abandoned. For reasons I
don't quite fathom, an absent owner leaves a
trio of horses adrift here, thus the "paddock"
part of the name. The horses must be at least
fifteen years old because they've been here for as
long as I've hunted this place. Maybe someone rides them or
takes them elsewhere at another time of the year, but during the
fall an arrangement of ill-kept barbed wire and sometimes-electric
fences keep them contained in the up-and-down pasture and the
surrounding grouse cover.

There were times in years past when the whole place smelled
of apples. Well, not always apples in a good sense—sometimes it
stank the vinegar smell of rotting apples. But not this year. It has
been a poor season for the wild apple crop everywhere in New
England, and the few that have appeared look like shriveled
warts.

Apple trees are part of the woods all through the Northeast.
Some are genuinely wild, others are the feral offspring of planted
trees, still others are old plantings in abandoned homesteads and

46

farms. Unlike so many other cultivated crops, apples seem to do just fine without human attention, and manage to hold their own in the competition for sunlight with the succession trees that spring up around them. Sometimes wild trees produce apples that look like those for sale at a farm stand, but mostly not. Wild apples are usually small and, if not bug-eaten, at least bug-sampled. Fortunately, the grouse don't care. They know groceries when the see them.

Without the farmer's attention, apples seem to be a truly cyclical crop. One year's boom crop seems to exhaust the trees, and regardless of weather and growing conditions, a hugely productive year is inevitably followed by what we're having now— a virtually apple-less autumn.

At the Thistle Paddock, Hanna and I work the top of the hillside orchard toward the far end of the cover. Along the way we pass through a break where I took a grouse a couple of years back. On the left there's a wall overgrown with blackberries. The bird came out of those brambles and crossed left-to-right at eye level as he headed downhill. The shot was fast and close, but for once I was ready, because three of the grouse's buddies had gotten up out of range moments before. It's tough not to half-expect a repeat as I pass through the break. I swing on an imaginary bird and can see it all happening again.

Walking through bird cover, I spend most of the time watching the dog run, and puppy Hanna—when she's hunting—moves with the same almost gliding gait that I remember being so characteristic of Hazel. What are the chances she'll develop into a bird dog half as good as Hazel was? The thought causes me to knock wood on the nearest tree. That would be more than luck; another Hazel would be a blessing.

At the orchard's end we turn and start to work our way back along the hillside. There's hardly a piece of level ground in the place, but this stretch is particularly steep. I've got my eye on Hanna as she pokes around in the brushy stuff above me.

Suddenly she's standing on a rigid point, transfixed by something just in front of her.

Every dog has to start somewhere. Maybe this is it.

I start toward her, then remember the camera and dig it out for what promises to be a memorable photo, especially since she's uphill from me and silhouetted in the sunlight. But before I can lay the gun aside, Hanna barks twice and retreats to me with her tail between her legs. Only then do I notice what she has been pointing: One of the horses is standing motionless, brown and shaggy and looking every bit as big as an elephant among the broken-down apple trees. He looks at us warily as we pass.

I've been startled by the horses here, too. You never expect them. But I don't think I've ever done any barking. At least, not out loud.

Here and there in the cover is an old spread-out maple tree— a wolf tree, some call it. The tree grew alone when this was an open meadow years before. Without the competition for sunlight that forest trees contend with, it developed its stout, spreading posture. Now the maple has shaded out the second growth that sprung up around it. But like a mother helping her children along, there are a few maple saplings thriving beneath her.

How old are these maples with the eight-foot boles? Two hundred years? Maybe three hundred? Where some men look at rocks and wonder back millions of years, I look at trees and wonder back centuries. Autumn in New England must have looked the same when the trees were seedlings. There were elms and chestnuts then, and, if you go back far enough, no stone walls. But the view was replete with the same colors, and hopefully, the effect on those who saw it was the same as mine is now.

Some puppies have a lot of point in them, and their propensity to strike an intense pose leads to a lot of false points. Stella was one such puppy, and there were times when it drove me crazy. Interpreting which points are real and which are false can be a challenge in the early going. Other puppies—including Hanna—aren't so overloaded with the pointing instinct. Not that they don't point, but they seem to have a better handle on it.

Hanna still dallies with mice and chipmunks, although not nearly as much as when the season started. And she has discovered that she REALLY likes the smell of birds. She regularly signals me just how much by wagging her whole body as she works scent. There's a bird nearby now, she tells me. All her actions are hurried, almost as if she's afraid the bird will jump before she can find it.

"Hut," I say, and walk to her. She stands, but lets me know she's got very important business to attend to and would like to get back to work as soon as possible. I push her rear end and hold her check cord while I repeat the "Hut" command. She stiffens each time I do the *push-and-hut* routine. She's not so impatient now.

Then, the moment of truth. I extend my hand and say in a near whisper, "Go ahead eeeasy."

She takes off like one of those circus performers shot from a cannon, but I've got hold of her check cord. She gets pulled up short, shaken by the ear, and replaced in the pointing position. *Where's that pointing tendency now?*

"I SAID EASY!"

After a pause, we try again. "Now, go ahead eeeasy."

This time she oozes ahead just as she's supposed to, but gradually accelerates until she once again approaches warp speed. The woodcock, who had been patiently waiting off to the right, flutters up only to sit back down again two hundred feet away.

Hanna didn't see the bird's flight, so I lead her downwind to circle within sixty feet of where the woodcock came down. I stand her up and then leave her on point for what seems like a long time—perhaps a full minute. I'm hoping some scent will drift her way, but the Electronic Scent-O-Meter hasn't been invented yet, so I can't be sure.

When I tell her to "Go ahead eeeasy," she takes a few tentative steps, then the woodcock finally decides that he has seen enough and takes wing, this time heading for Connecticut. I fire a shot in the air, but not at the bird. This one has been very cooperative, and good help is hard to come by.

Ah, patience, I tell myself.

Putting a check cord on a puppy-in-training seems like a good idea. Sparkey drags a length of rope behind him as he runs around, and when needed you don't actually have to physically catch the puppy, just intercept some part of the check cord as it flows by. It would all work fine if you were doing your training inside a gymnasium with a linoleum floor, but unfortunately we're out in the woods. If you've ever tried the check-cord idea, you know the rope is forever tangled or caught around a bush or stump, and you spend as much time cursing the rope gods as you do training.

At least I always did.

One part of the solution is to make the check cord out of cheap, plastic clothesline. It's not good for hanging clothes or much of anything else, but it makes an ideal check cord. Unlike the braided stuff, the smooth plastic resists tangling and flows past most hang-ups that would snag another rope.

The other element in the tangle-free solution is to use a check cord that's no longer than absolutely necessary. Lately, my check cords have run to the short side of twelve feet.

On the radio, the weather forecast divides the state into *east of the Greens* and *west of the Greens;* the Greens being the Green Mountains that form a north–south spine through most of Vermont. Today we're on the west side, and the day couldn't be lovelier. The sky is bright and frost-clarified, with the haze of late summer a thing of the past.

Autumn in New England is one of the very few things in nature that, upon first encounter by an outsider, is not at least vaguely disappointing. No matter what you've heard, the reality of The Color is better than what you're expecting. And it's coming fast. The swamp maples, particularly in the low areas, are already shedding their brilliantly crimson leaves. The ashes are distinctly purple, the black cherries are a cloud of maroon, and the aspens shimmer with chartreuse and clear yellow.

But they're all supporting players, because in the uplands the noble sugar maples are now coming to center stage. Most are golden yellow, but there are variations that run from fiery orange to peach pink. Some trees seem to turn all at once, but others blush from the outside in and appear frosted. The beeches and oaks have not yet gone over, and the birches and lesser trees are mostly past, but The Color is really about the near luminescence of sugar maples in sunlight. Because of them, for a lovely week or two our part of the world is the envy of the rest of it.

At a place called the Outback, the maples lining the roadside glow and tint the light with their autumn gold. There's a grouse drumming in the cover below the road, and I stand by the truck for a few minutes and listen. As always, the best I can come up with for the sound's direction is *over that way somewhere . . . maybe.*

This used to be a minor twenty-minute stop. Then, while chasing a grouse a few years ago, I discovered the extensive outback beyond where I had normally hunted. Some covers have obvious boundaries—a river or a mountainside or a row of houses—but there are a bunch of places in the same category as the Outback that are in need of further exploring. Of course, they're all far from home and I only visit them during the hunting season. I just don't/won't/can't allot the days necessary to push back the boundaries. Until the next maverick grouse leads me on a chase into the unknown beyond the fringes, the margins of the maps I carry in my head are destined to remain marked *Terra Incognita—Here Be Dragons.*

As Stella and I go in, a raven flies over. Unless you look hard, you'll think they're crows. Their tails and wings appear longer, or

maybe just narrower. An articulate person would say they are "attenuated." Ravens don't quite fit the crow silhouette. As often as not they're recognized because they croak an unmistakable raspy call. Usually they're solitary, sometimes in pairs, but they don't flock up the ways crows do. I regularly see them in Vermont, but they don't seem to come into Massachusetts. It must have something to do with the tax structure.

We work the cover, and after finding three woodcock along the swamp edge, Stella has a fourth point in some tamaracks. The golden needles cling to my flannel sleeves as I brush the "evergreen" branches on my way toward the sound of her beeper collar.

It's Stella's style that she stops on first encounter with scent, then relocates when I wave her on. She slinks ahead, and I wonder as always, *Is the bird running?*

Now she's pointing again well ahead of me, and I find her standing before a clump of spruces. Being right-handed, when everything else is equal I try to go to the right of a point so that I can shoot to the left, but there's a steep bank there and circling won't be feasible. Instead, I head directly toward the grove with Stella uphill and to the right of me.

At the end of a bold approach, during which nothing happens, I come to a stop, sure that I'll have to send Stella ahead again. Then the grouse jumps from beneath the nearest spruce. The trees are arranged in a wide C-shape with the opening facing me, creating a big, tall room with the bird inside. The shot is only twenty yards or so—nothing difficult if you just remember to hold above the target, which I don't. The second shot is equally easy, but I shoot right at the grouse a second time and it flies over the spruces and disappears.

A missed grouse can be a *fair miss* when the bird outflies the gunner's ability to hit it. Or it can be a *wasted shot* if the percentages are low. But a missed easy chance like this is a *Groaner,* in this case with a capital G.

Hold above those rising birds, you moron. Identifying and then failing to hold above a rising bird is something not from the left or the right side of my brain, but from the very bottom. I've been making the same mistake for thirty years. So far this season all my grouse opportunities have been of the harum-scarum variety: surprise shots and walk-ups. Here I finally get a pointed bird—but when I step to the plate, I can't hit the hanging curveball. I tell other people that if you fire twice, you must make two complete and distinct shots, yet here I've botched a perfect chance by making the same mistake twice.

These are some of things I say to myself as I walk around behind Stella over the next half-hour. I hate Groaners mainly because afterward I feel just plain stupid.

At the Deer Camp cover I park next to a shack with a padlock on the door. Deer camps, like this one, are scattered alongside roads all over the state. To someone with an uninitiated eye—someone for whom the term *deer camp* summons up a romantic image of a snug cabin at the end of a trail far back in the woods—these ramshackle hovels plunked too close to the highway seem like misplaced bits of slum. Sometimes they are mobile homes circa 1950. Others are obviously homemade affairs built of scraps and leftovers, and the only improvements ever made are the sort to keep the building erect. "If we fix it up too good, somebody'll just break in," seems to be the watchword among Vermont deer-camp owners.

There is highbush cranberry here with leaves that look like maple and with bunches of translucent crimson fruit that can be a magnet for grouse. But today the woodcock are in. Twice Hanna is working and about to bump a bird when I call her to a halt, flush the woodcock, then take the shot. What her retrieving lacks in style is more than made up for in enthusiasm. Afterward, I once more stand her up on point with the dead bird replaced at the spot where it flushed. It's a matter of faith that she's in the process of figuring out what I want, because right now, on her fifth outing, she doesn't seem to be making much progress.

With good reason there isn't a lot of literature written about the reality of yard training a bird dog—it's not high excitement. What it consists of is repetition of the most repetitive kind, and progress is incremental. I worked with Hanna in the yard on the belief that fifteen minutes each day trumps a couple of hours on the weekend. You teach "Heel" and "Hut," and you teach

"Fetch" and "Come," and the puppy progresses not always in a forward manner. Most of what I do is in Richard Wolters's book, *Gun Dog,* and I wouldn't try to amend anything he had to say because I couldn't do nearly as good a job as he did fifty-odd years ago.

From the very beginning—before I put her in the car to take her home from the kennel—Hanna was wearing a puppy collar. I went through several boxes of .22-caliber blanks at feeding times, which is cheap insurance against a gun-shy dog. And I never put a food dish in front of her without making her obey the command "Hut" as she charged toward dinner. The same with opening a door to let her out or in: she would "Hut" before I let her pass, and—no exaggeration—she learned the meaning of that command before she learned her own name.

All through the summer we took walks to the playground where she learned to "Hut" and to stay in front and walk at heel even though kids on the swings were calling to her and neighborhood dogs barked from their fenced yards. At the end of the summer we went into the woods for field training that mostly amounted to reinforcing "Hut" and transferring the "In front" command from the open spaces of the park to the grouse coverts.

When it came to birds, other puppies that I've trained were old enough to do some rudimentary work during the spring woodcock migration. But Hanna was a February pup, and was too young. Instead, we fooled around with some pen-raised quail in September. Although she pointed a few, I don't think that's a big deal.

My job is to help the dog figure out what to do with the birds that she smells, and I can't do that unless she'll stop when I tell her to. Of far more importance than birds is the training that will put the *invisible leash of obedience* on a young dog.

I've got the tape recorder out. The entry I'll make in the journal for the Deer Camp will read something like, "Used Hanna. She had forced-points on two taken woodcock—retrieved both.

Moved four others all along the west arm of the brook—no shots. Found no grouse, but the highbush cranberry is loaded this year." It's a matter of summing up ninety minutes of hunting into three or four sentences. No matter what I write, the unwritten part holds a story, too. That story is what happened when the things I write about weren't going on.

Sometimes, when I tell a particularly juicy hunting story, people will ask, "Did that REALLY happen?"

Maybe you'd rather hear about the other four and a half hours when I walked around watching the dog and looking at the trees? Oh, there's a lot to be enjoyed whenever any of us are outdoors. But every hunting day contains time that doesn't merit retelling. Even in a book like this, the listener/reader only wants to hear about the incidents that bear repeating.

When we finish hunting the Deer Camp it's coming up on 4 PM. When the autumn color is at its height, it's possible to be delayed an hour or more waiting to get onto the interstate. The main roads get crowded around sunset as the tourists head home. *Leaf-peepers,* they call themselves. So I either start for home now or wait until after dark.

We're all tourists at various times, but there's a difference between looking at nature through the tinted glass of a rolled-up car window as you drive along and actually getting out and becoming part of what's going on. When I'm hunting I've always felt that I am actually a participant in nature rather than just an observer on the outside looking in. It's a concept that I always have difficulty explaining to others, but it's no less true.

And at this time of year, pleasantly weary and with two tired bird dogs sleeping behind the seat, I'm never more certain that the world is a wonderful place. And I'm never more glad to be in it.

CHAPTER TWO

The Little Dog Laughed to See Such a Sport

Day Eleven: Indian Summer

"O suns and skies and clouds of June,
And flowers of June together,
Ye cannot rival for one hour
October's bright blue weather."

Helen Hunt Jackson

IN THE BACKYARD I notice that the moles have returned. I stomped their humped-up tunnels when I mowed the lawn late yesterday, and now there are several new mound-lines in the sod. Spike traps are ineffective because moles don't reuse their tunnels. They're after bugs and grubs that live in the grass roots, so in the past it seemed logical to use Diazinon to kill their food supply. And it worked: I got rid of the lawn grubs, and the moles tunneled elsewhere.

But then Sophie died of liver cancer, and I began questioning everything that might have caused it. The insecticide was at the top of my list of suspects, of course, along with the weed killers I had occasionally used. I stopped using flea powder in the kennel and threw away the tick collars.

The packages say the products are "safe when applied as directed," but I stay away from all that stuff now. Digging a hole and putting a good bird dog in the bottom of it is enough to make anyone reexamine his priorities.

And I'll keep stomping on their tunnels, but if the moles want to take over, God bless 'em.

Hanna and I stop first at Maple Spread, but there's someone else in the covert. I can hear the other guy yelling at his dog before I hear the dog's cowbell. And now there's a second voice, so there must be two men hunting behind a dog that doesn't listen very well, or, more likely, one who prefers to ignore the constant stream of voices behind him. I turn and head back toward the truck. Competing with other hunters isn't what I'm here for.

It's opening day in Massachusetts, and it's a Saturday, so I guess this sort of thing is to be expected. And the Maple Spread covert isn't exactly a secret spot.

Funny, but I'd bet the hollerers are the same sort of guys who'd tell me they wouldn't use a beeper collar because it'll scare away the birds. Maybe it does occasionally, but I've got to believe that incessant talking back and forth is worse. There are a lot of reasons to be quiet in the woods, but I don't like noise for any other reason than that I don't like it.

About noise: If being absolutely quiet paid dividends, then hunting in a light rain or a new-fallen snow would be hugely successful, but it doesn't and it isn't. Even in the best of conditions you can't hunt birds with dogs and be absolutely silent—the two are mutually exclusive. My dogs wear a bell or, when I need it, a beeper collar. And I do my share of whistling, mostly to let the dog know where I am, so there's no big effort to "run silent."

Instead, I try to control the noise I make and ensure that it doesn't call undue attention to me, the hunter. The dog is out in front, and birds should react to her. She's the one wearing the bell, after all. The small amount of disturbance I create will be just secondary commotion taking place in the background.

With a puppy-in-training you need voice commands. Not only "In front" and "Hut" and "Come," but you'll also employ the emphatic "Hey, I said IN FRONT!" sort of thing, as well as an encouraging "That's a good dog," when he does it right. It's a good idea to couple the basic verbal commands with a hand signal so that eventually all you'll need is an attention-getting whistle and then a silent wave of the arm. Hand signals—pointing at the ground next to you for "Come," waving your arm in the direction you're walking for "Front," and the traffic cop's stop signal for "Hut"—those signals will serve you well later in the dog's life when Sparkey starts to lose his hearing. That seems to happen to all bird dogs around their ninth birthday.

It's a mile or so to the next covert and the truck eases down what used to be a road. There's a sign that says PASS AT YOUR

OWN RISK. They're not kidding: the road is one of those grass-in-the-middle affairs that's hardly more than a couple of ruts.

Today, in my home state, it's Mount Tom that dominates the distant skyline rather Mount Ascutney. Since I'm in Massachusetts, I've got a trigger lock on the gun whenever it's in the truck. When that particular piece of antigun legislation passed, a lot of us said "Whew!" Considering some of the proposed alternatives, we felt relieved if all they wanted us to do is lock our guns when we're not using them.

But lock them we must.

Back when I was in grammar school, the teacher would regularly say things along the lines of, "If the person who threw the spitball won't own up to it, then the whole class will stay after school." Of course, the idea was to make someone tattle on the offender, who happened to be exercising his Fifth Amendment right to silence. It always seemed the teacher was punishing the class as a result of her not doing her job, which was to find out who threw the spitball or to prevent spitball throwing in the first place.

Sometimes, when I hear what's going on in regard to gun legislation, I feel I'm back in third grade again—we can't seem to stop crime, so we punish the whole class. I've always been a believer in being responsible for your own actions or lack of same, so the idea that something is society's fault implies that you and I, as members of the accused society, share some of the guilt with the criminals.

As an ex-liberal my opinion doesn't count for much. Although I'm hardly a right-winger, I would be very much in favor of finding out who the offenders are and then taking whatever measures are necessary, no matter how extreme, to make sure they cannot access the means to hurt other people ever again. I'm talking about not only guns, but cars, knives, blunt instruments, and spitballs.

At the Pass At Your Own Risk cover, Hanna and I hunt up through the abandoned pasture, and the song that was playing in my head the last time I hunted here comes back to me almost of its own volition. Why "San Antonio Rose"? I don't know, but I can't fight it. To make matters worse, I know all the lyrics.

The hillside is grown in gray birch and bittersweet tangles. We go up as far as the fence that delineates state-owned land. There are King Bolete mushrooms here, pushed up by the rain two days ago. They're heavy-stemmed and lovely, clean and bug-free when I break one. My father-in-law would be delighted. But I'm a half-mile from the truck with no means of carrying them out, so I walk on and leave them for the bugs.

There's good news and bad news in the area of Hanna's progress. On this her tenth hunt, she's getting the idea of what we're doing out here in the woods and has needed a lot less instruction during the past few outings. It's the sort of thing that sneaks up on you by degrees. She likes to pause in an erect pointing posture at the end of a cast, looking back at me as if to say, "When I find those birds, this is how I'm going to point 'em." She still stops now and then to investigate a particularly odoriferous mouse or squirrel, and she has a perverted fascination with coyote turds, but she does stay in front of me most of the time.

On the other hand, she's also getting independent. She's beginning to work out a little farther than I like. I've had to whistle her in a number of times, and now she's out so far that I have to chase her down.

"Not so far!" I hear myself say as I drag her back by the ear. It's just angry noise to Hanna: she doesn't know what that means. "In front" is what I should be saying. It's the all-encompassing command that means *Stay in range, Hunt to the front, Look back at me.*

After I catch my breath, we get started again. *Patience,* I tell myself.

The day is more cloud than blue sky, very bright when the sun finds a seam in the cumulous clouds to pop through, but then too dark for sunglasses when the clouds cover the sun again. Under the beeches the light itself is yellow when the sunlight makes the overhead leaves glow incandescently, then the same leaves shade the bright sky when the sun passes back behind the clouds again.

At the edge of some alders along the top of the hillside, Hanna almost has a point on a woodcock. When she starts to work scent I encourage her to go ahead, and she busts the bird. I bring her back and stand her up, showing her what she should have done.

Would she have pointed that bird if I had left her alone?

On my first couple of attempts training gun dogs, the young man that used to be me created two successive false-pointing Brittanys by encouraging caution-in-extreme whenever they found scent. That was a mistake. Now I encourage boldness. Of course birds are going to get bumped before any puppy can discover the right combination that makes for productive points. There is a William Blake adage that says, "You never know what is enough unless you know what is more than enough." Hanna's pointing instinct keeps trying to kick in. She just needs to be shown how to handle it.

In a cutover area, the goldenrod is still vibrant. It smells faintly of licorice, and the Queen Anne's lace unmistakably of carrot. In the warmth of Indian summer, a few bees still hum as they visit the sprays that haven't dried up. I keep checking unusual weeds and bushes for those mystery seeds from the grouse's crop in Vermont, but so far I haven't been able to make the connection.

There should be woodcock among the whippy saplings, but not today. After a half-hour we drop down and hunt along the brook, then return along the hillside by a different route, but if there are any woodcock here we can't find them. By noon we've flown only the one bird that Hanna bumped.

There seems to be an almost predictable mid-October lull in the woodcock migration. Perhaps the local birds and early migrants have departed and haven't yet been replaced by the main body of the population. Maybe it has something to do with the phase of the moon, although I've never put a lot of stock in the *migrate-by-the-moon* theory. The only basis I know of for the lull is empirical: that is, most years it happens.

We're taking a break, and the gun is across my knees as I sit on a deadfall. This is the second year I've hunted with the Beretta Ultralight over-and-under. It's a 12 gauge—something I thought I'd never use after thirty-plus years with various 20-gauge shotguns.

When it comes to grouse guns, William Harden Foster's description is as accurate today as it was sixty years ago when he wrote, "The gun must be of a design that is easily carried to the spot where it is needed, then it must be of a configuration to allow it to be used to maximum efficiency."

Of significance in his somewhat stilted definition is that the *carrying* part comes first; the best gun in the world won't do you any good if you're too pooped to do what it takes when the birds finally decide to fly. Thus, I had always opted for the lighter weight of a 20-gauge gun. And in truth, the 20 was usually enough.

But in a nod to the second half of Foster's definition, there could never be an argument that the 12 gauge produces superior ballistics. So when Beretta brought out their 12-gauge Ultralight, I had to try it. It wasn't that I wanted to hit more birds, just cleanly kill more of those that I did hit. And, in that respect, it worked. By using a bigger-gauge gun that carried as easily as my old 20, my percentages of clean kills on grouse improved significantly: 75 percent with the 12 gauge as opposed to 65 percent in my best years with the 20 gauge.

But then the stock broke.

One morning I unzipped the case and found that a piece of the stock the size of an oatmeal cookie had broken away just behind the receiver. The fracture was due to a flaw in the wood. I'm enough of an engineer to realize that when freshly broken pieces are out of alignment, an internal strain caused the break.

Since I needed the gun to complete the season, I made a repair that involved waterproof glue and sandpaper. It wasn't pretty, but at least the gun was returned to service.

The broken stock should have been no big deal. The gun was under warranty, and I planned to return it to Beretta once the season was over. It wasn't really anyone's fault. A gunstock is only a piece of wood, after all. Sometimes it's difficult to discern a good hunk of walnut from another with the San Andreas fault running through it. So in January I packaged the gun and sent it back to Beretta USA with a note and a dated copy of the sales receipt to verify my claim.

But instead of a new butt stock, I got a terrible runaround from Beretta, one that involved a bunch of testy phone calls and letters to the corporate president and out-and-out fibs being told by their service manager. Ultimately, they refused to honor their warranty. The gun had been abused, they said. Their opinion was based on the condition of the finish, which looked pretty much the way all new finishes do after an eighty-day season in the uplands.

So I tell everyone to be aware that although Beretta's shotguns are under warranty for a year, actually using such a gun for genuine hunting constitutes abuse and will void the warranty.

Absently, I run my fingers over the nearly invisible line of the repair. It wasn't a big deal. The break has been reinforced from the back side, the grip recheckered, and the stock refinished. I still really like the shotgun. It is, in truth, the embodiment of Foster's definition of a grouse gun: it's fast, it's light, and it kills birds efficiently.

Terrific gun, less-than-terrific company. It's a shame Beretta's warranty is no more durable than their cheap epoxy finish.

When Hanna and I get back to the truck there are swallows on the wires, sitting shoulder to shoulder, and a few individuals flutter up and sit back restlessly. They've flocked up in preparation for their migratory flight to who-knows-where. I know they eat only insects, so I'm surprised they haven't left earlier.

It's Indian summer of a relatively wet year in the middle of a dry decade. In the past few days The Color has come to western Massachusetts. It arrives in stages according to both altitude and latitude. Here in the Berkshire Hills, we're at least a week later than southern Vermont, and today the sugar maples along the road are putting off a golden light of their own.

If New England is the loveliest place to view autumn's change, it may have a lot to do with the sprinkling of spruce and hemlock in the hardwoods. The contrast of fiery color against the deep green makes it all the more lovely.

A maple leaf drifts by on the breeze, and when I look back at the swallows on the wires I find they've departed.

I stop in to visit Bobby Sazama. His mom and dad died several years back, but they were among the first landowners I made friends with when I started hunting all those years ago. There was always a percolator of coffee and a piece of pie waiting for me when I finished hunting their land. When people talk about things not being the way they used to be, I always think of Bobby's mom's apple pie. She used to put a few raisins in it, and her piecrust rivaled my mother-in-law's.

Bobby runs an auto-body shop out of the old stone barn on his dad's farm. He puts aside a disk sander and lifts his dust mask when I knock on the doorjamb. We stand around under the fluorescent light and catch up on happenings for a few minutes. I still have coffee at the Sazama place, but now it comes in a Dunkin' Donuts container.

It doesn't seem so long ago that Bobby would hunt along with me. It used to be the only time he'd get out. There was a day back in the 1980s when the woodcock were in. Hazel glided

66

from one point to another, and Bobby and I took turns shooting, passing my gun back and forth. We were still within sight of the house when we ran out of ammunition.

Another time, Amy pointed a grouse in some thick stuff. I told Bobby to get ready because I was going to drive the bird right by him. The bird went out as predicted, and I heard a single gunshot followed by several curses. When I wandered over to see what had happened, Bobby made a statement that pretty much sums up grouse shooting and all its vicissitudes. Here's what he said: "I was ready, but not THAT ready."

When I ask if he'd like to come for a walk today he only laughs. He's got the front end off a Buick Riviera, and there's a Dodge with newly rolled and pleated fenders waiting out in the driveway.

Hanna and I start down the hill past the old cellar hole and toward the fenced-in garden behind the barn. Hanna is racing full tilt—she doesn't see what's so obvious from my viewpoint—and runs into a woven-wire fence. She's thrown catapult-style onto her back. It's something that has happened just once to every puppy I've owned. Life is never quite the same afterward, and from that point on each puppy begins to look with the eyes as well as the nose. Eventually one of my dogs is going to break her neck doing it, but it seems to be a rite of passage that each puppy goes through.

If I had to rate the ten best woodcock covers I know of, the east-facing hillside down to the brook behind Bobby's place would be near the top of the list. There are old apple trees, and fields grown in gray dogwood and viburnum. There's a scattering of striped maple, sometimes called goosefoot maple because of the shape of its leaves, but the cover is more poplar than anything else.

In hunting stories it seems woodcock are always found in the alders, but for my money the poplar woods are where the woodcock are. There are several varieties in New England: quaking aspen, balsam poplar, eastern cottonwood, and big tooth aspen. From a bird hunter's standpoint it's all "popple" and it's all the same. It springs up quickly as shoots, grows tall after just a few years, and shades out the growth underneath. Farmers hate poplar because it invades fields and gardens and takes over in just a couple of seasons.

Today the hillside stands in brilliant puddles of fallen foliage. The clear yellow aspen leaves seem to universally carry a single diagonal stripe of green in autumn, even after they've fallen to the ground.

Hanna bumps a woodcock from some sumac just beyond Bobby's garden. The bird comes back overhead, and at my shot falls into a row of brussels sprouts. I lead Hanna to the spot, and after some searching she locates and retrieves the woodcock. I stand her up with the bird replaced under the sumac bushes. She points intently just long enough to realize that the bird is no longer alive.

When I look back, Bobby waves at me. He's been standing outside his shop, watching, and I feel more than a little bit guilty at being afield on his land on such a beautiful day while he's earning a living.

Hanna ranges out to fifty or sixty yards, and she's in sight most of the time even through what foliage remains on the aspens. She'll open up a bit as she gets more experience.

How far a bird dog should range is a matter of debate, and there are as many opinions as there are hunters. I know for sure that a pointing dog can work too close. A dog has to have freedom to maneuver if he's going to find and point the wary ruffed grouse. But *too far* can be tough to define. I like to watch the dog at work, so in my definition any dog is out too far when he's out of sight.

The idea of allowing the dog to wander out and find his own birds is based partially on default—it takes some doing to insist that the dog stay within a specific range. I don't subscribe to the theory that the dog knows more about where the birds are than you do. Oh, he might know how to find them when you get him into the area, but judgments about whether to look for them uphill in the oaks or down in the wet stuff are for you to make. You're the one with the brain, and the dog ought to go where you go and hunt in front of you. In that regard, puppies are always a problem. They want to go out in the skunk cabbage or run in the pines, not because they think that's where the birds are, but because they've never been there and it seems like a hell of a lot of fun to them at the time.

Controlling the dog's range is, in part, a matter of utilizing the command "In front." If Sparkey gets out too far, change directions and whistle him to the front. That's what I'm doing with Hanna today. But to stay in range and hunt where he should, the dog has to know where you are and which way you're going. He can physically come in, or simply look back at you occasionally. You really can't teach the dog to look for you—but you certainly can punish him for NOT looking for you. Sparkey will soon figure out that unless he keeps track of you he's going to get chased down and hauled back. It's an important component of *The Shotgun Method*.

Having said all that, Hanna is gone. She has been ranging out on the edge of too far all day, and now I've let my mind wander for a moment and don't know where she is. When I stand still to listen for her I hear only my pulse beating in my ears.

After spending the next two minutes whistling to no avail, I conclude she's lost.

What now? Go back? Go forward? An older dog usually doesn't really get lost because he knows about picking up his own scent trail and following it back. But a puppy—even one as smart as Hanna seems to be—probably hasn't yet figured out that trick. But I still think she's got a better chance of finding me than I have of actively locating her. I stand where I am and dig out an empty shell to use as a whistle; the shrill note will carry better than any whistling I can do with my lips. I sound off every fifteen seconds or so, and fight back the panic that keeps welling up over the lost puppy. Observing myself, I see a man under stress behaving with admirable self-control. There is a part of me that wants to run around yelling Hanna's name at the top of my lungs.

Finally, I catch sight of her running at the edge of the woods across a clearing. I holler "Hut!" and she stops, looking for me. I wave my hat, then whistle, and she makes a beeline across the field. While part of me wants to grab her ear and shake the stuffing out of her for getting lost, another part wants to praise her for coming back. Did she run off, or did she get turned around? At times like this I'm never sure what to do, so I make little of the incident and have her walk at heel until we get clear of the area.

When I send her ahead I tell her to "Stay in front now!" As if that's going to mean anything.

Hazel was a truly great dog, but she used to get lost at least once each season. After an anxious half-hour searching for her, I'd sometimes find her waiting for me back at the truck. The experiences evidently frightened her as much as they did me, so much so that in her declining years she rarely ranged very far, afraid of getting lost again.

We pass along the bottom and work the stream course. Once, twenty-five years ago, my Brittany waded the brook on a rainy day to point a grouse against the hemlocks on the other side. I got my feet wet, but made a memorable shot through an opening in the evergreens. When I turn and look uphill now, the trek back up the steep slope appears no easier today than it did then.

But halfway up, in an abandoned orchard, Hanna finds scent and races the edge of a clearing only to turn and race back again. She makes a couple of tight circles and starts off again and I'm about to call her to a halt when a grouse flushes from my feet. It twists to the left, flying low through the space between the rows of apple trees. My too-fast shot connects, but the bird only falters and keeps going. If you're like me, the gun relaxes as soon as you make a hit, and it's often tough to quickly get back into action for a follow-up shot. But this time the bird cooperates and stays in the open, and the second shot causes the grouse to veer sharply to the left and fly straight into the ground with its wings still beating.

The puppy has seen the bird come down and makes a hard charge at it, but once there she doesn't quite know what to make of the aimless ball of frantic motion that is the bird in its death throes.

I want to replace the bird and stand the puppy up on point, but the grouse still has a few stray wing beats left, and each time it shudders Hanna pounces and brings the bird to me. The grouse gets fetched a half-dozen times, and what we don't accomplish in pointing practice is more than made up for in retrieving.

There are New England asters growing at the roadside, and I pull over to cut an armload. When I mix them with a few sprays of goldenrod, the result is an Indian summer bouquet in deep purple and gold.

It's hard to believe that there aren't any woodcock around. I'm tired, and I've just hunted the best coverts on this tour and moved a grand total of two, but I still won't let it go. So instead of being reasonable and packing it in, I make a bad decision. The truck almost knows the way to the next stop on the tour. Hampden Basin is really a grouse cover that sometimes holds woodcock.

There's a bowl in the Hampden hills that I named the cover for. The slopes are grown to patchy grouse cover, but what makes Hampden Basin such a gem are barberries. The lustrous, lacquer-red fruits are among the most reliable of grouse foods. Barberries produce heavily and don't seem to be subject to the good-year/bad-year cycles that affect just about every other grouse food. The shrubs often grow in continuous oceans that

71

cover entire hillsides, yet they don't choke out the rest of the cover the way junipers do. Technically, they're an escaped ornamental rather than a native shrub, but grouse don't care. There's food and cover in barberries, and a hunter needs to go where the birds are. The bowl part of Hampden Basin is one continuous sea of the stuff.

Barberries have thorns—nothing big or serious, just small, short needles. And they don't really hurt very much, even though they will pierce the fabric of the toughest hunting pants. But whatever seriousness the thorns might lack as individuals they make up for in numbers: your legs can be scratched raw after walking through barberries. And the thorn points break off and hang up in the fabric of your pants and continue to scratch your legs long after you've left the last barberry behind.

Hanna is still full of energy, but I'm dragging. The bushes are thinly spaced along the hillside seeps where I've sometimes found woodcock in the past, but we come up empty.

With her thin puppy's coat, Hanna is no briar buster, and she works the thicker barberries timidly. We approach a stand of hemlocks and I hear a grouse flush ahead of us, then a second bird. I want Hanna to check for scent, but she's more concerned with avoiding the thorns.

We push on to a stone fence that borders posted land on the back side of a farm, and as I'm turning away one of the grouse we're chasing flushes from the other side of the fence, staying low. No shot is possible. The bird sat tight as I passed and was probably pointable, but Hanna was behind me, still queered by the barberries. It would be easy to holler at her, but she's just a puppy. I show her where the grouse took off, and when she gets a whiff of the bird she comes alive again and suddenly the thorns are forgotten.

I grin at her antics, but still, I'd have liked a decent chance at that grouse.

We work along the stone fence far enough to put us beyond the barberry ocean for the trip out. Hanna has had enough exposure to the briars for one day. As we turn away from the wall, the second grouse flies from a tree in front of me and also heads for the posted land. I'm less than ready, and although I turn and have the safety off, I'm never on the bird and he slips away unsaluted. There's nothing to do but curse.

There are more and more shots that I'm not quick enough to make. Perhaps it's a by-product of getting old. Or maybe, at least today, it's a matter of being too late in a hunt that was already too long. I glance to where the bird came from, and all that's left of a shot I was too slow to make is a single vibrating branch in the hemlock.

By the time we get back to the truck I'm exhausted. Hampden Basin might have been a good choice for the first stop of the day, but it's hilly enough to be a poor choice for the last. When I was a kid of twenty-five I didn't give a damn, but lately it's always a mistake to continue hunting when I'm tired. Now I'm worn out to a point where one night's sleep won't revive me. Sometimes I could kick myself.

Then again, there's a grouse and a woodcock in the cooler, and a bouquet of Indian summer asters so purple they almost hurt the eye. In the truck, Hanna sits looking out the windshield at me, ready and eager to be off to the next covert.

On the way home the lovely autumn colors along the roadside continue to glow even as the light fades.

Day Thirteen: Just Around the Corner

> *"Few battle plans ever survive first*
> *contact with the enemy."*
>
> Sir Winston Churchill

RON CALLED last night. He wanted to get my impression of how the bird season is shaping up so far. We spoke of the woodcock flight and what the grouse are feeding on. But "Where are you

73

finding them?" was a question I answered in general terms. I have to be careful with Ron. Although he's my hunting partner when we hunt quail in Kansas, he's as close as I come to having a grouse rival. There are some specifics about coverts and grouse that are best not revealed.

I won't grind out my own statistics until the season is over, but Ron agreed with my gut assessment that grouse numbers generally seem to be down from what we saw last year. Just what might be the reason for the reduction in the grouse population gets confusing, and I don't want to get into a discussion that borders on the *great quantum grouse cycle theory*. If the New England grouse cycle is a religion, than I'm afraid I'm an agnostic— maybe even an atheist.

It has been a terrible year for apples and grapes, and there doesn't seem to be a signal food this season—something that the birds seek out. It's easy to get a false-negative reading on grouse numbers in a year when the signature foods are down.

I asked Ron about the mystery seeds I found in the crop of the Vermont grouse, but my description didn't strike a note with him.

"How's the puppy coming along?" he wanted to know.

What could I tell him? She's a puppy. Her first point is still somewhere in the future, but she's showing good progress and at times actually seems to be hunting for something. She's not a runaway and most of the time she listens to me. She's right where I would expect her to be three weeks into the season. In truth, all Hanna lacks right now is experience.

Partyka is one of the few covers I have left close to home. Isolated by a bend in the river, it was an abandoned field when I first hunted here. It has since grown up in stands of popple and alder and some big-but-avoidable thickets of blackberry canes. Flighting woodcock favor the overgrown field, and more than once I've salvaged an otherwise ugly day by spending an hour here before quitting. It's not big, but in its favor it's only a few minutes from the end of my driveway.

The day is moist, which brings up the breath-catching leaf mold smell in the woods. Hanna stays close in the thick cover. I'm feeling smug over this marginal success when a land-mine woodcock takes me by surprise. In the thick alders there is a moment when I'm sure the chance is gone, but then the bird reappears thirty yards out as it crosses a cleared area. Woodcock in the open aren't difficult, even at that distance, and I knock the bird down.

Hanna is whistled in and brought into the clearing to make the retrieve. The bird is lying in plain sight. I go through the find-dead-bird routine with Hanna, but after a minute of un-inspired searching she wanders off. I call her back and show her where the bird has fallen, and at my insistence she picks it up without any eagerness.

So much for feeling smug.

I can train for performance, but there isn't much I can do about enthusiasm. Although I don't immediately realize it, the puppy is telling me something.

Minutes later in the same alders, I bump a second woodcock and knock that one down as well. I corral Hanna and lead her to the spot, but she's more interested in returning to what she had been doing. After some searching I see the woodcock crumpled on the ground and bring Hanna to it. Although she picks it up and delivers it to me, it's only after I all but put the bird in her mouth. I toss it out and send her to fetch, but she only gives me a whipped-dog look. The whole performance is pathetic.

"What the hell is going on?" I hear myself muttering as we start out again. *Maybe I'm pushing her too hard.*

I try to make dog training a two-part affair: demonstration first, then enforcement, which is what I'm doing here. But when I get the sort of cowering reaction that Hanna is giving me, usually it's because the dog doesn't know what I want of her. *Maybe I'm on the wrong track? Perhaps I've got to go back to the demonstration phase.* I spend the next ten minutes considering how I might retreat and start over again.

Hanna is about to show me.

We work along the river where the autumn red of the sumac seems almost luminescent, then push into another stand of twisted old alders. It's slow going—alders aren't meant for critters that walk upright—but Hanna finds a woodcock on her own. While I'm watching, there's a moment when it seems she might point the bird. But any point requires a modicum of cooperation on the part of the pointee, and this bird won't hold still when the puppy presses too close. The woodcock bounces up and heads to the right. I have the safety off but the bird manages to beat me by flying into the sun—for the next few minutes a constellation of green spots swims in my vision.

I have no idea where the bird went, but after a moment's consideration I fire a shot into the air. That brings Hanna charging through the weeds, eagerly looking to me for instruction.

"That's more like it." I scratch her ears for a few moments before returning her to the place where the woodcock flushed. As I've done before, I plant one of the dead woodcock from my game bag and stand her up on point in front of it. But she's as impatient as a little kid. "I know I know I know," she seems to be telling me.

Alders add nothing to the autumn spectacle. There are still some green leaves hanging on in the upper branches—enough to almost hide a flushing woodcock—but once summer ends their foliage seems to rust away, and most it now lies in brittle curls on the ground. Except for the branch tips, the trees are bare.

In the weeds beneath the alders the puppy finds another woodcock. Her tail starts going and she can't seem to move fast enough. Although I holler "Hut!" she's already pushed this one beyond reset, and he's up and flying before she can stop. The woodcock pretends he's a grouse and stays low, twisting through the branches, and I need two shots to put the bird down. Hanna is excited, and when I lead her to the area where I marked the bird down, she searches eagerly until she locates the woodcock, then makes the retrieve with all the gusto that was lacking in her first two.

When it comes to training bird dogs, I'm a great believer in the idea that judgment trumps schedules. But sometimes—like right now—I need to remind myself of that fact. The whole business of "shooting a few birds for the puppy to get her pumped up" has obviously run its course a lot more quickly than I would have predicted. With some dogs it takes a few weeks, sometimes more. But now that Hanna is actively finding her own birds she wants nothing at all to do with those I shoot without her help.

Hanna has let me know that it is time to shift gears. She has had a series of *almost-points,* and it's becoming obvious that her first real point is just around the corner. So from now on, if she wants woodcock, she'll have to point them before I'll shoot. The limit is three birds, so I'll have to miss-on-purpose any others she finds.

We head down to the river, more to get the puppy a drink than out of any hope of finding another bird. There is no real cover along the greasy clay bank, just the verticals of cut-leaf maples and black willows, all of a size that can endure the weeks of flooding each spring. Occasional tangles of old flotsam hang in the trees' lower branches as testimony to the river's disposition. A pair of mergansers swims out from the bank, then splashes along their own reflections as they take wing.

Hanna is in the water and glides out until the current begins to take her, then quickly returns to the calm shallows. Like Hazel, she swims well, with none of the panicky splashing characteristic of my other setters.

77

In literature, rivers have been used as allegories for just about every human experience. This one flows by on its way to join the Connecticut, and I stand and watch the current for a long moment. I can understand the principle of water evaporating and forming clouds, then condensing and falling as rain. I can also understand that same rainfall moving across the land and collecting into brooks and streams, then flowing back to the sea. What I can't get my mind around is the magnitude of what's in front of me. I'm looking out at hundreds of tons of water flowing by me every second—an amount measured in cubic acres of water.

The two just don't equate. Translating abstract ideas into reality doesn't always work out to scale, and sometimes the enormity of things just won't fit into the confines of my mind.

The river serves as a reminder. The mind can't always stretch far enough to accept the actuality of something, whether it's as boggling as geological time or as mysterious as a dog scenting a woodcock or just the incomprehensible vastness of a watershed. The fact that the brain goes into overload in trying to grasp the reality of such things makes them no less real.

I can intellectually understand the physical actuality of it. Emotionally, though, it won't go down. There's nothing to do but admit that the dimensions of my all-too-human mind limit my imagination. I guess that's faith. Or, at least, the definition of faith.

Hanna alternately stands and shakes, then lies back down in the shallows. Hazel used to have the same habit. I whistle to Hanna and we start back uphill.

The pause in the migration, if there really was a pause, is over. Today, October 17, it's taken just a half-hour's hunting to fill a three-bird woodcock limit. I don't even have to check my hunting journals. For this place, thirty minutes is about right. The birds are moving in again.

It wasn't so many years ago that the limit was five, but even that could seem ridiculously stingy when you'd hit a flight and the dog hardly moved from one point to the next. It's all a function of perspective, and the effect is the same everywhere. I've hunted in Texas, and at the day's outset a Texas bag limit of twelve quail always seems infinite. On most days it might as well be true, because you don't even come close to taking a dozen. But sometimes the dogs point three coveys before noon and things go as they're supposed to with regard to shots made on covey rises and single finds. When you check your game bag, you find that other plans have to be made for the afternoon.

It never balances out. Some days you get lucky and take three grouse with three shots, but most days you're not offered three makable opportunities. In the vein, I've heard men equivocate and say the extra birds they're shooting on a good day make up for the times they weren't able to fill their limit, but even they know they're not convincing anyone. It's what a hunter does once he has a limit that separates the sportsmen from everyone else.

In a small birch stand Hanna has located another woodcock. She kicks up dead leaves as she stops and starts and changes directions several times. Before she can get her engine over-revved, I shout "Hut!" and she manages to stop without flushing the woodcock. By the time I walk up to her she's pointing.

It's happened before, and I find myself again wondering, *Does she now scent the bird more accurately than when I called her to a stop a moment ago? Or, more likely, has the pause given her an opportunity to think with her brain and her nose rather than her feet?*

Whatever, it's a point, albeit another in the "forced" category.

I lay the gun aside and go through the staunching routine of pushing on her rear end and stroking her tail. When the bird flushes I have hold of her check cord and let her know that my vote is cast for the steady-to-wing-and-shot proposal, although that's an election I won't win for a while.

Any concerns that I might be overpressuring Hanna have obviously been a misinterpretation of her reactions. It now seems equally obvious that my decision of twenty minutes ago was correct: no more woodcock shooting unless she points. Her first honest-to-goodness point is still in the future, so I won't be pulling the trigger a whole lot, but it's apparent that she's now ready for what that particular lesson can teach.

I dodge the blackberry thickets and make my way back up the hill toward the truck. Out in front, running at top speed, is the happiest puppy in the world.

Day Fourteen: A Hurrying Wind

> *"To me education is a leading out of what is already there in the pupil's soul."*
>
> Muriel Spark

THINGS CHANGE.

The leaves are falling. There is a bit of rain in the wind gusts, and the wet hurries the leaves down all the faster. Other days might be just as breezy, but today is so much more dramatic because the wind has something to blow around. At times the effect is the same as being in a snowstorm, with yellow and brown leaves swirling around as I pass. Like snowflakes, no two leaves are quite alike, and, again like snowflakes, they're destined to "melt" and be absorbed by the soil.

I had planned on a full day's hunting, but if these sprinkles turn into showers I'll have to cut it short.

Hanna works uphill through the cover in front of me. She has already tested my resolve not to shoot

woodcock she hasn't pointed. There were two birds on the alder flats below that she bumped, but in truth I wouldn't expect even an experienced bird dog to point much of anything in this wind.

We're passing through a narrows that's a bridge between the downhill alder runs and the hillside above. Ahead of me Hanna casts into cover off to the left and stops out of my sight. I wait a moment, then go to see what's happening and find her rigid on her first unassisted point.

Some ballplayers spit on their hands before stepping up to the plate. Others adjust their hats and hitch up their pants. My own nervous tic involves partially opening the gun to be sure there are shells in the chambers. It makes no sense, of course—I know the gun is loaded. Two brass heads peek back at me when I look into the chambers. There's nothing left to do but take a deep breath and step into the batter's box.

The woodcock is just a few feet in front of Hanna and pops up to twist through the overhead branches when I approach. There's a windblown shot and a retrieve, and for the first time there isn't a need for a this-is-how-I-want-it-done lesson afterward.

Part of me wants to holler "It's about time, for cryin' out loud." But fortunately the other part of me—the part that wants to get down on his knees and welcome the puppy home—wins out. Hanna licks my face and mucks up my glasses, and it's easy to believe she's as pleased by the whole business as I am.

In dog training, things tend to happen episodically, and today we're starting a new episode. Hanna has now pointed one-in-a-row, and I'll never again be entirely satisfied with anything less. As a bird dog she's not *there* yet, but she's not below the horizon any longer, either.

When we start out again the Chief Inquisitor sarcastically asks, *Why are you carrying a camera in your vest pocket?*

Of course, I brought it to record Hanna's first point on film, and I momentarily regret not pausing to take a photo. But photos are just souvenirs and rarely capture things the way you remember them. I'm usually disappointed in the pictures I take—there are always unnoticed branches and weeds that got in the way. Instead, I've got an indelible memory of Hanna standing with all four feet solidly on the ground, peering ahead as though she had X-ray vision. I had a front-row seat for that. Some things you don't forget.

There was a time when I used to view bird hunting as a *triptych*. You've seen them—they're those medieval altarpiece paintings on three connected panels. In my version of the hunting triptych, the gunner was featured in the prominent middle section with the bird and the dog relegated to lesser roles in the wing panels. The gunner, by the way, was always me.

But things change. The gun and all it signifies isn't nearly as central as it was when I was a young man. On the triptych as I imagine it today, the shotgun and the hunter have been demoted to one of the side panels. The bird dog has become a far more important component in the mix. For that matter, so has the bird. There was a time past when birds were little more than targets, but thirty-five years of following bird dogs around the New England woodlands have given me an education—not the lessons of the academy, but something more eminent. The dog and the bird give meaning to each other, and like some lacy aquatic pondweed that looks like nothing at all when taken out of the water, each needs to be in his own element to have dimension and form. Disconnected and by itself, each section of the triptych doesn't mean very much.

Things change, and sometimes for the better. I like the view from over here on the side panel.

The sprinkles turn into windy showers. Parked at the next covert, I sit for twenty minutes looking out through the rain-streaked windshield, trying to recall the first-point occasions of my other dogs. I've got each *first-grouse-point* event in full Technicolor, filed and labeled in a prominent place in my memory, but those early woodcock points all seem to run together.

I hear from the Inquisitor again: *Indelible memory my foot.*

There's no two ways about it, I should have taken a photo. Oh, I've still got my photographic memory, but lately I'm often out of film.

The next gust plasters a flurry of wet leaves against the windshield, and it becomes obvious that today's hunting is called on account of rain. I have the windshield wipers doing double time on the drive home.

It may be one of those cosmic coincidences, but later, when I put Hanna's supper in front of her, it's the first time I'm not feeding her puppy chow. I had been weaning her for the past ten days by mixing the remaining puppy food with regular chow, and today is her first on just the adult stuff.

It's fitting. Things change.

Day Sixteen: October on the Ground

> *"Hunting makes coffee taste better in the morning and whiskey taste better at night."*
>
> Robert Ruark

WHEN I STOP at the end of the drive at Peter's house, his setter comes out to greet me. She jumps up on the door of the truck and peers in the open window, smiling her open-mouth dog's smile. Her name is Kelly, and although she always seems glad to see me, I don't flatter myself. I'm sure it's a matter of a dog equation that amounts to "When this guy shows up, we always go hunting." I scratch her ears while Hanna makes jealous noises behind the seat.

Peter wants to see what I've done with the puppy, so we're going to hunt together today. The idea took some thought before I agreed. Early on, when a dog is learning to stay in range and hunt to the front, another person can create a distraction that works against progress. But maybe Hanna has reached a stage where the presence of another hunter won't distract her. We put both dogs in the dog crate in Peter's truck and drive off.

In hunting stories, the fellows are supposed to chat about the flight of woodcock or the attributes of certain shotguns or loads. Sometimes they discuss hunting ethics or gun safety, or the pros and cons of certain breeds of bird dogs.

I don't know about you, but I don't have any friends like that. The people I shoot with and hunt with tell dirty jokes and talk about the Red Sox, or trout fishing, or playing golf, or the way the skeet vest fits the woman shooting on the next field. Oh, sometimes a missed shot is acknowledged, but usually it's just a way of razzing one another. We say polite things about each other's bird dogs, mostly in the form of left-handed compliments, things like, "A good dog like that deserves a better owner."

We drive a rutted nonroad and park outside the Overlook. Peter's dog is not happy about being left in the dog crate, and she can be heard complaining as we duck under the wire fence. There's a stretch of cow pasture that has to be crossed to get to the cover. In the distance the cattle spot us and assume we've come to feed them. They begin a mass migration in our direction, one that gathers momentum as it rolls along until it borders on a stampede. Peter and I double-time toward the far fence. In the past whenever Hanna has seen me running, I've always been after her, and now she cowers in the belief she's done something wrong. I hurry her along shouting, "Come on come on come on."

We make it to the far fence ahead of the herd. I'm not sure if they would have trampled us, but it's just as well we didn't have to find out.

There are often woodcock immediately along the top of the cover that borders the fence, and to prove it one jumps after Hanna has run by. We watch the bird twitter away, and after a long moment I explain, "She doesn't have her nose on yet."

Peter nods, but the whiteface cows peering over the fence seem disgusted.

I had hoped it wouldn't be necessary today, but I put Hanna through the routine of standing her up on point where the bird flushed. In truth, I'm not even sure if she's at fault—she just plain didn't smell the bird.

Hanna cooperates, if not patiently, then races ahead when I whistle her on and bumps another woodcock.

Now I'm embarrassed. I find I'm handling Hanna a little more roughly than necessary when I stand her up a second time.

Careful, I tell myself. There's the third-person factor at work. When you see your dog's performance through the eyes of someone else, things you might ordinarily overlook are suddenly magnified. I have a friend who swore off field trials when he realized that the only time he got mad at his dogs was during competition.

Hanna pointed a woodcock three days ago—one woodcock. There have been a couple of others since then, but even so, she has missed more than she's pointed. I'm a fool to automatically assume that she'll be perfect. A few points do not a bird dog make. I nod in agreement with my own thoughts.

We head downhill along the edge of the pasture fence. On the other side, some of the cows follow our progress, bumping each other and making heavy sounds that can be felt as much as heard.

On the slope the ash trees have long since lost their leaves, and there's a noticeable thinning today among the sugar maples. Here the leaf fall continues. In the morning light they come down like snowflakes on a dead calm day, drifting and silent. The effect is the same, too, because the fallen leaves seem to cover everything and collect upon branches and logs. My passing creates a small disturbance that sets them in motion again.

At the bottom of the hill we duck back under the fence to work the birches that have sprung up among the juniper clumps in the wet flats. Although a few yellow leaves persist here and there, the overhead branches are now bare. We are still shadowed by several young cows, but most of the others have found more important things to attend to.

Pete whistles a signal and points forward. The brush is thick, and when I come up alongside him, Hanna can be seen standing under a little crab apple tree pointing like a veteran. I wave Peter ahead and move to take hold of Hanna's check cord. The woodcock isn't where the puppy says it is, and after some wandering in the general area Peter finally kicks up the bird. Feathers fly at his shot, but the woodcock continues on and disappears into the pine woods ahead of us.

"We'll find it," I offer.

Pete shakes his head. "That wasn't a tough shot. I could've done a better job for your puppy."

"It's hard to shoot well with that many eyes watching you." I nod toward the bovine audience immediately to our rear. I would have supposed that Peter's gunshot would have spooked the few remaining cows, but they continue to stare at us.

Maybe it's luck, or maybe it's a matter of my having seen it happen so many times before: We follow the woodcock's flight line into the woods and Hanna comes to a point at the first logical spot. Under her nose is the woodcock, lying with its wings outstretched and its head down.

Woodcock aren't difficult targets, and they regularly fold when hit. But once in a while, as Peter just did, a gunner will fringe a bird with a pellet or two and it'll keep flying. Once hit they seem to die quickly. I'd bet a roll of quarters (and usually win) that any woodcock that keeps flying after leaving feathers in the air can be found dead on the ground within one hundred yards. My advice on how to win that bet is to keep the dog in close and follow the line of flight for a few minutes' walking time. Once the leaves are down and a bird can be watched after the shot, it's amazing how many of them fall or make an "emergency landing" after just a short flight.

As we hunt, Peter is on my left. When hunting two men abreast, the ideal would be if one partner was left-handed, but it doesn't often work out that way—there aren't enough southpaws to go around. Since both Peter and I are right-handed, I'm unsure who has it worse. The one on the right has to unnaturally point his gun away from the other guy, while the partner on the left constantly wonders if there's a gun pointed in his direction.

We joke about it, but muzzle control—that is, paying attention to where the gun is pointing at any given instant—has always been the essence of safe gun handling. Anything else finishes in second place.

Hanna works the cover well, and if she is distracted by Peter's presence she doesn't show it. Peter, for his part, says little and remains all but invisible. We get one more woodcock point before we're through at the Overlook pasture, and this time it's my turn to miss. It's one of those shots that's so easy I want to pick up my head to see the bird fall. In target shooting, there is an adage that says, "When you peek, all you see is a missed shot." It applies equally to a woodcock spiraling out of the birch tops; all you see is the bird's rear end going elsewhere.

During the hunting season I operate out of something that looks like, for want of a better term, an old-time doctor's bag. I believe it's properly called a *Gladstone*. I've got my sunglasses in there, a tape recorder, extra film, pen and notebook, a spare dog bell, choke tubes, a first-aid kit, and anything else I might need while hunting. It's my kit bag. Today it was easy to throw it on the floor of Peter's vehicle and mindlessly believe I had everything I'd need.

Not necessarily so.

In the glove compartment of my own truck I keep two boxes of ammunition. During the course of a day I replenish the loops in my vest from those boxes. This morning, however, my truck is parked in Peter's driveway, and my ammunition is still safely stowed in the glove compartment.

When the day started there were ten shells in my vest. Now I'm down to eight.

Peter is refilling his own vest with yellow shells. He's using a 20 gauge, so there's no mooching ammo off him. He, too, knows all about dumb mistakes, and laughs.

At the next covert, Hanna stays in the crate and we use Peter's dog, Kelly. It takes some doing to hunt dogs as a brace, and Peter and I have given up trying. The adjustment that the dogs need to make is the sort of thing they usually have to grow into. I've had a couple of successes with an old dog and a puppy complementing each other's style, but it was at best a fleeting experience and was the exception rather than the rule. Typically, when you put two viable bird dogs down together you get a field trial, with each dog trying to outdo the other. In grouse hunting that sort of thing is nearly always counterproductive. So instead, we take turns—or rather, the dogs take turns.

If ever there was dog that defined the phrase *pointing fool,* Peter owns her. Kelly is out of Bondhu stock, and at an age when other dogs have long since given up backyard games, she still creeps up on robins and doves and points them just for the hell of it. Kelly runs hard and works her birds well, and has done so since she was a puppy without much handling. I'm sure Peter thinks I'm too strict with my dogs, and for my part I think he's not demanding enough with his. The dogs don't seem to care as long as we take them hunting.

We're hunting the Tower, or what's left of it. This used to be a wonderful cover with hillside orchards straddling a swampy valley, but thornbushes have choked out the best of the place.

These "thorns" are properly known as multiflora rose, although everybody I know calls them thornberry. It grows in clumps, and it'll reach out and grab your hat as you walk by. Being a type of rose, what looks like clusters of bright red berries are actually "hips" that are a staple in the grouse's diet. For years thornberry grows as a thicket around which a hunter can navigate, but then the time comes when individual thickets begin to overlap ever so slightly and the cover quickly becomes impassable. Not *all but* impassable, not *nearly* impassable, but *absolutely, totally* impassable. I cursed and struggled with the thorns for a couple of seasons, but I've now concluded that birds that fly off into the thornberry ocean are safe from me.

On the plus side, I suppose, is the fact that nobody's ever going to shoot out the Tower as long as the de facto thornberry refuge remains. Short of a fire, the only solution to the impenetrable thorns is to turn a herd of goats loose and come back next year. This place would require a big herd.

With Peter's dog searching the cover in front of us, we skim the edges as we hunt past the orchard grown to thorns, then cross the brook and work the more open cover on the far side. There's bittersweet here, and a nice birdy section along a field of planted Christmas trees before we turn back and work the farther pasture edge on the return.

There's an unannounced shot. When I turn Peter's way he's looking skyward, searching the treetops.

"A grouse," Peter begins and ends.

The tops of the hemlocks along the brook are twined with bittersweet, and the bird must have been feeding aloft. This is part of the unique, three-dimensional aspect of grouse hunting—not too many other game birds come out of overhead trees.

"Which way?"

Peter motions uphill and we start up the side of the valley. We pass beneath some gloomy thick hemlocks. On a bright day, sometimes I get the feeling that the defeated darkness has retreated to places like this.

89

We top out and turn to the left. Peter elects to stay downhill as we follow the valley's rim. I'm on level ground on the top, paralleling his course. The dog breaks out and casts in front of me, then points abruptly in front of a clump of blueberry bushes. I whistle to Peter—our signal for point has always been the wolf whistle—and in reply he waves me ahead. I walk just five steps before the grouse runs out of nerve.

It often seems a grouse knows what's about to happen and does everything in its acrobatic power to dodge the shot. This bird, a young hen, seems to know she's been caught in the open and needs to get back into the valley evergreens. She veers sharply left on a compound rising curve and folds at my shot. Her momentum carries her into the hemlocks and she falls well down the slope beyond the little stone fence and barbed wire that defines the lip of the hill. I call Peter's dog and send her to where the bird lies, but Kelly is no retriever and after a sniff she starts off in search of something else worth pointing.

Peter walks to the grouse and brings it uphill to me.

"Did she have it pinned?" He's asking about his dog's performance.

"Solid. And she warned me to shoot quick, because the bird was going to flush your way."

"Smart dog."

I'm sure you have at least one friend like Peter. None of us are all of one piece, but Peter is something of throwback to an earlier generation. There is a part of him, a part he wears very comfortably, that seems enduringly locked in the past, a past of straight deals and straight shooters. He's an easy person to be with.

The hen has a full crop, and still has a single bittersweet berry in her mouth. We were pretty sure we were chasing the bird Peter had a shot at, but it's nice to have this confirmation.

There are three more grouse on the back side, but they thunder out unseen and cannot be relocated in the evergreens.

The birds all seem to be in trees today, and I don't have an explanation why. Pete's dog stops to sniff an accumulation of grouse turds as we pass through more hemlocks on the way back out. At least one bird must have roosted here. It's tempting to translate such observations into clues, but I've stopped. Grouse move around. Some days you'll find a dozen birds in a stretch of cover, then you'll come back a week later and find zero in the same stretch. The reverse is equally likely. They haven't migrated or been shot out, they're just somewhere else doing something else.

My dad knew a lot about the habits of wild pheasants, and could accurately predict where they'd be early and late or what they'd do in cold weather or on frosty mornings. I've been chasing grouse around for half a lifetime, and if there's a pattern to their habits I haven't gotten a good grip on it yet. Oh, I've picked up a few nuggets, but if I was supposed to replicate the sort of wisdom my dad had about pheasants, I'm a failure. One certain conclusion is this: an accumulation of grouse turds means a grouse had his rear end over this spot sometime since the last rain. Period.

We return along the edge of a low pasture where the thornberries are still in separated thickets. There are shagbark hickories along here. Their bare branches hold an eerie posture, twisting down and then curling back up again. Like all nut trees, at the end of the summer they simply shed their leaves. Here and there a leaf will turn a dirty yellow for a day or two, but mostly they just dry up and fall off. Once on the ground, a treeful of fallen leaves doesn't amount to a decent pile of crumbly brown remnants. Evidently, nature forgot the hickory when the invitations were sent out for the party that is autumn in New England.

At the edge of the pasture, Peter's dog finds a woodcock. We approach her point, hoping for a grouse but expecting a woodcock, and when the bird flushes Peter takes it cleanly. I mark the bird's fall and go to make the retrieve, but almost immediately Kelly points again.

"Tell her to hang on until I can find this bird."

The woodcock is not lying where I marked it, and Peter leaves his dog and joins me in searching the heavy grass. Finally he spots the bird. It is suspended a few feet off the ground, caught in a thornberry bush. Even with Peter's assistance, it takes some careful arm maneuvering to reach in and extract the bird from the thorns. I'm thankful for leather gloves and long sleeves.

Kelly is still on point when we return, but has lain down. It's been a long five minutes. I move in front of her, but nothing develops. Peter makes a walking imitation with his fingers when I glance back at him. "The bird has walked out," his pantomime says.

I wave my arm in a reply that says, "Send the dog ahead."

Kelly moves forward, then slows to a creep and points again after crawling under a thornbush at the edge of a thicket. People dream of a dog with a choke bore nose—one who points birds at some unbelievable ranges of a hundred yards or so. That may be okay out west where a hunter may have to get off his horse and load his gun before walking in. I've shot behind a few dogs like that. For that matter, in open cover when the wind is right all of my own dogs have had some long-distance points—never one-hundred-plus yards, but at least forty or fifty. It's remarkable, but whatever the advantage of such long-distance pointing is, it's lost on me. In a typical woodcock cover, a point without the bird immediately to the front doesn't hold much meaning. Hell, there are a bunch of places where even I could go on point and give odds that there'd be a bird somewhere within the next one hundred yards. That's little help. No, a New England gun dog has to find birds and then SHOW the hunter where they are.

And now Kelly has done just that, but neither Pete nor I particularly wants to struggle into the thorn thicket to flush this one.

After a pregnant pause, Peter breaks radio silence. "It IS your turn."

Like a kid making up the rules to an invented game, I tell Peter, "It doesn't count if the bird falls in the briars."

There's a little space beyond this first bush where the bird might be. Hunched down, I walk backward until the branches catch my back, then roll outward as I step beyond the bush—sometimes you can shake the thorn's grip by rolling away. I've nearly unlatched myself when the woodcock flushes. The gun comes up and I have a good sight picture, but never fire. The bird would have fallen in the expanse of thornberries, and I'd rather pass.

Peter grins. "So much for your turn."

A minute later Kelly points a third woodcock beneath a hickory, and this one flushes right back into my face when I walk in. I turn and take the bird cleanly. When I reload, the number of empty shell loops serves to remind me that there are just six shots left for me in the day.

We put Hanna out at the Forgotten covert. It's not a big place, just a twenty-minute walk along the bottom of a hill down to a pond that some beavers engineered a few years ago, then back up again. All along the downhill slope there are small springs—*seeps* would be a more accurate term—that create mini-swamps favored by woodcock. We'll hit those on the return trip.

We're not out of sight of the truck when Hanna finds a bird in some birches along a stone wall. In the moment before she points her back legs seem to go weak and she sets up with her rear end lower than her front—an imitation of the style Hazel displayed on her woodcock points. In the brushy cover the bird eludes Peter's shot and passes well to the front of me.

As an aside, I should say that when I'm running low on ammunition, acting conservatively is nonproductive. I don't know about you, but that sort of thinking just hampers the flow of my shooting. The only approach that works for me is to continue to shoot as if I have two boxes of ammo in my game bag, and when the shells run out I open the gun and go home.

Having said that, I'll add that this longish crossing opportunity is the sort I would normally pass up, and I would have if Peter hadn't yelled, "Take that bird!"

I hate excuses almost as much as I hate missing. After the shot, Peter asks if the bird is down. My stock answer is, "I threw him back."

In this case, I threw him back twice.

We work the rocky edge of the hill down to the beaver pond, hoping for grouse but finding none. A pair of black ducks flushes close to us as we approach, then circles back over to have a look at the sort of guys who pass up sucker shots at jumping ducks.

When we start the return trip we find that a few woodcock seem to have thought the hillside seeps were a good place to stop over. Hanna bumps one, then works the scent of another. She doubles back on her trail, then takes a left and eases ahead ten feet before coming to a point. Up until now it seems she has only pointed the birds she has run into, so the fact that she found one ON PURPOSE is significant. Hanna is beginning to happen to the woodcock rather than the woodcock happening to her.

There are two birds in front of her. They get up not as a genuine double, but as a report-pair, and I take one with each barrel.

Once Hanna has retrieved the second bird, Peter, who deplores unnecessary talk in the coverts as much as I do, pauses to pay the dog a compliment: "The last time I saw your Hanna, she was sight-pointing a wing that you dangled in front of her with a fishing rod. It's getting easy to forget that she's just a puppy."

I'm flattered.

We already had four woodcock when we started at the Forgotten covert. I've even got a pair of shells left when our collective limit is filled.

About limits: It's always a mistake to expect that sort of success—or even enough shots to have filled a legal limit. In hunting, failure is the norm. It's a real and usually unavoidable part of what we're doing out there, and the common bitterness of it makes the occasional success all the sweeter. Things don't always work out. None of us routinely shoot as well as we know how, the scenting conditions aren't always ideal, it's too hot or too cold or too wet, we turn the wrong way or the sun is in our eyes or the waterproof boots aren't. Some days you get chicken, other days, no matter how hard you try, you get only chicken feathers.

There was a time when failure was hardly ever noted in outdoor writing. Nash Buckingham was a case study of that particular style. Nothing ever went wrong in his stories—the weather was always ideal, birds were always killed cleanly, and there was always another covey over the next hill. On the rare occasions when someone actually missed a shot it was a lesson used as a path to a greater success. Robert Ruark may have been the first outdoor writer to make more than a passing mention of failure being part of hunting. Then Gene Hill came along with a self-deprecating style that trumped Ruark's, and in a rush to imitate Hill's success the entire outdoor-writing world quickly became a celebration of missed shots and botched opportunities. These days, nobody wants to write about accomplishment; indeed, success is out of fashion and politically incorrect. If it appears at all in a modern hunting story, it has to be a function of luck, not something a hunter earns through practice and hard work.

As a case in point, I read a letter to the editor recently that said, "[So-and-so] wrote of taking a limit of grouse two days in a row, and had photos to verify his hoggishness." Wow. The guy being scoundrelized took a legal limit, but it has become popular to label as a game hog anyone who takes more birds than he can eat at one sitting. It's not that today's sportsman is incapable of success, it's just that he's not allowed to be successful without feeling guilty about it.

But let's pay reality the compliment of acknowledgment—nobody goes afield with the intent of failing. Fruitful expectation is the stuff that propels all of us forward, and the thought that you might actually be successful enough to take a limit is part of those expectations.

Hunting is about having fun, after all. If shooting birds wasn't fun I wouldn't do it, nor would anyone else. But it IS fun—so much so that as soon as I do it, I want to do it again. That's not a crime or a sin; that's fruitful expectation. I'd be the first to agree that total numbers of birds taken are not all-important, but I at least want SOME. A few too many outings with too few birds, too many missed shots, and lousy dogs will find the outdoorsman spending his time elsewhere, no matter how much "communicating with nature" he does while he's out stomping around.

That's what I think. Not that my opinion counts for much.

We bump a fourth bird that Hanna has missed, but then she points again beneath some alders. For once the superb woodcock camouflage doesn't work, and the bird can be seen sitting patiently in front of Hanna's point. When Peter flushes the bird I hold tight to Hanna's check cord to keep her from breaking, and we watch as the woodcock pops straight up, making squeaky-toy noises, and heads for parts unknown.

Back at the truck we sit on the tailgate, sipping lukewarm thermos coffee while the dogs sprawl in the fallen leaves and the afternoon sunshine. October is on the ground all around us, and in the distance a grouse can be heard drumming a salute to the season.

I shouldn't feel this good. All I've done, really, is walk around and get tired. Oh, I shot the gun, knocked down a few birds, and watched a young dog fulfill the promise of her breeding. Peter and I haven't shared more than a few minutes' conversation in the past four hours. All this on a fall day in the middle of my life.

So why is it that I'm so happy?

I don't have a definitive answer. What I know for sure is that when the sky turns the infinite blue of October I'll continue to follow my bird dogs knowing there is no place on earth I'd rather be, and no other thing I would rather be doing. Nothing else comes close.

CHAPTER THREE

Between the Fall and the Snow

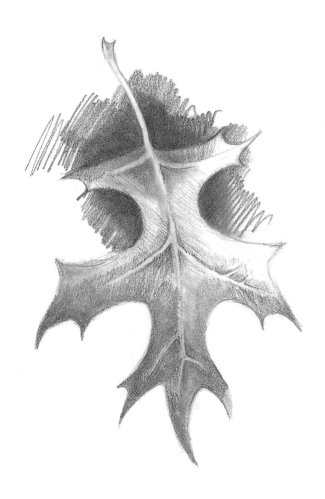

Day Eighteen: Stay the Course

"Experience, like a pale musician, holds
A dulcimer of patience in his hand."

Elizabeth Barrett Browning

THE MORNING IS overcast and dull when I pull off the road and
park outside of Tripwire. I spend a minute to scribble a reminder
to myself on a Post-it note: "Pick up flowers." If I stick it to the
steering wheel there's a good chance I'll see it on the way home.
It's Susan's birthday.

This covert is a half-mile of aspen woods that provides a
textbook example of forest succession that took place while I
was watching. Thirty years ago, when I was a young man and a
pheasant hunter, Tripwire was a recently abandoned tobacco
field grown to weeds. In this part of the world tobacco is mostly
shade-grown wrapper leaf for cigars. The "shade" in shade-
grown is provided by cheesecloth netting, so it all requires an
elaborate arrangement of poles and steel support wires across
the entire field.

When I first hunted pheasants here, the posts and overhead
wires were still strung up across the eighty acres that a tobacco
farmer had decided wasn't worth the effort any longer. Untended,
things had begun to break down even then, and it was easy to
find a fallen wire to trip over.

One day, while looking for roosters, my dog kept pointing
woodcock. I thought it was unusual to find so many of them out
in an abandoned field, but a closer look around revealed that the
"field" had begun to give way to sumac, gray birch, and poplar.
In the clumps where the young trees had grown tall they had
shaded out most of the weeds and grasses beneath them. The place
was becoming a woodcock cover.

That was years ago, and the land continued to change. The
aspen forest flourished and Tripwire became a bona fide hot
spot. It took only fifteen years or so for the fast-growing aspen

101

to mature, then the birds went elsewhere. Oaks and white pine took hold in the shade beneath the aspen trees.

During the 1980s, a developer thought he was going to do something with the land, but quit after bulldozing a dozen acres. The aspen came back up in the cleared area almost immediately, and the woodcock began returning. Then the place was bisected by a run of high-tension wires, and the cutting that took place produced plenty of edge cover—and plenty of woodcock.

In spite of the changes and the passing time, the steel trip-wires persist, springy as ever and none the worse for a coating of rust. After all these years it would seem they'd have wasted away, especially since several abandoned cars in the near corner of the cover have all but decomposed during the same time period. But the wires endure, and they'll still manage to trip you if you let your guard down. It's easy to do—when a dog is excited and busting birds and you need to get a hand on his collar quickly, the tripwires are far from your thoughts.

Hanna has adopted one of Hazel's old traits—she likes to reach down and grab her bell in her mouth when we start off. Today, she runs around like that for a minute until she encounters a woodcock in a stand of sumac hard against the wall of thick stuff at the edge of the aspen woods.

With the bell still in her mouth she stands on point. I go to her, figuring the woodcock will flush toward the clearing to the right, but the bird sneaks out low and disappears into the aspens before I can catch more than a glimpse of him.

Woodcock, when they're in the relative dark beneath the forest canopy, seem to prefer to flush toward light; usually an opening where the sky shows through the foliage. But like nearly everything else about woodcock, that tends to be a percentage bet rather than a sure thing. On a quiet and gloomy day like this I'm not betting on anything.

Sometimes there are grouse in Tripwire. They come out of the bordering oak and hemlock woods to feed on the bitter-

sweet that grows in several extensive tangles along the back of
the covert. We head off in that direction on the premise that any
woodcock will stay put while we see if the grouse are visiting
the bittersweet. The reverse is not necessarily true.

As we're passing through an opening, a woodcock takes flight
in front of Hanna. It must be the same sneaky bird we flew out
of the sumac, which would explain his jumpiness. Woodcock
usually don't hold well for an immediate second flush. Even so,
I call Hanna in and stand her up, then do the trick with my hat
thrown in the air. She seems to be mildly interested, but is glad
when I whistle her ahead. She pays no attention to my hat lying
on the ground.

In the aspens the leaves are down, or at least 95 percent of
them are. The oaks will be the last to change; they're still green,
but the leaves are leathery and dark. Throughout the uplands the
vibrant greens of June are a thing of the past. Only the ferns remain springlike in those low areas the frost has skipped over.

Up ahead, the first of the bittersweet tangles show bright
orange through the vertical aspens, and several blue jays fly up
onto the lower, branches as we approach. Grouse aren't the only
birds that seek out bittersweet berries.

The growth gives the false impression of being a glowing
mass of orange, but there is nothing orange about bittersweet. The
berry is tomato red and the husks are a dull yellow color. It's an
illusion—no solid orange color could shimmer as this mixture
does. In painting, that trick is called *broken color.* The romantic
painter Delacroix made it famous, and the impressionists played
it and played it and played it.

Hanna slows and puts her nose down as she works scent
among the tangles, and when she points I approach with the gun
at ready.

Grouse—gotta be, I'm thinking. But she softens as I walk
abreast of her, and after a moment she moves ahead. A glance at
where she was pointing reveals a puddle of woodcock crap on
the fallen leaves. Up ahead, about a hundred feet away, Hanna is

pointing again, and again she softens as I get to her. She's standing by another white splash. When I send her ahead she bumps the woodcock she should have known would be there.

Some guys claim they regularly have woodcock run from their dog's point. I won't say they don't, but running is not part of the woodcock's modus operandi. As evidence, just compare their legs: a pheasant is built to run and runs like hell; a woodcock, with scrawny little legs, trusts to camouflage as its first line of defense. Oh, I know that on occasion an individual woodcock will walk away from a dog's point. I've been there and seen it happen, but not very often. Similarly, once in a great while a baseball pitcher will hit a home run. There are, after all, exceptions to every rule. But for the most part, pitchers pitch and woodcock sit still and trust their camouflage.

As further exculpatory evidence in the running-woodcock argument, whenever one of my dogs seem to have such a runner, she moves from one puddle of woodcock crap to the next, just as Hanna did moments ago. Admittedly, I'm no expert on the defecation habits of woodcock, but it seems logical that a running bird is not going to crap a dozen times in a few minutes. Rather, it's an arguable conclusion that the bird isn't running at all. Instead, it's feeding, and what the dog is following is not the fresh trail of a running bird, but old trail the woodcock left behind as it sauntered around probing for worms beneath the poplars.

I've often made the argument that the maze of strong scent a woodcock lays down is actually part of an evolved defense strategy against four-legged predators. And I'd further speculate that the puddles of crap are an integral part of that stratagem—they play the part of decoy woodcock. I don't know if I've ever convinced anybody with my argument, but that's my story and I'm sticking to it.

Whatever the purpose, each puddle must have a world of scent coming from it, because even an experienced dog will point woodcock crap once in a while.

There are no grouse in the bittersweet today, but Hanna mishandles another woodcock before we're clear of the tangles along the back side. Young dogs like to put their nose down in the leaves and get a snootful of that strong footprint odor. Of course, a good dog is supposed to keep his head high and home in on the bird's body scent. I've tried to teach that, but mostly my dogs have taught me that they'll put their noses where the scent is and figure out for themselves how to find woodcock-the-bird rather than woodcock-the-smell. It's a sooner-or-later, inevitable sort of thing that just takes a little experience, and Hanna is on the steep part of the learning curve.

Somebody told me that a stand of aspens is almost always a clone; that is, each tree is an aboveground extension of the same root system, so it's all one plant. The way new shoots seem to jump out of the ground after the trees are cut lends credence to the clone idea.

For the past several seasons the cutover area beneath the high-tension wires has grown up until it's now incipient woodcock cover. Given how these things work, the power company will soon come along and brush-hog it all to smithereens in order to keep the right-of-way open. But for now, at least, the new growth holds promise.

Hanna is working scent in front of me as we hunt beneath the wires. I wait, expecting a point momentarily, but she decides she's mistaken and moves ahead. Two woodcock pop up, heading in alternate directions. I go to the puppy and stand her up, but there's woodcock crap on the ground all around us. When I send her ahead a third woodcock flushes barely five feet away. In outdoor stories like this, the dog trainer is supposed to smile when that sort of thing happens. Although I'm showing my teeth, nobody is going to mistake my expression for a grin.

105

A minute later Hanna has found more birds. She nearly points, then changes her mind and moves to the right. From the left, not one, but two woodcock pop up. When Hanna stops-to-flush, a third bird jumps from the same vicinity.

"Go ahead eeeasy," I tell her, and a fourth gets up.

Can this be the same dog that Peter complimented so highly the day before yesterday?

Hanna works scent, stutter-steps indecisively, almost points before changing her mind, and bumps more birds. At one juncture there's an opportunity for a triple when three birds get up together and fly off lazily against the overcast sky.

We started in beneath an erector-set sort of structure that serves as a tower for the high-tension wires, and by the time we've worked the two hundred yards or so to the next tower we've flown eighteen woodcock without a point. There's simply too much scent for the puppy to unravel, and she can't seem to home in on just one bird among the multitude.

It's important at this stage of Hanna's training that I not shoot woodcock she hasn't pointed. Okay, but this is torture.

Steady, boy, I tell myself. *Stay the course. It isn't like she's not trying.* This morning we were barely out of the truck when she pointed a woodcock, so it's not a matter of her having forgotten how.

At the end of the run it's time for a break, and I spend a minute on one knee, scratching Hanna's ears and telling her she's a good dog. Hanna is eight months old today. Sorting out scent when conditions are overloaded with the smell of dozens of woodcock seems a lot to ask of a puppy, particularly in light of the fact that she was innocently piddling on the cellar floor just five months ago. It's not hard to imagine that she's as frustrated by all this as I am.

The birds flew in every direction, so we might get some points on reflushes if we give them some time to sit—twenty minutes or so should do it. It's a matter of allowing the birds to fall back to sleep. They're nocturnal feeders and fly-by-night migrators, so they sometimes snooze through most of the day-light hours. The idea that a hunter wakes up a woodcock when he walks in over a point might serve to explain some of the crazy things the bird does when it flushes.

We hunt the far pine edges and chase a grouse around for a half-hour. There are expanses of gray birch trees here, all of them bent double with their tops touching the ground after having been distorted by a spring snowstorm a few years back. Their posture is never anything to write home about, but these particular pretzel-twisted birches make an impenetrable thicket. If we ever had a chance to relocate the elusive grouse, that chance evaporates when the bird retreats into the birches on its second flush.

As we return to the aspens, a hawk is soaring overhead with a half-dozen crows after him. He seems oblivious to his harassers, and it's easy to admire his stoicism.

There was a time when I tried to become a hawk expert who could identify something other than redtails and sparrow hawks. Then I discovered that some species had light and dark morphs, winter and summer color phases, adult and juvenile plumages—enough variations to baffle even a genuine ornithologist.

Hawks are supposed to be the great enemy of grouse, but grouse have little to fear from buteos—the broad-winged, soaring hawks. Harriers and falcons might be considered candidates, but they are not woodland hunters. Accipiters are. Of that group, goshawks are famously linked to grouse predation in a knife-is-to-throat relationship, but they're scarce to rare throughout their range. The jury is still out on the Cooper's hawk, a more com-mon accipiter, but outweighed by an adult grouse. Owls seem to be a greater threat, particularly barred owls that often hunt in daylight and are very common in the Northeast.

As we return to the vicinity of the power lines a woodcock takes flight ahead of Hanna and disappears beyond the gray treetops.

107

"So much for the idea of resetting these second-flush birds." Things must be bad if I'm talking to myself out loud.

But then, within sight of the power-line clearing, Hanna skids into a point without first working ground scent. She stands there firmly, pointing what has to be one of the birds we flushed, sitting in a pool of its own scent right where it landed.

When I circle to the right, I stumble on a tripwire and inadvertently shake bushes in both directions along the line it makes through the cover. Of course, the woodcock in front of the puppy takes flight. He crosses left-to-right, pretending to be fast, and goes down at my shot.

When I send Hanna to make the retrieve, for once she doesn't come directly back to me. Instead, she prances around delightedly for a few extra moments with the woodcock held high, and when she sits to deliver the bird her wagging tail fans away the dried leaves on the ground. Anyone who pretends that dog training doesn't include the dog's own feelings hasn't been paying attention.

My journal entry for October 22 will show that we moved twenty-four woodcock by day's end, which is more a calculated estimate than an accurate count. What's not a guess is that Hanna had six woodcock points. Five of them came after the nightmare under the wires. It would have been easy to allow myself to become angry with her when she was bumping birds and, of course, she would have reacted to that anger. Instead I was patient, albeit in a teeth-gritting sort of way, and a difficult situation became a lesson for the puppy.

I'm not sure if the young man that used to be me would have held his temper. That fellow, when last I was him, was an impatient SOB. He would have ended up with a cowering dog for the rest of the morning. A few too many angry mornings and he'd have a cowering dog permanently.

There is an overused baseball cliché that says a pitcher must *stay within himself*. I've never really heard anyone define what that means, but I assume that when a ballplayer tries to do more than he's capable of, he is no longer pitching *within himself*. To a degree, this might be applied to dogs, but is far more accurate when applied to dog OWNERS. We all must be forgiving of a percentage of honest mistakes, and try to realize what's possible and what's not.

Though some would have us believe otherwise, progress isn't always a straight line upward. Be patient and stay the course.

And pay attention to the notes you leave yourself. Otherwise, you'll forget the flowers on your wife's birthday and have to run back out to the florist's before she comes home.

Not that anybody I know did anything like that.

Day Twenty-Three: Calendar Pictures and the Evening Star

> *"There have always been two major problems: Man and man, and man and earth, his environment. Neither stands alone, and the false solutions always turn out to be the ones that ignore that eternal kinship."*
>
> Hal Borland
> "Winter Sky"

LAST YEAR I BOUGHT some maple syrup from an old Vermont farmer. It was in December and a foot of snow covered everything, but even so it was apparent that his dairy farm was a lovely arrangement of stone walls and pastures that looked like an illustration from a Thornton Burgess storybook. Out back there was a nice woodcocky-looking swamp grown to soft maple and alder. When I asked him then about hunting his land, he invited me to stop by anytime.

Anytime has come.

Once the truck is parked I stick my head into the barn and several outbuildings before finding the farmer in a garden behind the house. He's talking with another man, and returns my wave.

"When I looked out in the barn and asked those black-and-white cows where you were, all they said was 'Moo.'"

Mr. Snow, as I later find his name to be, gives me what passes for a blank look. "You won't hear them say much more than that."

I have to listen closely because he speaks a near-foreign language called *Yankee*. If you've been to Vermont or anywhere in northern New England, you'll know the way he spoke that sentence. It came out sounding like, *Y' want hea 'em say much mo 'en 'a-at*. That is, if you can say all that without moving your lips.

When I extend my hand I get a firm handshake in return.

"I spoke with you last winter," I say. "I took home some of your syrup, and left you some of my money. I'm pretty sure I got the better of the deal."

Both men laugh. We visit for a few minutes and talk about the weather and the state of the fall garden they're examining. The other man turns out to be old Mr. Snow's son. Then it's time for the crucial question:

"If I assured you I could tell the difference between a partridge and a Holstein cow, would it be okay if I hunted the woods behind your pasture?"

"Oh, we don't mind you hunting," the son says. "But make sure you take down your tree stand. We've got guys banging nails into trees out there and then leaving all that junk behind—"

Old Mr. Snow cuts him off. "What d'ya think he was talking about when he said he could tell a Holstein cow from a pa'chige? He's a bird hunter, ya dumb cluck."

It's hard to keep from laughing. "Dumb cluck." I hadn't heard that expression since I was a little boy.

I've never met the fabled *typical Vermonter*—the one who says "You can't get there from here." Instead, virtually all the people I've met are friendly, generous, and open. I try to be the same, and have had a twenty-year run of success so far.

There's a rutted road that leads to where they've asked me park the truck. Along the bordering rock wall the sugar maples stand knee-deep in golden pools of their own leaves, looking for all the world like a calendar picture for the month of October. When the day arrives that I can't hunt any longer, I'll still come up here, if only to paint Vermont during the autumn. Even after the leaves are on the ground, the shadows are deep and cool on a starkly sunny day such as this.

There's an electric fence all around the pasture, but Hanna and I dodge that and head into the woodcock cover. In the maple swamps the trees are as bare as January—there's hardly a leaf left aloft. The ground is muddy where water seeps out of the hillside, and passing cows have made deep holes in the mud. Here and there dense balls of red berries on withered stems are all that's left of last spring's jack-in-the-pulpits.

Just beyond some standing water, Hanna points tentatively with her backside low. I whistle to her to go ahead, but she only becomes more staunch.

After a brief struggle in the mud, I walk to and beyond the place where the woodcock should be, but nothing happens. If grouse are professionally nervous, then woodcock are professionally patient. Somewhere in front of Hanna, this one continues to wait. I kick the nearest bush then walk back and kick a few more, still without result. When I let my guard down is, of course, when the woodcock gets up. What would have been a makable shot now becomes a hurry-up affair that's cleanly missed.

But the bird is a short-hopper and drops back down just a hundred yards in front of us. Hanna has seen the bird land, and, after looking back at me for a long moment, she goes directly to the spot and points again. She doesn't realize it, of course, but she's imitating Sophie, who was a specialist at that sort of thing.

Sophie was never a chaser. Instead, she always paid attention to where the flushed bird came down. She would circle and point—a point that spoke more of her powers of observation than her bird-finding ability. As evidence, sometimes she'd mark the bird behind a certain bush, then would lose track of which bush it was and point in the wrong place. But the performance was always fun to watch.

We're in some skinny swamp maples now, and at the flush this woodcock finds some flying room beneath the overhead tangle of branches and twists off through the tree trunks. I follow the bird's flight with the gun down, waiting for a shot that never develops.

There are spruces and tamaracks interspersed with the alders along the back side of the swamp. Just beyond another boggy cow path Hanna works scent, then cuts sharply to the right and, after a few steps, points again. Among the evergreens, the bird bounces up too close. I rush the shot and miss. Woodcock are slow enough that most are taken by shooting directly at them and letting the size of the pattern make up for whatever small lead needs to be addressed. But when the bird is as close as this one, the shot pattern hasn't opened up, and when it whizzes past the woodcock floating twenty-five feet away it can't be more than the size of a grapefruit. It's just as well I didn't hit the bird.

That one's gone, but sometimes woodcock can be found in pairs or trios, and I make a habit of working the dog in a tight radius around the spot where we've found a single. This time that tactic pays dividends, and Hanna points the bird's partner at the other end of the little spruce grove.

When it's possible to tell a hen from a cock I try to give the hens a break, and this one seems as big as a chicken when it flushes—definitely a hen. I follow the bird's flight with the pretend-pistol that is my extended finger. As always, I'm surprised at how much time I would have had to make the shot.

Unlike pheasants or mallards, telling the sex of a woodcock on the wing is not a well-defined sort of thing. Mostly it's a matter of size comparison—the little ones are usually males, and the noticeably big ones are ALWAYS hens. But sometimes you just can't tell. Grouse are easier—there's a distinctive ratio of tail to body size, and you need only get a halfway decent look at a flying grouse to determine if it's a hen or a cock.

We sit for a minute at the logical turnaround spot in the cover. So far all I have in the game bag are three empty shells. Hanna is having a good day even if I'm not. She has pointed four of four woodcock, and I haven't had to say a word to her other than "Good girl."

There's an ancient white oak out in the middle of the cow pasture. It might have grown there in the open for two hundred years, and its massive, twisting, near-horizontal branches give it a flat-topped spreading posture characteristic of old oaks. It's beautiful in its own gnarled way.

Trees can be recognizable at a distance. Elms are famous for their vase shape, and basswoods take on the form of an inverted heart if they are left alone and given room to spread. That seems to be the dual criteria for a tree to attain character: give 'em room and leave 'em alone. Pin oaks, horse chestnuts, beeches, hickories, sugar maples—all have a distinctive growth pattern.

Rather than a tombstone, I'd like to have a tree planted over my ashes. It doesn't really matter what kind, just as long as it's far enough away from buildings and power lines so that nobody will have to chop at it. That way, it can spread out and grow into something that'll give passing tree fanciers a little bit of pleasure. I'd like that.

We're returning back along the pasture edge of the swamp, following the zigzags of a stone wall and avoiding the electric fence strung along the top of it. Within sight of the truck Hanna strikes scent again, and she works up onto the wall. She stands for a moment, then turns to an indiscernible woodcock sitting close

113

on the wall's near side. As her tail comes up into a vertical point-ing position it strikes the electric fence and with a high-pitched yelp Hanna leaps forward. The woodcock flushes, and for a moment, before the law of gravity takes over, both bird and dog are in the air at the same time.

Hanna gives the wire fence a wide berth for the rest of the trip back, but seems none the worse for wear.

The undergrowth in the covers has thinned as the successive frosts have killed it off, and the going is easier. At this time of year grouse seem to migrate back into the coverts from the bor-dering hinterlands. I don't know whether it's the cold weather or a lack of cover once the trees are bare, but the numbers of birds I find always goes up after the leaves are down.

This time between the leaf fall and the snow is heaven, but I call it *November*. Oh, according to the calendar the actual month of November won't begin for another few days, but for me it started when the leaves were finally down. And it's over once there's snow on the ground, no matter what the actual date might be. In between is the time that all bird hunters wait for—good scenting conditions, easy walking, clear shots, and temperatures cool enough so that you can hunt all day. That's November.

The next stop is the back side of a mountain that I call the Alps. It's behind my friend Pierre's place, and because I call his land Switzerland, what borders it ought to be the Alps, right?

On the drive up I have to stop where a yellow birch has fallen across the road. Backing down is out of the question. This is a situation like you see in the *Road Runner* cartoons—the nar-row road clings to the hillside with a steep drop-off to the left. My truck's outside tires aren't quite hanging on the cliff's edge like they do in the cartoons, but almost.

If the tree were as big around as my arm I could probably move it out of the way, but this one's in the thigh-sized category, so I've got work to do. There's a bucksaw in the back of the truck, and it takes just a few minutes to clear the road. And if I'm going to the trouble of cutting up a windfall, the wood is going onto my woodpile at home. I'm always surprised at how heavy fresh green wood is, and how much water it must contain.

It sometimes amazes me that in a day of hunting I probably step over enough firewood to heat my hometown for a month. But who's going to go into the woods and lug it out? Since I no longer heat with a woodstove I barely go through a cord of wood each winter, all of it burned on the hearth. As such, my requirements for firewood run more to quality than quantity.

For me, hard maple and beech are the ideal—both woods burn brightly and well, they split easily, and they are in ready supply here in New England. Hickory is supposed to be wonderful fireplace wood, but breaking it down always seemed like more trouble than it's worth, even when I borrow a hydraulic splitter. Birch and cherry are nice, and although the old adage says, "Ash green is fit for a queen," those hardwoods are all out of favor with woodstove owners whose sole interest in firewood is BTU content. Universally, those folks like oak because of its superior heating potential and the fact that it'll burn all night. Oak is common in southern Vermont, but is all but unknown in the northern part of the state.

Not so long ago, a man might spend most of the winter in his woodlot, cutting and hauling the following year's supply of fuel. Back then, a snowless winter would be a major disaster: sleds were virtually the only means of transporting cordwood or anything else in the backcountry, and without snow nothing moved. According to historian Eric Sloane, a sled-load was a *cord,* which was a chest-high pile of four-foot lengths—a convenient yet stable stack when loaded onto oxen-drawn sleds, which were usually eight feet between uprights.

In the truck, Hanna has been watching me clear the road. She's impatient to get going, and makes noises that aren't quite barking to let me know it.

115

There is an expanse of honeysuckle on a hillside at the Alps. It can grow thick and be all but impenetrable in places. It's brittle and bushy with translucent red berries that grouse occasionally eat but hardly favor. About the only good thing I'll say about it is that it doesn't have thorns. There isn't much mountain laurel in Vermont, but this stuff replaces it as the "state bush" because it seems to be everywhere.

Today the grouse are in the honeysuckle, and Hanna twice works scent before a bird rumbles up nearby. I've got the safety off each time, but can't seem to catch more than a glimpse of the bird.

When it comes to dogs pointing birds, woodcock cooperate by holding still. Grouse rarely do. Pointing a grouse takes some experience, and doing it on a regular basis takes a lot of that commodity. Hanna has been working grouse scent all season long, and on a couple of occasions she has pointed *gone* after the bird has flushed, so she's getting closer all the time.

Now she's working again. There's a scattering of broken-down apple trees in the honeysuckle, and Hanna works to a gradual stop as she approaches one, then sprints ahead and flushes the grouse that was crouched on the far side. The bird stays low and is screened at takeoff. No shot is possible.

Hanna could have pointed that grouse, but ran out of patience at the last moment. She gets hauled back by the check cord and stood up where she paused before making her mad dash. I walk around and throw my hat in the air and fire the gun. Twice. I don't let her move, and show her that I'm angry.

"You gotta point that grouse!" I holler at her, just in case I haven't made it clear.

The bird seemed to have headed for a little stand of pines that juts out into the honeysuckle field. We circle to the left so that the breeze is in Hanna's face and approach the pines. Hanna puts her head in the air and works quickly through some dried goldenrod toward the pines.

Getting a grouse to hold still for a point requires two diverse attributes in a bird dog: the bird must be approached with enough *speed* so that it is afraid to run, but with enough *caution* so that it won't be frightened into taking wing. Speed and caution don't usually go together, but in this case the twain have met. Hanna points.

When I get abreast of the puppy there's a brief scramble in the dried litter beneath the pines, then just a fleeting shadow as a roll of thunder announces the grouse's departure. There's nothing to shoot at, but I fire the gun toward the treetops just to make some noise.

In the grouse-point column, Hanna's total now is exactly one. That means she's got 427 more to go to equal Amy's record. I scratch her ears and tell her she's a good girl, and then clear up something I said earlier:

"I didn't mean just that PARTICULAR grouse, Hanna. You've gotta point others, too." I shake my finger at her as I tell her this.

Don't ask me who I'm trying to amuse. Hanna looks back at me and her ears get one last scratch before she's sent ahead.

Since I joined the computer age, I don't hand-write the pages of my hunting journal any longer, but every puppy's first point has always been a red-letter day, so I'll have to do some coloring on this one when it's printed out. It's a shame I couldn't have taken the bird for her. This is like a ground-rule double: you're glad to have the extra-base hit, but at the same time you're disappointed that the runner on first couldn't score.

I shake my head. Most of the time you don't even get a shot at a flushing bird, so there's no reason to be disappointed. In the past I've been luckier than I have a right to be—on four of the six previous puppy's-first-grouse-point occasions I've managed to shoot the bird for that particular dog.

This morning I spoke to Pierre by phone, and he invited me to hunt his land. He lives at the very top of a mountain. Sometimes he accompanies me, but he won't be home today. Pierre is Stella's greatest fan. On his piece of property she once pointed more woodcock than Pierre had shells to shoot. We met when I knocked on his door and asked permission to hunt his posted land.

My mother, who is French-Canadian, once told me that Pierre's last name means "little doll." His name is *Cattin*.

When I mentioned this to Pierre, who is Swiss-French, he laughed in astonishment.

"Your mother must be Canadian-French," he said. "In French, *catin* means 'prostitute.' That's why I spell my name with two *t*'s. It's just like those Canadian-French to make a joke like that."

Gee, what do you say then?

Later I got back to my mother on that, and she did some backing and filling: "Well, literally that's what it means, but in common use everyone knows a *catin* is the sort of doll that a child plays with."

I should have known better. The French vernacular is rife

with that sort of thing. The figure of speech that means "He won hands down" is *Il arrive avec le doight dans le nez*. That translates literally to "He arrived with his finger in his nose."

The half of me that's French thinks that's pretty funny, but the other half is still scratching his head.

There's a place to park next to Pierre's garage, and a handy garden hose to run some fresh water for Hanna. Hunting Switzerland intelligently involves spending every downhill step in a wise manner, because in the end you've got to come back up. I've badgered Pierre about it, but so far he hasn't installed the escalator I've been asking for.

There's a knoll with some apple trees on it, and the switchback downhill course that I've planned skims the edge. I'll make several passes down along the east face, follow the stream along the bottom, then hunt the margins back up along the south slope and walk the road for the steepest part of the return trip.

I'm still thinking out the path I'll follow when a grouse flushes from the knoll, crossing in front of me like a station three high-house that you might see on a skeet field except that there's a lot of down-slant in the bird's line of flight. The chance is fast but well seen; I'm able to deliberately swing through the bird and it tumbles in the air at my shot.

When you've got time, take your time. I'm congratulating myself, but I also know that on surprise grouse shots like this your instincts take over. You don't have time to think things out, so those instincts had better be well trained.

There's a stream at the bottom of Pierre's mountain, and there are four woodcock in the alders along the bank. Hanna points two of them for me, crowding each bird so close that the flush takes place seemingly under her nose.

Also along the stream is a large, gray paper bulb of a white-faced hornets' nest, grown over and around several low tree branches. The leaves that concealed it all summer have deserted their post, and by now so have the hornets, I'm told. But I'm not going to find out. A platoon of hornets once built a nest under the eaves of my house. That nest was about the size of an apple. This monster along the brook could hold a brigade—maybe an entire hornet division—and I give it a wide berth.

There are several brooklets flowing down the side of the mountain to join the stream at the bottom. We follow one of them back up on the return trip. There's an open flat where some long-ago farmer built a rock dam across the flow, but all that remains of his little pond is a shallow gully grown to blueberries.

As we pass, Hanna looks into that gully, and her appearance is more of surprise than any attempt at a point. A cock grouse thunders up, heading nearly straight uphill. Although I previously mentioned that most woodcock are hit by shooting right at them, unfortunately for me most grouse are missed for the same reason. You can't shoot directly at a grouse and expect it to hold still until the shot gets there. You've got to lead them, sometimes by a lot.

None of this is news. Still, too often for my own pride, when the bird comes thundering up I forget what I know how to do and shoot right at it. The earlier cross shot was a consummate challenge, but this is the negative reciprocal of that one—the kind of dumb mistake that keeps me from getting too cocky.

We start out in uphill pursuit. There is a deep, thorny valley in the hillside where the grouse seems to have retreated. Hanna checks out the edges, then moves down into the valley until the thick-growing briars keep us from going any farther. The grouse, if he knows what he's doing, has withdrawn into the thorns at the head of the valley and is safe from us. More power to him.

We backtrack out and walk up the edge of a mowed pasture that borders Pierre's land. We've got a long uphill walk in front of us, and I follow the stone wall along the contour of the hill. That line takes us past the head of the thorny valley, and when Hanna pokes into the edge of the briars the cock grouse comes blasting out, boring straightaway across the pasture toward the woods beyond. It's a station seven low-house shot in the open and I take my time and drop the bird. Hanna is so delighted that she seems to be dancing as she makes the retrieve.

Sometimes circling a grouse will cause it to lose track of you, and when you appear from another direction the bird believes you represent a new threat. Inadvertently, that seems to be what happened here. The cock grouse outsmarted himself and kept running into the thorns until he couldn't run any farther. Then when we passed by out in the pasture he thought he was surrounded and had to flush. I wish I could say that it was planned that way. Sometimes the fish jumps right into the boat.

Ten minutes later when I step out onto the road I can see the truck in the distance, parked in the shadow of Pierre's garage at the top of the hill. I've nicknamed every truck I've owned Silver, but, although I whistle, none of them ever came running. That trick only worked for the Lone Ranger. It's a long walk back up the hill.

As I'm driving home down Route 100, the road curves and heads southwesterly. The lavender afterglow of the cloudless sunset illuminates all I see through the windshield. At the top of my field of vision something catches my eye as it flies past. It's a woodcock, buzzing along in the twilight toward the woods looming darkly beyond the field to the left. I pull the truck to the roadside and watch until the indigo dusk swallows the bird. For a long moment I sit with my hand on the gearshift, hoping for another glimpse. The evening star winks in the twilight just above the thin sickle of the moon, inviting a wish. In autumn, I don't bother making wishes because on days like this it's evident I'm living out what I'd be wishing for: a puppy's first grouse point, a pair of grouse in the cooler, a new woodcock cover found, a dozen empty shells in my game bag.

Still, I habitually allow my sense of time to spoil my pleasure. Too often I think in terms of *just three weeks of the season left*. I wish I could be more like my dogs and believe that autumn would last forever, or at least not worry about the reality that it won't.

121

Day Twenty-Five: Spring Ahead, Fall Backward

> *"Patience. A minor form of despair*
> *disguised as a virtue."*
>
> Ambrose Bierce

ON THE BACK porch, I take another look at my watch before ringing the doorbell at Mrs. Aaron's. *What if she's still on daylight saving time? Is this too early to be banging on her door? No, it's the other way around—it's later than ten o'clock.* They changed the clocks last night, and people everywhere are slightly out of step today, including me.

Before I can figure out what time it really is, Mrs. Aaron opens her door. She must have seen the truck pull up.

"I was wondering when I was going to see you, Steven," is her greeting. "My, but it's almost November."

In return I say some nice things, and ask about her children and remark about the construction of the new front porch, which is well under way. Then, as always, I go through the formality of asking if she'd mind if I hunted on her land, and she replies, "Of course not."

I've been exchanging Christmas cards with Mrs. Aaron for twenty-five years. There are a couple of my books on her shelf and I've been introduced to her grown children, but by and large our relationship is one that finds me standing on her porch with my hat in my hand two or three times each season. Her land is posted, and I'm the only one who hunts there because, she's told me, I'm the only one who ever asked. She's never taken any of the birds I've offered her, and she likes the fact that I pick up litter along her road. And that I say thank you.

Both dogs are behind the seat today, and they're peering out the rear window of the truck. As always, Mrs. Aaron waves at them, but they never wave back.

Hanna and I start in along the brook behind Mrs. Aaron's pasture. The morning is cool and bright blue, with a sky full of cirrus clouds that are supposed to be harbingers of coming storms. They're those high wispy clouds that can drive the painter in me nuts because they can only be suggested, never painted accurately.

After all the years of hunting here, the area holds more than a few memories, not all of them good. Once a few years back I reminded myself in the most graphic manner to quickly reload after shooting. It was a windy day and I scratched down a grouse with my second barrel, and fearing a down-but-not-out runner I immediately started after the bird with the gun open. The grouse had been one of a group, and the others started coming up. . . . This is painful. Do I really have to go into it again?

But today I manage to get by the little swampy hollow without reliving that nightmarelike moment of fumbling with loaded shells and empties while what must have been the covert's entire grouse population flew off one after another.

There's nothing on the near side of the brook, but as soon as we cross and negotiate the rusted barbed-wire fence on the far side, Hanna sets the tone for the day by chasing up a grouse from some evergreens. As I've been doing all year, I corral her and bring her back to where she should have pointed, but she's pumped up and unwilling to hold still for the lesson until I shake her by the ear a few times and shout "Hut."

A little later, Hanna chases a low-flying woodcock, then runs up the bird when he settles back in. *What's the matter with her today?* I ask Hanna that very thing as she gets put through the stand-up routine, but if she knows the answer she won't say.

Oh, she knows how to handle birds; she just isn't doing it. Some fellows will spend time in the off-season planting birds for their dogs—dogs that are four and five years old. The fellows have missed the point. The whole idea of using planted birds is not to teach the dog to point—well, maybe on the first half-dozen times it is, but once the dog knows HOW to point he doesn't need the sort of rudimentary lesson planted birds can provide.

The real opportunity that controlled situations with planted birds offer is the chance to handle your dog while he's on point.

Talk to Sparkey, stroke his tail, walk in front of him, pick him up and move him to the side—do everything you can to promote staunchness. Whether Sparkey remains staunch is not the major issue. What the issue IS is that you've demonstrated to the dog just what it is you want him to do on point, and in the future you'll have a basis for correcting him when he proves less than staunch.

When we hunt the hemlock edges on the return trip along the brook, Hanna seems to be making believe she can't hear my whistle. *She's regressing. She was better than this last week.* Every puppy is going to have off days—progress is not always a straight line ever upward. *The Shotgun Method* of dog training has days like this built into it, but it's mandatory that I, the trainer, don't put up with less-than-acceptable performance. I'm dealing with a puppy, after all, and if it seems she's acting like a teenager it's because she is.

Her routine of pausing in a pointing posture at the end of a cast, something I once found so cute, only grates on me today. Impatiently, I whistle her on.

There are a couple of occasions when Hanna ranges out so far that it seems she has gotten lost. I move out quickly and whistle her back. When it happens for the third time there's no *maybe* about it—she's misbehaving, and I run after her and haul her back to where she should be. In a bit of convoluted logic, I can't physically make Hanna stay in range, but I can punish her for not staying in range. That's field training, and Hanna has supposedly mastered all of this already.

After two more repetitions, I'm exasperated and put the puppy at heel for a while.

Some might argue that I'm not teaching the dog anything by having her walk beside me. I'd be the first to agree. But the only things I've ever done with a dog while I was angry are in the regrettable category. I know enough not to fall into that self-made trap again, so everything gets put on hold while the trainer cools down a bit.

Not only am I out of patience, I'm out of breath, too. I'm not the athlete I used to be. For that matter, I'm not so sure I ever was. Someday they'll find me in the woods dead of a heart attack, and it's a safe bet that it'll happen while I'm running after a free-spirited puppy-in-training. Before I kill myself, maybe I should smarten up and learn to use an electronic shock collar in these situations. I own an old Tri-tronics model that's good for what it's good for—it gives the dog a long-range kick-in-the-pants. Lately the new ones are compact versatile devices that many trainers swear by.

I've had this argument with myself a hundred times. When it comes to basic training, Hanna has to be shown what's wanted of her, and it's hard to believe that can be accomplished with an electronic push-button two hundred yards behind the scene of the crime. So I run after the dog. I don't know any other way. I'm not saying it's for everyone, but it works for me.

Back near the road in some sassafras saplings where there's always woodcock, Hanna finally points. As I've been doing all season, I give the soft, two-note "Go ahead" whistle to firm her up, but instead she elects to interpret the signal literally and charges forward to flush the bird. Worst of all, she looks happy about it. I clench my teeth.

There is a sense of relief when Hanna is put back in the truck and I let out Stella to hunt the far side of the road. *Sanity at last.*

Did I have similar troubles when Sophie was a puppy five years ago? Or Stella eleven years back? I keep trying, but really can't recollect. Oh, I remember Sophie all right. What I don't recall accurately is the order that things happened; how old she was when she learned this and that; the amount of patience I needed; the times she regressed and I worried that she wasn't making progress.

There have been a lot of puppies. Before Hanna, the line stretches back to an earlier time when I had hair and arches and the first lady's name was Lady Bird. But with the passing years who can remember anything other than a few incidents? Each new pup is sufficiently different from the one before so that time schedules and set formulas apply only generally, not specifically. With *The Shotgun Method,* training progresses through a relatively brief period of just a few months. Since there's five years between my puppies, I can't remember much of it in a time-line sort of way that would be useful now.

In my vest are a couple of beer cans and a plastic Coke bottle that I picked up near the bridge crossing. It's an unfortunate truth, but the number of people who'll throw litter out a car window far exceeds the number who'll bend over and pick it up. I do what I can, but I'm not an outright anti-litter crusader, and I certainly don't stop to cart out an old washing machine that somebody dumped along a back road.

It seems like an ironic joke that town dumps were created so people wouldn't throw their rubbish out in the street. Now they charge you money to bring your trash to the dump, so is it any wonder people take their unwanted stuff for a ride and come home without it?

Like most sportsmen, I pick up discarded cans and bottles while I'm hunting. It goes in the back of the truck to be properly thrown out later. If picking up litter isn't part of the outdoorsman's ethic, it should be.

Stella and I spend an uneventful hour hunting on the far side of the road. She points two woodcock, both passed up, before it occurs to me that I might not shoot a single one over her this year. I've been saving all the opportunities allowed by my three-bird limit for the sake of the puppy. With that in mind, on the way out I take a little male woodcock that Stella points within sight of the truck. She makes the retrieve, and I make a big deal of posing her with her bird for a picture. She's happy, and in the resulting photo Stella can be seen smiling a dog's smile with her mouth open.

At the truck, I break out the sandwich from the cooler and have lunch even though it's still early. My stomach forgot to change its clock.

If you're a hunter, you know it's aggravating to have to get up an hour earlier to go duck hunting, and have to quit an hour earlier when you're out after grouse. The simple solution, of course, is to adjust the times we go to bed and get up, but all of us live lives governed by clocks, and it's easy to feel we're getting gypped out of an hour's hunting time.

I've yet to hear a convincing reason why, in the twenty-first century, we continue to go through an obsolete exercise that was originally designed to give overworked farmers more time to toil in their fields. How many mistakes are made and how much money is lost because of the twice-a-year nuisance of switching between daylight saving and standard time? For that matter, the hour's sleep I'm supposed to save is usually spent resetting all the clocks in my house.

Mrs. Aaron is raking leaves in her front yard, and returns my wave as I drive past on the way out.

For years I wrote hunting stories and changed the names of people who let me hunt on their land. Mostly it was a privacy matter: I didn't want anyone else banging on Mr. Sazama's door and saying, "Steve Mulak sent me." But Bobby Sazama's father is gone now, and there's a part of me that knows he would have been thrilled to see his name in print in *Sports Afield* or *Gray's Sporting Journal*. Mr. Cooney's false teeth used to click when he talked, and I loved his place so much that I changed his name to Hancock when I'd write about hunting there. Mr. Cooney is gone, too, and in the town of Hampden there's now a high-end housing development on the cover that I used to call Electric Fence.

Landowners deserve our collective applause. Most land in New England is privately owned, and it would be easy for any landowner to say "No" when permission is requested. Many do, but some, like Mrs. Aaron, seem glad to have people share that part of the outdoors that she pays taxes on.

New England has a hundred Mill Rivers, or at least it seems so. Naturally, there's a Mill Street in every town, as well as a Canal Street and a Race Street, all of which speak to an earlier time when this hilly part of the world was powered by its rivers.

Along the Mill River we pull over at the cover I call Cyprus. Right where I park the truck is a grove of birch trees. On the biggest of them, a strip of bark has been torn away and the resulting scar looks like a map of the island of Cyprus. It's not the sort of thing that jumps out at you.

The frost has killed most of the wildflowers, but there's a bunch of closed gentians that are still going strong among the birches. They're in clusters, a deep purple wildflower that's one of nature's mysteries. The flowers never open, but remain in a form that appear to be buds until they wither away. They propagate, but I can't even hazard a guess how. Their foliage looks a lot like zinnias. There are enough of them so that I don't feel guilty about cutting a small bouquet for Susan.

We get started, working the meadow edges along the river. Hanna runs ahead without being told, suddenly an independent cuss today, and I'm left mulling over the *why* of it. Certainly, there's a part of today's regressive performance that's skewed by my own expectations. It's a matter of perspective: things I might have put up with just a month ago are no longer to be tolerated.

On a bigger scale, that perspective is the reason most of us are pleased with the work of our puppies but disappointed in the same dog when Sparkey becomes a two year old. We discount a puppy's errors and celebrate his successes, but a year later we have conveniently forgotten all the mistakes we overlooked and now expect perfection. In truth, it's the same puppy grown a year older.

Twenty minutes later I'm still absorbed in my convoluted thoughts when a grouse breaks out of a clump of gray dogwood off to the left. When you stop paying attention you usually pay the price, and that's the case here. Hanna had been working scent, but I simply didn't have my antenna up. The bird flushes in the open, a flat, quartering left-to-right shot, but I'm slow to react and when I finally get on the bird he enters the shadows and is momentarily invisible. Of course, when you lose sight of the target your first reaction is to put your head up—at least I always do. If I would just continue my swing and keep my cheek on the stock there'd be a chance for success. But that's easier said than done, and the shot passes above the bird.

It is an unfortunate truth that spectacular shots are usually the result of screwing up a routine chance, then recovering in time to make the far more difficult second shot. Here, I've screwed up the routine shot, and there's a moment when I'm sure the grouse is gone. But then he appears again as he tops some hemlocks, offering what seems to be a trap shot—a station five with maximum angle on it. A gargantuan lead, keep the gun moving, and the bird falls.

One definition of someone who is a good shot involves the idea that he never pulls the trigger without fully expecting to hit the target. That leaves me out, because I'm genuinely surprised on what was a too-long shot.

Hanna retrieves the bird and is bringing it in, but in keeping with the retrograde theme, she drops the grouse about fifty feet from me. She hasn't done that before, but considering her performance today it might have been expected.

Problems with retrieving can be difficult to correct because the dog is doing something that is mostly right. I used to be afraid to take action, fearing the dog might think, "Okay, he doesn't like me bringing the bird back to him. Maybe he'll be happier if I bury it."

But force-training provides an instant, remedial lesson package that can take the dog back to where you started and show him the right way. With the bird held in front of her, I say "Fetch." Hanna reaches for the bird as she's been trained to do, but then drops it when I back away. She gets a slap under the chin, and the bird is again held out for her to take. "Fetch" means *take the bird*. It also means *don't let go* and it means *bring it here*. When the dog drops the bird, the command is not "No, Sparkey, don't do that." "Fetch" means *do everything right—the whole package*.

Some men argue that they want no part of forceful training methods. They train their dogs with love. Okay.

But the real test of any training method is the result, and more often than not trained-with-love Sparkey is well loved, but mostly untrained. At best, he cooperates. Oh, he'll do okay as long as he's having fun, but Sparkey will prove that he's NOT trained whenever he's told to do something he'd rather not do. I love my dogs, too, but they are easier to love when they are properly trained.

We sometimes forget that dog training is animal training. Animals aren't thoughtful or mean or noble or in any way good or bad people. The point is, they're not people at all. They're animals. The real challenge is to love your dog, but not forget that he's an animal when it comes to training.

Now Hanna carries the grouse as she follows me, and I finally stop and allow her to sit. I hold out my hand and give her my own customized release command, "Thank you."

Hanna's body language seems to say she's glad that's over, and she casts to the front when I whistle her ahead. I'm not one to equate dogs with humans—not on any level—but I'll admit that they have very visible emotions and, like us, are often governed by them. Today was Hanna's day to see how much she could get away with, and her antics have left me in bad humor.

Like so many of my coverts, Cyprus is no secret. Other people hunt here. There are several deer hunters' tree stands along the river. Usually I hardly notice them, but these are conspicuous because the hunters have left an accumulation of junk at the foot of their selected trees—beer bottles, plastic wrappers, cigarette packs. Later, I find where they've had a bonfire and drank the balance of the case of beer they hauled in. They seem to like Rolling Rock. The mess is disgusting, and after a frustrating day with Hanna my tolerance is approaching critical mass.

Hanna is at heel on the dirt road back to the truck when I run into three guys heading in. They're in camouflage and are carrying compound bows. I've got just enough of a mad-on to confront them. "Are you guys part of the Rolling Rock gang?"

They're all kids in their late teens or early twenties. In return I get three blank stares.

"A bunch of slobs are making a mess back in there." I pull out a couple of green beer bottles from my game bag. "They've left their trash thrown all over the place."

People in a group can be a lot braver than they are as individuals. One of them nearly shouts at me, "What's it to you?" Actually, his exact choice of profanity doesn't deserve to be repeated.

"I'm a bird hunter. I use the woods too. You guys have every right to make a mess out there, but I have every right to call you slobs for it, and that's just what I'm doing."

The shouter takes a step toward me, his eyes showing red in a painted-on mask of camo green. "You think you own the woods?"

To avoid sputtering, I summon up a small smile. "No, I USE the woods. It's you guys, leaving a mess for other people to clean up, who think you own the woods." There's a moment when we glare at each other, then I add, "I'm not looking for a fight, fellas. I'm just asking you to pick up after yourselves."

In the movies, it works. The kids say, "Gee whiz, we see your point. We'll do a better job." Then we all shake hands and laugh.

Unfortunately, this is real life, and a far cry from the movies. The kids' stream of profanity continues, and in the shower of invective they make allusions to what they'll do if they see my truck parked at the turnoff when I'm not around.

I've seldom mastered the art of saying just enough, as people in novels seem to manage so effortlessly. Ordinarily I'd get into a shouting match with these kids, but for once I'm wise and turn and walk away.

The episode with the Rolling Rock crowd sours my mood further, and even Jimmy Buffet on the CD player can't improve my outlook.

It's Stella's turn when I park outside the Greening covert, but she's limping and seems tired when she gets out of the truck. During her life she has had two different major surgeries on her hind legs, and after exercise there are times she apparently becomes just plain sore. I put her back in the truck and slip an enteric-coated aspirin down her throat. It'll help her rest easy for the remainder of the day.

What remainder? It's now half past three, and sunset by the revised time schedule will be at quarter of five. The days get progressively shorter during hunting season. It's a shame, because hunters progressively get into better shape. It ought to be the other way around—not that we'd get in worse shape, but that the days would get longer when we're capable of hunting more hours.

In Greening, Hanna and I chase a grouse around that won't let us get within fifty yards of him. There are no woodcock down on the trackless flats where I once got turned around and nearly spent the night when the markings on my small compass became illegible in the failing light. There's plenty of woodcock sign and some of the puddles appear fresh. Apparently a flight was here for a while but moved out last evening. Hanna slows several times as we pass through the area, but she never actually points. She's a long way from being erudite on the subject, but the past several weeks' worth of woodcock lessons at Tripwire and other places have done her some good.

We're making an uphill turn at the far end of the cover

when she works to a point before a rotted log. She has a woodcock. Her tail is high, but her back end is slightly crouched. As I'm making my way toward her a bird jumps from the other side of the log—an easy climber that I take with a single shot. Hanna sees the woodcock fall and, after a glance back at me when I bark "Fetch," she moves out and makes the retrieve.

But she doesn't bring me the bird. Instead, she tiptoes back to where she was standing in front of the log and, after dropping the dead woodcock, goes back on point.

It takes me a moment to digest what's just happened. My thoughts run to things that begin with *You never know. . . .* When I walk forward another woodcock flushes, this one ten feet in front of Hanna's nose.

After the shot and the retrieve, I put the two birds on the log and sit and scratch Hanna's ears and tell her what a good girl she is. But I remark, too, about what a lucky boy I am. Here's an eight-month-old puppy who has just demonstrated that she not only knew that the first woodcock was not the one she was pointing, but was also smart enough to figure out what to do about it.

Lucky boy, indeed.

It has been, up to this point, a day without melody; Hanna's regression and the need to continually correct her, a spectacular shot demeaned by a sloppy retrieve, then the incident with the Rolling Rock chowderheads. There hasn't been a lot to like up until now.

Hanna sits smiling at me. The dog's interaction with humans is based far more on emotion than intelligence. I don't mean they're not smart, but what originally got dogs into a relationship with Cro-Magnon man back fifteen thousand years ago was their capacity to be a friend.

Dog training is demonstration and then enforcement, and to do it successfully you have to strike an emotional balance in both dog and trainer—not too stern, not too laid back, with plenty of pleased excitement when the dog does well. And when the dog is disappointing you, enforcement can be a big task. Be patient, reprimand the dog when needed, but don't get mad about it.

Having said all that, showing the dog you're angry sometimes makes sense, but losing your temper never does. You can fracture a pup's emotions with too heavy a hand and cause him to retreat somewhere he can't be reached.

Patience is at the heart of every dog-training decision.

Thankfully, today I had just enough.

Interlude: Russet Feathers

> *"If the only satisfaction to be derived from the sport lay in killing birds, I would have quit the game long since."*
>
> Burton Spiller

THE GUN HAS BEEN cleaned and put away and now the cellar smells pleasantly of WD-40. The dogs are back out in the kennel, having finished their supper. And I've logged in the details of the day's hunt on the computer, to be later transcribed into this year's hunting journal.

On the workbench, today's woodcock are lined up alongside the three from yesterday. They've been chilling in the refrigerator for a while, and it's time to get busy with the game shears.

One of these days I'm going to shoot a banded woodcock. There's plenty written about various woodcock banding programs, so I know it's plausible. But I've looked in vain for a band on the leg of every woodcock I've taken for the past thirty years. What I do find upon close examination is a lot of shot-up feet. Woodcock fly with their legs dangling and their bill down, so such damage is inherent.

Woodcock seem to charm everyone who pursues them, and I'm no exception. They're not typically tough targets, but they zig and zag until we all feel like power hitters standing in against a tricky knuckleball pitcher. There's a lot of muttering and head shaking that goes on in the game of woodcocking.

In other parts of the country, the woodcock—maybe even more than the ruffed grouse—represents all that is genteel about the traditions surrounding eastern upland shooting.

When I hunt in Kansas or Texas the folks there, knowing I'm a woodcock hunter from New England, expect two things of me: One, that I'm crazy enough to be a Red Sox fan, and I don't disappoint them on that count. But they also expect that I would hunt behind classic pointing dogs, use a side-by-side, and wear tweeds. My English setters are of traditional bloodlines, so I guess I'll have to plead guilty there. But the westerners are disappointed to see me with an over-and-under and wearing clothes from Cabela's and L.L. Bean's.

That second set of expectations, of course, stems from the body of high-sounding prose that originally delineated the traditions of upland gunning in this part of the world. Since I'm a traditionalist, some people expect me to dress like one.

One thing that remains unchanged across a century of American woodcock-hunting heritage is that you can have a good time without beating yourself to death. The challenge of the sport needs no exaggeration. The woods in the Northeast have a basic hospitality in their makeup. Whenever I'm outdoors, no matter where in New England I might be, I've always had the feeling that I could walk home from right here and probably have a good time along the way.

Thinking of the hunting experience and what it's all about, there really is very little *hunting* in my memories of going out. Mostly, it's the myriad things that make up the adventure: personalities and places, skies and weather, flora and fauna, roads taken, sights seen, sounds enjoyed. Those things are what outdoor writers write about, whether they're telling a story about woodcocking in the Home Covert, casting for salmon on Maine's Penobscot River, or horsebacking after elk in the Rocky Mountains. It's the fun of the adventure that really counts. Catching fish or shooting birds is certainly a large part of it, but only a part. Maybe that's why preserve hunting never appealed to me and why good-quality gear always has.

The best stories are about people, and the best hunting stories are about people who just happen to be hunting at the time. It follows, then, that classic outdoor pieces are still fresh and vibrant several generations after they were written because they concern themselves with readily recognizable people acting like real human beings while they are hunting or fishing. Model-T Fords, double-guns with exposed hammers, fly lines made out of silk and catgut—none of those timepiece details seem to slow the reader down if the author was skillful enough to bring us into his tale.

Universally, the good writers all knew that people essentially are the same no matter the time period: Some are rubes, some are SOBs, and some are sportsmen we wouldn't mind hunting with. The characters created by these writers are all recognizable, and their stories were, and continue to be, wonderful.

Unfortunately, some would-be outdoor writers imitate the style rather than the essence of the classics in the hope that some of that wonderfulness will rub off on them. Calling grouse "pa'chiges" and referring to a woodcock as "that little russet feller with the shoe-button eyes" sounds okay coming from Burton Spiller, but not from a man so young that he's never seen a loafer with a penny in it, let alone buttons on shoes.

The fact that editors go ahead and publish these meek attempts at imitation answers their own question as to why originality is such a rare commodity.

I have the shears going now, and it doesn't take long to remove the breast from each bird. For years I puzzled over the handedness I sometimes saw in cleaning woodcock. Like a fiddler crab, some would have a distinctly better developed right side to their breast, others seemed to favor the left. Those muscles, of course, are connected to the bird's wings, so it didn't seem logical that they would develop unevenly. Then I finally began making a more detailed examination. In every case, the distortion of the breast muscle was the result of the wishbone being broken by shot and the resultant contraction of the muscle on that side.

The breasts are rinsed and then go into plastic freezer bags. I like the kind called Ziploc Double Guard. They'll protect birds for at least six months without allowing freezer burn. They're not the cheapest on the grocery shelf, but they work. Tragically, I had to throw out some grouse a few years ago. I used an "el cheapo" brand, and after a few months freezer burn had made the meat inedible.

If ever there was an invention that would let me catch and release a game bird, woodcock are what I'd use it on. In truth, they're not very good to eat. It must be a matter of individual taste, because there's a lot written on the subject by people who think woodcock-on-the-plate are something terrific. But they're not for me.

If you've never had one, I can tell you they taste like liver. There are a bunch of foods that I disliked as a kid but have now acquired a taste for. Liver and woodcock are not on that list. Thankfully, I know a few landowners who will take the birds I offer, and I have several acquaintances who think they're a delicacy.

Each year in March or April I hold my annual Spring Woodcock Feed. All the birds from the previous year are cooked and fed to my friends. We drink a lot of wine, and when it's over the freezer is empty.

If you actually like woodcock, I'm here to tell you that I'm envious of you. And, also, that you are well served by most of the cook-'em-with-bacon-and-onions recipes you'll find in every game cookbook.

I've included below are three recipes that I alternately use at the Spring Woodcock Feed. They're for those of us who like everything about woodcock except the flavor. That flavor needs a little "adjustment" before you put knife and fork to a woodcock. These three recipes will make them palatable, although hardly the sort of thing you wake up in the middle of the night craving.

Spicy Hot Woodcock Fillets Over Coals

Cut the fillets off the removed breast of each bird. Marinate the meat in a 50-50 mixture of red wine and balsamic vinegar, with a lot of garlic and onion added. A few hours is good; overnight is better. Then, just before they go on the grill, slather them in Chinese hot oil and give them 30 seconds to a minute on a skewer over the coals. They don't need a long cooking time—the marinade has already broken down the structure of the meat.

The only crucial factor in this recipe (as well as in the following Speidis recipe) is to make sure ALL the meat is covered during the marinating process.

Woodcock Speidis *(Speed-ease)* Over Coals

Again, cut the fillets off the breast of each woodcock. Make up a marinade of 1 tablespoon of meat tenderizer, 6 finely chopped cloves of garlic, 1 teaspoon of pepper, lots of finely chopped parsley, 2/3 cup of cooking oil, 1/4 cup of vinegar, 1 teaspoon of salt, and 2 teaspoons of basil. (Note: It is possible to use too much vinegar in the marinade, so measure carefully.) This is enough for twenty woodcock. Marinate the (thawed) fillets overnight. Skewer the meat and broil on an outdoor barbecue as you would a shish kabob. Like the Spicy Hot recipe, they don't take long.

Woodcock with Texas Toast and Tex-Mex Gravy

This one comes from the late Sam Clements of Amarillo. It was originally a dove recipe, and will prepare a dozen woodcock, give or take a few.

Use the skinned breast of the woodcock, bone in. Wash the birds and leave them wet. Dust the meat in a paper sack with some flour and black pepper. Use more pepper than you'd think.

Heat $1/2$ stick of butter and an equal amount of cooking oil in a skillet. Get the combination as hot as you can without burning the butter. Brown the flour-covered breasts for about $1 1/2$ minutes on each side.

Now turn the heat down to a small simmer and add in $1/2$ cup of sherry or port. Simmer the birds for about 10 minutes with the lid on. Remove the lid, turn up the heat once again, and rebrown the birds for $1 1/2$ minutes on each side.

Remove the birds to a warm place for a few minutes. Pour off any of the remaining liquid in the skillet and discard. Scrape the solid goodies from the bottom of the pan to loosen them, and add 3 cups of milk to make a gravy. Add a lot of black pepper. Warm the gravy-to-be over medium heat. Don't let it boil. When it's thoroughly heated, add a mixture of half-milk and half-flour to thicken. Just add a bit at a time and really stir. About $3/4$ cup will do the trick.

Put a couple of birds on a slice of rye toast that you've had your assistant make while you were attending to the gravy. Now pour the Tex-Mex gravy you've just made over the birds.

And the final line in all three recipes is: Call the woodcockers to supper and stand back and tip your hat.

Day Twenty-Eight: All Saints' Day

> *"Dull November brings the blast,*
> *Then the leaves are whirling fast."*
> Old Nursery Rhyme

ABOVE MY DESK the October calendar page has been turned against the wall, and a new month stares out at the world. It's November first. If you had to guess and circle a day on next year's calendar when the woodcock migration would be at its height, November 1 would be a good choice. In the past, wonderful things have happened to me on this date. There was a triple limit of grouse, woodcock, and pheasants when I was twenty-six back in 1973. In 1979 Hazel had her first grouse point. In 1988 I took a one-shot woodcock double over Amy. November first always seems to be a spectacular day, if not weather-wise then at least as far as hunting expectations go, and today is no exception. Later, when I listen to my own voice on the tape recorder as I recorded the day's events, the expectations of All Saints' Day is evident in my voice, even to me.

Along a side road I dodge the potholes for a half-mile, and finally pull over next to the Connie Mack covert. There was a legendary baseball player and manager by that name, and there's a sign as you enter town saying he was born here. What Connie-Mack-the-covert consists of is a series of overgrown fields and surrounding edges that combine to add up to a prime woodcock area. It's one of the few places I hunt where I've never seen a grouse. The only thing I can attribute it to is the complete absence

of conifers anywhere nearby. Everything else is here in abundance—water, a variety of preferred foods, cover with plenty of understory. But no evergreens.

There are a bunch of woodcock in the spindly birches. Hanna bumps the first, then points the next, but that bird is clearly a hen, and I point my finger at it and say "Bang" as she climbs up through the treetops. Hanna crowds too close to the third and pushes him up, but the fourth bird is well pointed and missed cleanly once it tops out.

When hunters write or talk about their bird dogs, they always seem to mention the cliché wherein the dog gives them a dirty look after a missed shot. In truth, I've never known any of my dogs to react in such a derogatory way, even though I've given them plenty of reason to. Although all dogs at times display human traits, I've always felt that "The Dirty Look Story" was a bit of a stretch, something that takes place in the imagination of the self-effacing hunter.

Having said that, I can tell you that my dogs regularly do something that might be similarly interpreted. The gun goes off but no feathers fly, and still the dog searches for a dead bird. It's tempting to interpret their actions as sarcastic, but I know it's just a matter of faith—the sound of the gun has come to mean *dead bird*. Hanna now continues the long tradition and searches the ground beneath the birches like a kid looking for Easter eggs.

"No bird, Hanna," I holler, but I never worked much on that one—I don't have a command for "Never mind." When I finally get the puppy to move on, I'm sure she wonders why we're giving up so easily. I wish I believed in something in life, anything, the way my dogs believe in me.

Once in a while a woodcock will fly low, weaving between tree trunks, but usually they'll behave as these are doing: they rise to the top of the covert, however high that might be. You'll seldom find them in growth higher than thirty feet or so—not that you should go around measuring the height of trees to find woodcock. It becomes a matter of the bird being able to climb out and have some flight room. Here, in the close-growing birches, each bird seems to go straight up through the dense overhead branches before flattening out above the treetops.

Minutes later, Hanna points another woodcock in the shadow of an old fireplace and chimney standing by itself among the gray birches. This time I manage to provide her something to retrieve. There's time to tell Hanna to "Hut" as we both watch the bird falling back to earth to bounce down just a few feet from us.

We're obviously in a flight of birds, and I'm in no hurry to fill out my woodcock limit. Although Hanna points three more, I pass on each chance, hoping for a double opportunity that never comes.

The numbers are getting complicated, so before they start falling out of my ears I dig out the notepad and mark "8 flushes, 6 points, 1 bird, 2 opportunities." I keep track of this sort of thing for the sake of the hunting journal, but there's a lot going on and it's tough to keep changing numbers in my head and still have room to think. Once written down, I don't feel the need to keep a running total right in the very front of my brain.

Hanna and I work the woods on the return swing. I'm try-ing to believe that we'll find the first-ever grouse at Connie Mack, but today isn't the day. Our search takes us along the wood margins where beech trees still hang on to their leaves. The color seems to have leached out of them and they look more like faded newspaper than the polished gold of a week ago. Yesterday, in Vermont, I drove through the village scene I had started paint-ing a few weeks ago. When I earlier left the picture half-finished, I had good intentions of coming back to it once the autumn color was on the trees, but now the tress are bare and it'll have to wait until next year. Autumn's brilliant flame dies too quickly.

We move on to the Junkyard.

My one and only legitimate grouse double was taken here fifteen years ago. The story sometimes rambles on, but I'll abbre-viate it. Hazel was on walking point when a grouse flushed ahead of her and tried to double back along the edge of the cover, offering a front-to-rear shot to the right. No thinking was involved—I shot the bird. Unnoticed until after the trigger had been pulled was the second grouse, flying a parallel course just beyond his partner, and that one was taken with the tight barrel. It happened so quickly that I stood for a moment wondering if I had imagined it all. There were no feathers in the air, no witnesses, only the two empties and a wisp of smoke coming from the open barrels. Then Hazel brought in the first of the pair and it was all reality.

Honest to goodness MAKABLE opportunities at a double— that is, a pair of grouse that gets up together and is in range— are about as common as finding a buffalo nickel in your change. You can hunt all season without getting an authentic chance. So understand that having Hazel retrieve two cock grouse to me on that cloudy, dark morning was not to be taken lightly. I hung the birds in a twisted little hawthorn tree and posed the dog next to them for a photo that still hangs over my desk. Hazel is under a stone in the backyard now, the Winchester Model 21 side-by-side in the photo is long gone, and the hawthorns were bulldozed away a few years back.

But the bright memory still resonates. A grouse double is not the sort of thing easily forgotten.

There's an uphill briar patch in an abandoned pasture on the back side of the Junkyard. The good cover makes a horseshoe around the field, with briars on the inside of the U-shape and open woods beyond. After we chase a couple of long-distance grouse out of the swamp below, we start up one side of the horseshoe.

Ahead of me Hanna stutter-steps and points and moves ahead and almost points again before deciding to move on cautiously. Now she's running, but then the whole stop-and-go process is repeated again. There's a definite direction to her faltering progress and it's obvious that she's following something.

Grouse aren't in the same class as pheasants, but they do run. I have several theories on that, some of which conflict with each other, but the fact remains that the infantry method is their preferred means of escape. When danger is detected, a grouse will usually sprint to the nearest "hide cover" where he can sit tight and discover what's going on behind him. When a hunter walks up a bird, chances are it's from the back door of one of those hide covers. Oh, he'll take wing when surprised or when running isn't a feasible alternative, but ordinarily the flight option is a grouse's ace in the hole—he can always fly if running doesn't work out.

What that means, then, is that a running grouse that keeps running either is wounded or, as in this case, has lost track of where his hide cover is.

Somewhere up ahead I hear a distant grouse flush and assume the bird Hanna was trailing has elected to go with the flight option and has departed for parts unknown. Then, in the moment when I relax, the bird is suddenly a silent gliding blur coming right at me.

As I turn to take him going away, he climbs with a burst of speed and dodges behind a screening pine limb. The shot is right where it should be, but it's unclear if the bird fell or continued. When I run ahead a few steps there are feathers still hanging in the air like a three-dimensional punctuation mark where bird and pattern came together. With my extended finger, I retrace the bird's flight path. *Okay: If the grouse was hit there and was flying in this direction at breakneck speed, where should he have come down?*

Unfortunately, my answer is *Out in the briar patch*.

The briars are mostly blackberry canes. To speed things along, I carry Hanna as I break my way out to an estimated spot where the bird fell. There's a single ethereal bit of feather fluff on a branch about twenty feet away. Closer investigation turns up another few bits of fluff and two complete breast feathers on the ground where the bird struck. Hanna gets a noseful of scent and burrows into the blackberries when I tell her to "Find dead bird."

Unfortunately, it'll be the first of five hundred repetitions of that command during the next twenty minutes.

It's slow going. Although Hanna has learned a thing or two about thorns during the past month, she just can't make any headway. Each time she seems to have something, I break in to her and start lifting the tangles out of her way. Down on my elbows at ground level it becomes evident that underneath is another world, a maze of openings and natural passages where the blackberry canes have grown and fallen for decades.

There's been a hole developing in the index finger of my left glove for the past week or so. I didn't think much of it, but now, in pushing the briar canes aside, one of them hits me just right (or wrong, depending on whom you're rooting for) and a thorn goes deep into the tip of my finger.

Thorns are part of hunting. Each time I dry off after a shower the nap of the towel routinely catches on thorn points that are working themselves out of the hide on my legs. It's not a big deal, but this one is. I can't know it at the time, but it'll hurt enough to put that finger out of commission for months. The thorn won't work its way back to the surface until Saint Patrick's Day.

Every year there are times when my persistence squeezes just a bit of luck out of a bad situation and I'm able to reach a wounded grouse hiding in a rock wall, or the dog picks up a scent trail when hope is fading. Unfortunately, this isn't one of those occasions.

I hate lost birds like turkeys hate Thanksgiving. They bother me for days afterward. I've done everything possible to ensure clean kills, including switching to a 12-gauge gun last year, but nothing short of staying home and not hunting is going to completely eliminate lost birds. From the very beginning this one had something of the inevitability found in a popped-up fastball's fall back to earth. It's a shame and a waste.

After twenty minutes in the briar patch, it's time to admit defeat and move on.

Back at the truck I take a break on the tailgate with a cup of coffee and a couple of Susan's cranberry muffins, but I can't stop chewing on the lost grouse. I went all last year without a lost bird, and had just one the year before. A year when you lose only one is something to feel good about, though not on the day you lose it.

During the fifteen minutes or so that I'm sitting there, three cars stop and ask if I've had any luck, and I'm afraid I don't hide my sour mood very well. I wouldn't think three cars used this back road all day. Where were these guys back in 1985 when I had a grouse double to show off and was wishing someone would come along?

When I pull up and park at the Barking Dog covert, the dog that gave the place its name is barking in the yard of the house* across the street. He speaks in complete sentences: "Roof roof roof roof." Then, after a moment's thought, he adds, "Roof roof roof, roof roof." When Hanna gets out of the truck he continues his conversation, but starts putting exclamation points at the ends of his sentences.

From past experience, I can tell you that as long as my truck is parked on the road, Barkley will continue his running commentary. I've gotten turned around in here, then regained my bearings by listening for the direction of the barking in the distance. Obviously, there's nobody home at the farmhouse—who would put up with nonstop barking? I don't understand it. Anti-bark collars work, but people think they're cruel. Never mind the amount of cruelty heaped upon the neighbors by years of incessant noise. We don't want to hurt Barkley with an electric shock that'll shut him up in a day or two.

For that matter, people take puppies to veterinarians and have their tails docked and their ears clipped, they have dewclaws removed and have the dog neutered. But any talk of snipping a dog's vocal cords meets with incredulous looks of disbelief—how can you even think such a thought? Cut his nuts off, sure, but don't you dare snip those vocal cords.

We work the slope of the far valley at Barking Dog. The brook is downhill to the left, and above me to the right the hemlocks grow thick before the land flattens out into open woods. In this otherwise apple-less year there are a few fallen apples under the trees along the hillside. They're nothing a human would bother with—little, wizened buggy things—but wild animals aren't fussy. The flesh of the punky apples has turned brown where they've been sampled, and a few are showing creamy white, indicating something has been at them within the past five minutes. A lot of creatures eat fallen apples, but these seem to be pecked rather than gnawed.

I've no sooner reached an obvious conclusion than Hanna strikes scent and works upslope. A hen grouse gets up well in front of her and heads over the hemlocks. The bird is out too far for a shot, but the gun is halfway to my shoulder as I watch the bird depart. Before it is out of sight a roll of thunder announces a second bird, this one a cock with a steel-gray tail maybe twenty-five yards to the front. I fire more quickly than needed, and the bird seems to be to the left of my aim at the shot. He continues on, apparently unhit. I say something through my teeth that I'd rather not repeat, but then the bird does something weird. Instead of following the hen over the hemlocks and out of sight, he veers to the left and downhill toward the brook where the cover is more open.

When grouse react as a pair they have a natural reluctance to fly in the same airspace. It may be a strategy to confuse predators and ensure that at least one will survive. (It's also the reason chances for doubles are so rare.) But this was strange—grouse try to screen themselves from ground predators, and this bird didn't. His partner behaved normally, but the cock slid downhill in plain sight.

Did I hit him?

I take a good look around to verify my bearings. We'll look for the hen grouse later. For now I whistle to Hanna and we start down toward the brook and after the cock.

There are some still-leafy oaks here, although the leaves have all turned a color reminiscent of a vanilla caramel still wrapped in cellophane. Hanna casts ahead of me at a run as we near the brook, then she down-shifts and narrows her search and as quickly as I can say it she reels into a point. She's still firm when I walk up to her. A quiet, two-note whistle tests her point—it's the signal to "Go ahead."

She eases forward in an imitation of a snake, twenty yards or so into a little eroded washout of rocks and ferns. When she points, her tail is straight up and her neck is barely long enough to constrain her head, which wants to go even farther forward. No doubt about it: she has the bird.

It's tempting to say a bird dog on point is a magician, but then I'd have to qualify that and explain that I don't mean the sort of charlatan magician who will fool you with sleight of hand, which is entertaining but never believable. In Hanna's case, the magic is real.

No pussyfooting here. I walk to her right and go to where the grouse should be, then turn and start back toward Hanna. The bird boils out of some rocks and flies by me like a twin-engine plane with one engine out. There's time to follow him with the gun lowered until he is out twenty-five yards or so, then put him down. It's the same steel-gray cock.

The bird's strange initial reaction and now the labored second flight is evidence enough that the grouse was carrying a pellet or two from my errant first shot. It's good to have this one in hand, but I'm certainly not shooting my best today.

After Hanna retrieves the bird, I stand her on the rocks at the head of the washout and place at her feet the first grouse taken over one of her points. Almost as if she knows I'm taking her picture, she picks up the bird and stands with it until I click the shutter.

We climb out of the valley and through the hemlocks, and look for the hen where she should be.

Grouse don't fly far. The fact that their breast is "white meat" indicates that there is limited blood flow to those muscles; thus, they have little endurance. As a result, there's a not-very-definite distance of *one grouse flight* that varies with the cover and the situation, but it's something you get a feel for after a while. In this case, my guess is about two hundred yards.

In that vicinity there's a stone wall and some isolated evergreens, but I'm putting my money on a raspberry thicket that has grown up around a fallen monster-oak.

Hanna goes to one side of the deadfall and the hen blasts out the other, offering a left-to-right crossing shot that's almost too close. I put a woodcock lead on a target that needs a grouse lead, and know even as I pull the trigger that I've missed.

After a moment spent cursing my shooting, I consider, *Could Hanna have pointed that bird?*

The answer is *Maybe.*

There are a lot of grouse that just plain can't be pointed. Overly cautious grouse don't often hold still. They run, they flush out of trees, they make a living being wary of everything that moves in the woods. I've heard of dogs that could consistently point one of every three birds found, but I've never actually seen one. My best grouse dog pointed 29 percent in her best season. That was Stella in 1992. Hanna, currently with a grand total of four grouse points, is hardly in the category where I should be disappointed in anything she fails to do in regard to grouse.

Shooting at pointed grouse is nice, but if *woodcock rules* were applied and hunters only shot at birds the dog pointed, the grouse population would be fairly safe from me in particular and the grouse-hunting public in general. Hunting literature is full of stories about old-time grouse hunters who only shot birds over point. That makes for nice reading, but the reality has always been that almost everybody takes them as they come.

Here's why: Skeet, a game originally intended as grouse-shooting practice, comes out of the same era as the classic grouse-hunting literature. It was co-invented by William Harnden Foster, a man who authored one of those classics. But if a hunter only shot birds over points, then why would he need to practice anything other than low-house seven and its variations? If skeet represents grouse shots hunters took back in Foster's time—and it does—then all the crossing shots and incomers indicates that they were taking them as they flushed, just as you and I do.

The percentages seem to break down into functions of three. A grouse hunter needs to flush three birds to actually see one; he needs to see three to get a shot at one; and, at best, he hits only one out of three. Do the math. On average, you need to move twenty-seven birds in order to sit down to a grouse dinner. Of course, there are no guarantees in those statistics. Some days even though you move a dozen you never get close to a bird. On other days you can't hit anything and although you have plenty of opportunities you still have canned beans and franks for supper.

Having said all that, bumbling a wide-open, left-to-right opportunity on a bird I knew was there is all the more painful, even with the pleasant weight of the first grouse in my game bag.

For a minute I stand looking into the slate-violet depths of leafless woods where the bird disappeared and consider my chances. The hen flew into open woodland. The trees are tall and there's virtually no understory—it's essentially a park. There are a lot of reasons not to chase birds in that situation. On a lucky day, you might get within sixty yards of a grouse, but more often than not it flushes one hundred yards away and flies to Blinkville. Then there's always the idea that a bird chased too far out of its home range is vulnerable and might not find its way back. One grouse out of Barking Dog seems enough for today.

The woodcock migration is at its peak, and Hanna has pointed a bunch of woodcock in every cover. I've been passing up the single birds she finds in the hope of getting a chance at a double. But the end of the day is arriving right on schedule, so on the way out when Hanna points staunchly in a stand of popple, I take the bird and scratch her ears when she makes the retrieve. Not a hundred feet farther she points again with a posture that indicates another woodcock and I take that one as well.

With a limit now in possession, Hanna points for a third time. It's a chance to get in a little training. She won't be able to chase this woodcock if I've got hold of her check cord. Of course it's the double I've been waiting for all day, and of course the chance would have been in the piece-of-cake category.

Would it have mattered if I had shot a couple of extra woodcock? My own version of the right answer is, *To me it would have.*

Hunting is a game played by and large without benefit of referees. It is a private, solitary experience, and, as with other solitary games, the most important rules a hunter follows are those he imposes upon himself. If there can be a real difference between hunting and simply killing, it must exist in the attitude of those who hunt.

On the plus side, Hanna stood firm when the birds fluttered up, and she never put a strain on the cord. I pat her on the flank. "Good for you, Hanna."

November first has turned out to be one of those days when, after much anticipation, a hunter can fathom the true meaning of anticlimax. A lot of grouse flew, but I shot poorly and botched a couple of makable shots. There was a lost bird and might have been two if Hanna hadn't bailed me out.

I shake my head, listening to my own thoughts. *What's the*

matter with me? For the most picayune of reasons, I've fallen into an unappreciative mood. To hell with expectations. There's a grouse and a pair of woodcock in my game bag, a third woodcock in my truck, and a bunch of empties in the right-hand pocket of my vest. It's November and I'm aboveground and walking upright.

And the puppy had a good hunt. She's back on track after a rough outing a couple of days ago. I didn't realize it while it was going on, but now it seems evident that for the past two weeks Hanna was in that twilight zone between *puppy* and *bird dog*. And she is, I remind myself, only eight and one-half months old.

When I whistle to Hanna she pauses to look back at me, then we start back up the brook toward the truck where Barkley the recreational barker is giving voice to his impatience.

CHAPTER FOUR

Pretzel Logic

Day Thirty-One: Showers Possible
Throughout the Day

> *"My Sorrow, when she's here with me,*
> *Thinks these dark days of autumn rain*
> *Are beautiful as days can be;"*
>
> Robert Frost

IT'S NOVEMBER 6—half-past the hunting season, more or less. Before Vermont begins the deer rifle-season later this week, I'm going to try and make a pass through my coverts north of Bennington.

On the road into the first stop I pass a tractor with a manure spreader coming the opposite way. Mr. Richland is the driver. I stop the truck on the shoulder and wave as he passes, but the tractor's brakes aren't in the best of shape, and it takes him a hundred yards or so to come to a stop. After a short run down to where he's pulled over, I ask him, "Did the moose come back?"

There was a young bull moose that made a pest of himself when he fell in love with several cows in Mr. Richland's dairy herd last year. For a brief time his farm was featured on every evening newscast.

Mr. Richland scowls at me for a moment before recognition sets in. "Oh, hello Steve. For a minute there I thought you were one of those darn tourists again." He actually says *darn*.

People thought the whole moose–cow affair was high humor, and Mr. Richland had some problems with sightseers invading his pastures and outbuildings while he was trying to make a living. I've teased him about that being the price of celebrity.

When I repeat my question, Mr. Richland spits out a stream of tobacco juice and offers a few opinions about the bull moose, none of which bear repeating on the evening news.

The farm is posted, but when I sought him out years ago Mr. Richland was only too glad to allow me to hunt the covers on his land. And he's no fool: he has always taken the grouse I've offered him. He once told me that he was sure a partridge was a bird the locals shot alongside the road, and a grouse was one of those birds the city boys from Massachusetts shot at while it was flying. I think he winked when he said that, but I can't be sure.

"You'd better get a move on," he advises. "It's fixin' to rain."

"Naw. The weathermen only said there'd be a few sprinkles."

Mr. Richland glances up at the gloomy western sky, then we have what amounts to a full-blown, Vermont-style argument about the weather:

"It's fixin' to rain," he repeats.

There are overlapping sets of muddy tire marks on the paved road leading down to the pasture where Mr. Richland has been back and forth all morning. At the barway I park well beyond where the tire tracks make their turn—manure spreaders some-times don't know when to stop spreading.

A few sprinkles are falling when I let Hanna out of the truck and put her through the one-minute drill. She's eager to get going, but I make her "Heel" and "Hut" several times as we walk the edge of the pasture toward the cover beyond.

The weather report predicted a possibility of showers throughout the day. A few raindrops I can handle, but hunting in the rain is no fun. The air is heavy and smells of rain and manure newly spread, but almost as a reward for my faith in the weather-men the sprinkles stop as we enter the brush and trees beyond the pasture wall.

The cover is as familiar as only an old friend can be. Stella had her first grouse point in here, and just up the road is where Hazel got lost later that same year and I realized that her hunting career was over. If Stella is twelve, that must have been eleven years ago. And up on the cobble is where Amy nearly ran off a cliff and pointed a grouse hiding just over the edge.

It's all pretty much the same as it was the first time I hunted here. It's the opposite of a place like Tripwire, where things grow so rapidly that they're different from one season to the next, with some corners getting better as others grow up. There's an ebb and flow of natural succession in the life of every grouse covert, but the tide seems to change more gradually in places like this. It must have something to do with the fertility of the soil, or lack of same.

There's a thickly overgrown ravine that I've always called the Nightmare Area, and Hanna points a pair of grouse among the low-hanging grapevines. First one, then the other thunders out somewhere in front of her as I fight my way toward the point. Even with all the leaves down, neither bird offers as much as a glimpse. Sometimes you can follow a grouse by sound alone, but this isn't one of those times. Without a definite line to follow, it becomes necessary to make one up. *The birds must have followed the edge of the cover toward the low swamp,* I tell myself.

So do we. All the skunk cabbage is frost-killed now, and when Hanna charges out into the swamp she nearly gets stuck in the deep mud. She comes back out looking like a police car— black on the bottom and white on the top. We work the edge to a logical conclusion, and when I whistle to the dog and begin a loop back it starts to rain.

It seems obvious I'm going to get wet, because the rain is immediately more than sprinkles. It's the sort of steady rainfall that my dad would describe as *a nice rain.* Being a farmer, he meant that it was coming down at a rate that would soak in and do some good rather than a downpour that would run off and cause erosion: *a nice rain.*

We're looping back toward the truck when a grouse blasts out of a pine tree. The gun comes up but the sight picture never develops, and before I can adjust the bird is gone. George Bird Evans wrote impatiently of hunters not being able to tell one grouse from another and counting reflushes as new birds, but he must have been a better man than I am. This grouse might be one of the two from the Nightmare Area—it's conceivable that the bird might have flown over here—but who can know for sure?

Up ahead, the puppy points in a brushy stand of gray dog-wood. *The grouse's partner?* Hoping it is, I go directly to Hanna and when a woodcock flushes I overreact and shoot too quickly. I can see the pattern's near-instantaneous path through the falling raindrops, above and in front of the bird. If this were a baseball game, the commentator would say "That off-speed pitch had Mulak out on his front foot. Holy cow, did he look foolish on that one."

If you're at all like me, you shoot okay on woodcock when you're expecting woodcock—that is, those occasions when you're after woodcock and the dog points and you're prepared for a woodcock flush. There's a lot to be said for having the confidence of knowing you've got the right gun, chokes, and load for the bird you're after. But there's also something to be said for having the right frame of mind. Southwestern Vermont is not devoid of woodcock, but in truth it's not the migration hot spot I once hoped it would be.

And when you're in a fast-ball count and the pitcher throws you that changeup—or worse, the knuckleball—we can all look pretty foolish.

Holy cow, indeed.

Unlike winter, there is no sense of malevolence in an autumn rain, but a half-hour in the steady downpour has left me soaked right through to my underwear. Thankfully I've got spare clothes in the war bag. Back at the truck I root around until I find an old towel to sit on, then drive down the road and park out of the rain under a highway overpass. I'm standing alongside the truck, having taken off the wet stuff and wearing little more than goose bumps when Mr. Richland drives by on his tractor. He's got on a raincoat that consists of a plastic trash bag with holes poked into it for his head and arms. He waves, but doesn't stop to say "I told you so."

Or maybe he would have if he could have gotten the tractor's brakes to work.

It feels good to be dry again.

There was a time not so many years ago when I was in a constant search for good-quality waterproof hunting gear, particularly rain pants. But I've stopped looking. It's not that I've found the right stuff, but rather that I don't hunt in the rain anymore. At least, not on purpose. Sprinkles, mist, or just wet woods I can handle, but when it's raining I go home.

In mildly wet conditions, I seem to be able to remain comfortable as long as my torso stays dry. Toward that end, my outerwear of choice is a roomy anorak. It's made of modern Supplex nylon, not the old hard-finish material that sounds like a grouse flushing every time a branch rubs up against it. It doesn't rip easily and it keeps the wind out. Whatever you decide to wear underneath—be it a flannel shirt, a wool sweater, or a tuxedo jacket—it will be protected from branches and thorns. You can use as many layers as the temperature dictates, and wear the anorak on all but the warmest days of the season. And since the nylon is water repellent, it'll keep you dry in anything short of the steady rain falling here today.

On the way back down U.S. Route 7, I drive through Manchester. On a rainy weekday, the crossroads the locals call Malfunction Junction isn't the sticking point that it can be on weekends, and I breeze right through. Not so long ago the town was typical Vermont—maybe a little tonier than most because of the Orvis Company's store and the Equinox Hotel—but there was woodcock cover right across the river. But it doesn't look like that famous Rockwell Kent painting any longer. The town has lately turned into *Outlet City,* complete with traffic gridlock and all the problems of any tourist destination. I hope the good people of Manchester got what they bargained for.

Passing through, I can't help but glance at the new condominiums across the brook. They went up during the off-season two years ago, and sit on top of some alder runs I used to call Unknown Bridge. Although it was at no time hugely productive, at least it was close to the cheap motel where I used to stay. But as I drive by, I find myself echoing the sour grapes routine: *I used to hunt there, but it's no big loss. I never did much good.*

What a smart-ass I can sound like at times, even to myself.

About progress: No matter if it's grouse cover or not, there is a part of me that feels a mild shock whenever I see new houses going up in roadside woodland. Somehow, without sensible reason, the emotional part of me assumed all that was over with since so much has been done already. I wonder, sometimes, if men who claim to love the outdoors don't really just despise the things civilization has done to it. These days, most New England grouse cover is abandoned land—land that was once cleared for human use of one sort or another. That it would make good acreage for development today should come as no surprise. It once appealed to a long-ago developer for the same reason.

At home, with just a few exceptions, I don't hunt in the Connecticut River Valley anymore, even though I live there. I fought it for a while; I still had a few coverts left within a half-hour of my driveway, and I rationed my time in them until suburbanization forced me out. People routinely build houses in the woods, then complain when they hear gunshots. Research done at Remington Farms demonstrated that No. $7^{1}/2$ shot cannot be made to go seven hundred feet no matter how the gun is elevated. Unfortunately, the sound travels a lot farther than the shot ever will. Hunters would get into a lot less trouble if their gunshots sounded like *plink* rather than *ka-BANG!* After all, who has ever called the cops because they heard a bow hunter shooting behind their house?

But the spread of houses is inexorable. A few homes in the wrong place can summarily end hunting in an entire covert. If I live long enough, I'm certain I'll see a housing development in every one of my grouse spots. None of the coverts I've lost actually belonged to me, therefore you lost them as well. Too bad for all of us.

As I head farther south the rain turns into spotty showers, and I've got the windshield wipers on the intermittent setting. There's nothing pressing waiting for me at home, so I get off the highway and make a protracted return trip along the back roads. With the leaf fall now complete, I poke along through almost colorless scenery that appears like an ink wash over a continuous pencil sketch. I keep hoping a new covert or two will jump out in front of the truck.

Not long ago I had a conversation with a retired game warden. He had been a grouse hunter in years past, but had lately taken to chasing pheasants. The reason, he told me, was "There just aren't many partridge around any longer."

The warden was sure he was right, even though it was a year when I was finding plenty of birds. What happened, I would later figure out, was that when his grouse coverts matured and became unproductive he didn't bother to find any replacements.

So I wander the back roads gazing out through a rain-blurred windshield, trying to prevent the same thing from happening to me. My idea of Hell is to be in a situation where I have to spend autumn days driving around looking for places to hunt when I should be hunting.

Well, maybe not Hell, but that's Purgatory, for sure.

I like to say that there is something of a *house-that-Jack-built* relationship that you must put together before you can sit down to a dinner with grouse as the main course: "Here is the bird that flew from the dog that pointed the grouse that picked at the apple that fell from the tree that grew by the brook that flowed through the covert that Jack found by studying his topographical maps."

161

You can find grouse covers on topo maps if you know what to look for. You begin with the salient fact that the only grouse food you can find on a map are apples—orchards carry their own symbol on the map key. Certainly, commercial orchards aren't what you're looking for. No self-respecting grouse is going to hang around where they mow the grass and spray for bugs every couple of weeks. What both you and the grouse are after are those overgrown-but-still-producing orchards where the farmer gave up the ghost a decade ago. If you have two versions of the same topo map, sometimes orchards that show on an older map aren't differentiated from the surrounding woodland on a later edition. Find that and you've hit the jackpot.

There are some gaps in my collection of topographical maps, so today I'm reduced to following a road atlas where mountains are shown as sketchy haystacks seen from above. Here and there I've penciled in the names of some of the roads from previous explorations, although in Vermont a lot of them simply have numbers, as in TH-104. I assume the letters stand for *town highway,* but it might mean *tourist haven* or maybe *tough hoeing.* You never know. Mostly I explore, and only later I'll check the map and my mileage notes to find out where I've been.

When looking for new coverts, there is a road classification that doesn't show on the maps. Other than the highways, there are the fifty-miles-an-hour roads with a stripe down the middle of the asphalt. Then there are thirty-miles-an-hour roads, paved, but narrow and without the stripe. Then the macadam gravel roads that are, at least in Vermont, in pretty good shape. Those are the twenty-miles-an-hour roads. They have ditches on each side and you have to slow down and put your tires on the shoulder when you encounter a car coming in the opposite direction. All the good coverts I've found are off the twenty-miles-an-hour roads—you're never going to find anything worthwhile that's easy to get to.

As I'm meandering, the cover looks good in several places, but there are posted signs along both sides of the road. They get thicker the closer you get to a ski area, and in some places in Vermont they're more numerous than the FOR SALE signs. But then, as I travel around a bend and past a homestead, the cover gets birdy looking, with a nice balance of understory and second-growth birch and maple. And there's a power-line clearing cutting through at an angle.

I pull onto the shoulder and have a discussion with myself: *It's not really raining anymore, and the anorak has pretty well dried out. But the woods are wet, and I'm wearing whatever dry spare clothes I brought along. Okay, I'm going to get wet, but it's not really cold outside.*

Hanna casts the deciding vote. She wants to go, and is glad to be out of the truck again. She's back to carrying her bell in her mouth when we start in, and it seems strangely silent for the first minute.

Unfortunately, the cover turns out to be a mirage. It happens a lot of the time. What looks inviting just isn't so hot once you get into it. At other times the good stuff peters out and what you can see from the road is literally all there is. Or once inside, you see houses peeking through the trees on the far side of the cover. I don't want anything to do with quasi-legal places—I have enough of them already—tight covers where you can't shoot in this or that direction because of the houses. Or grouse-only places where, because of a questionable legal status, I won't risk the noise of a gunshot at anything except a grouse, and even then it better be a pretty good opportunity.

But you have to keep searching. Baseball players, even the pros, fail most of the time. Just think of how many at-bats sluggers have between home runs: The best ratio is something like eleven to one. Since they get paid to hit the ball out of the park, that's a lot of failure for every success. And I'm no Babe Ruth of bird covers, just in case you didn't know. In truth, if I can find one really good new place to hunt each year, I'm doing well.

Lately I've had to change my tactics: all the easy-to-find places close to home have been found or are gone. I spend a lot of time asking for access to posted land. I knock on doors, I write letters, I make phone calls. Sometimes it works, and sometimes, no matter how hard I try, the answer is "No."

Mrs. DeWitt owned some land that I coveted, and although I wrote her two letters and left messages on her answering machine, when I stopped by and asked permission, she said, "I'd rather you didn't."

Other people have said, "There's plenty of woods just up the road." Woods and grouse cover are not necessarily the same thing, of course, but I know a "No" when I hear it.

Another man said, "A guy went through there with a bird dog and cleaned the place out a few years ago." I didn't argue. He didn't want me on his land, and there wasn't much I was going to say to change his mind. When I think of all the things I might have said, after wishing I had, I'm always glad that I nodded and left.

Things don't always work out the way you planned. But spare me the lame excuses, please. In the end, I think we'd all prefer Mrs. DeWitt's answer.

At midday a hunting dog needs a little something to eat. Certainly not anything that's going to fill the stomach—bloat is a too-real problem in working dogs—but something to keep energy reserves up. I've settled on a tuna-fish-can-sized portion of meat. This one is called Mighty Dog. Hanna attacks the canned meat like a kid with a candy bar on Easter morning when Lent is finally over.

In Vermont, little towns that show on the map are sometimes nothing more than a gathering of a few houses at a crossroads. Often, if a person were to drive into town looking for a cup of coffee or a tank of gas, he'd be disappointed—there's nothing there. Oh, maybe a house trailer pretending to be a post office or a town garage where a lone highway truck is parked, but that's all. Vermont is full of towns like that.

As I'm climbing the hill out of one such town, the cover across from an old cemetery intrigues me. My pant legs are wet, but other than that I seem to be in good shape, so I pull over and have a look.

After another brief argument with myself, I get out of the truck and make a pass into the woods. Disappointment quickly sets in—the cover turns out to be a confused series of brooklets and boggy areas. My feet are wet when we come back out onto the road twenty minutes later.

Although the opposite side of the road doesn't seem as promising, having already gotten wet I make a *What-the-hell* decision, and Hanna and I start in.

As we parallel the cemetery I can't help reading the gravestones. Many are all but illegible, the chiseled writing having been worn nearly smooth by the passing of time; or is it the acid rain? In the far corner is one worth pausing for: the man who lies here was a captain in the Continental army. A right-hand salute is in order as I pass.

Beyond the graveyard is an alder swamp where beavers have been working. The swamp empties into a stony brook that we follow through a mix of hardwoods and pastures with plenty of old apple trees sprinkled in for good measure. Once the leaves are down, I'm always amazed how much smaller my covers become, but this place goes on and on. "Oh boy, oh boy," I keep repeating out loud.

Along the way I hear two separate grouse flush, and although I have the safety off each time, neither is seen. Hanna, with a different perspective than I, runs ahead a few steps at each bird's flight and provides me with a clue as to where they've gone. Interpreting the actions of a nonsteady bird dog is not recommended procedure, but I follow Hanna's indications and unfortunately only succeed in hearing the birds flush again somewhere ahead of us.

As we're following the brook, a pair of mallards at alder-top height glides over and dumps in just ahead of us. I motion to Hanna to come in, and shut off her beeper collar.

In the inside pocket of my vest I keep a pair of duck loads—steel No. 4s. They'll kick like a mule in the Beretta Ultralight, but I exchange them with the shells in the chambers. The way the law is written, to be completely legal I'd have to get rid of all the lead shot I'm carrying, then go back and get it all out of my truck as well before I try to shoot these ducks. To hell with that. I have three different duck stamps, the season is open, and I'm making an attempt to be legal. That's as close to full compliance as I'm going to get.

In the wet, there's no rustle of leaves underfoot and it's possible to move silently. I tell Hanna to "Hut" and begin to slink ahead, hoping to jump the mallards.

If a dog is 100 percent reliable on "Hut" you don't need a "Stay" command. Unfortunately, Hanna is still learning, and when I turn around she's immediately behind me, advancing in an imitation of my own surreptitious approach. I take Hanna back to the spot where I gave her the "Hut" command and repeat it. As I do, of course I hear the clatter of wings as the mallards spring into the air up ahead.

There's nothing to do but shrug. Some things just aren't meant to be.

We work the other side of the brook on the return trip. I'm reflecting on the lack of woodcock in what is obviously woodcock cover when I hear a grouse get up ahead. I have the gun up, but the bird beats me with the old up-and-down routine: he rises, then abruptly dips back down into the alders again.

"Damn," I hear myself say out loud. The sound of that spoken curse brings up the bird's partner, a hen that tries the same trick.

I have a good lead on the bird and fire through the thick stuff and wait, but hear nothing at all.

I'm a great believer in hunter's intuition—that is, if you THINK you've hit a bird, you probably have. But I'd like some evidence. I hurry ahead and look for feathers in the air and on the ground but discover only some bright green wounds in the alder branches where my shot pattern struck.

After hanging my handkerchief on a tree to mark the spot, I call Hanna to start her looking. When she comes in she's already carrying the hen grouse.

I'm flabbergasted. Alone, I wouldn't have found that running bird. How many grouse like this does a dogless hunter lose each year? None of the estimates are encouraging.

When I scratch Hanna's ears I ask her if the can of Mighty Dog had anything to do with this retrieve in the wet, but she just smiles back at me. If she knows she's not saying.

It starts to sprinkle again. There's an old pair of penny loafers at the very bottom of the war bag, and stuffed inside of them is a pair of wool gym socks. With the hen grouse weighing pleasantly in the game bag, I can hear those dry loafers calling to me even though I'm still a fair hike from the truck.

Two sets of wet hunting clothes and pair of boots that'll take a day to dry seems a fair price to pay for a bagged grouse and a new covert of the grade-A variety, maybe even A-plus. I'll call this place the Captain's Graveyard.

As I pass on my way out, I salute the Revolutionary War captain's grave a second time.

Interlude: Out of Action

ON SATURDAY after an all-day hunt—an indicator day on which I hunted Hanna for the first time without a check cord—I lift her up onto the cellar workbench with the intention of combing the stick-tights out of her ears.

Yikes! Her right eye seems to be coming out of her head. It's protruding the way I've seen a duck's eye bulge after I've rapped its head on a tree trunk to finish it off.

When I call the vet's office OF COURSE it's after business hours, and OF COURSE the vet is not there. The recording says to call the Rowley Animal Hospital for emergencies—that's the local ASPCA clinic. They're expensive. After chewing on the problem for a few minutes I come to the obvious conclusion that whatever is wrong with Hanna needs immediate attention, and the sooner the better. So I bite the bullet and phone Rowley, and the girl on the phone says to come right down.

A young lady-veterinarian takes care of us. They're all young and female these days. It's true. There must be a law that now keeps people of male persuasion out of that profession. This vet appears young enough to be on the high school soccer team, and it's difficult at first to take her seriously. But in less than a minute she has pinned down what's wrong. She opens Hanna's mouth and when the dog yelps, she begins her explanation.

It's a retrobulbar abscess. That's an abscess formed behind the eye socket that is forcing the eyeball to protrude. When the dog opens her mouth, the hinge part of the jaw squeezes the abscessed area and causes pain. Inside my head, the metaphorical light goes on: *So that's the explanation for the seemingly random yelps I've been hearing (and ignoring) from Hanna over the past couple of weeks.* I'm told the abscess formed because a piece of something that the dog was chewing on—a sliver from a stick, perhaps—migrated up the tooth root and formed an infection. It has to be opened and drained, and the dog has to be put on antibiotics.

"Can't we get away without surgery?" I ask.

No, she tells me, because there is a need to match the antibiotic to the specific bacteria that are causing the infection. And the abscess has to be broken.

"When does all this have to be done?"

Her answer is right now. I'll leave Hanna and they'll start her on a general antibiotic, then anesthetize her and go in and lance the abscess.

There's no choice to make, really. I drive home with Hanna's collar on the seat beside me and wonder how many days I'll be without her.

The surgery itself turns out to be only $42. But anesthesia is $140, and the antibiotics come to $119. Then there's the exam, admission, hospitalization and the total is up to $409. I remind myself that there was no choice.

There was a time when I used to say I'd been lucky with bird dogs because I really hadn't spent a lot on dog repairs. For most of my adult life I had no unplanned dog surgeries or broken bones

169

and, with the exception of my first Brittany who had a love-hate relationship with porcupines, my dogs managed to avoid serious field injuries. Plus I had Dick Hersman for a vet. He had a no-nonsense approach to treating dogs, and shared my opinion that autumn was for hunting. Since a bird dog has only a scant few autumns, he often patched up minor injuries so that my dogs could keep hunting. Life was good.

But then Stella came along, and that star-crossed dog required two leg surgeries in three years. Then Dick Hersman died a young man, and I went through a series of vets over the next few years. Some were primarily interested in selling retail products, others were never there when I needed them, and still others believed dogs should be pampered like the spoiled children of rich parents.

People on the outside looking in just can't imagine this sort of thing when they buy a puppy. Instead, they fall in love with the classic images of hunter and bird dog gone a-hunting together: lovely points, wonderful retrieves, mutual love and admiration.

Even if they can steel themselves against the initial cost of a well-bred dog, which is on the plus side of five hundred dollars these days, are they prepared for the rest? Oh, they can afford puppy chow and a collar, but the visits to the vet during the first year alone—office exams, vaccinations, heartworm pills, a spaying operation—can look like the annual budget of a small European country. And if they don't already have a dog, then there's all the other dog things: leashes and beds and kennels and feeding pans, to say nothing of the incalculable collateral damage to lawn, shrubs, doors, car interiors, and anything the puppy can fit his baby teeth around.

And then, from out of the blue, there are things like a retro-bulbar abscess—four hundred dollars on a Saturday evening without thinking twice.

I know all that. I'm not rich by anybody's measure of wealth, yet I have not just one but THREE dogs snoozing in the kennel.

Thankfully, it's only paper money.

Day Thirty-Two: Hunter's Moon

"Fresh October brings the pheasant,
Then to gather nuts is pleasant."

Old Nursery Rhyme

FROM HER POSITION behind the seat, Stella uses her snout to give my right hand a hefty nudge. It's a habit of hers, almost as if she were saying, "Hey, if you're not doing anything with that hand, how about scratching my ears?"

I hope to get in a late-afternoon hunt with Old Miss Belle. She has had an enteric-coated aspirin before we left the house, and she's feeling pretty frisky right now. Hanna will be out of action until Thursday while she recovers from her surgery, so until then I'll put in short days with Stella close to home.

Along the way I drive past the Poland Brook Wildlife Management Area. There was a time when I loved this place, even though the state of Massachusetts stocks pheasants in the mowed fields at the far south end. Poland Brook had overgrown farm areas that attracted woodcock, and there was good cover in the low hills and along the brook. I say "was good cover" because the state began a program of brush-hogging the sumac and scrub alders to make more room for pheasant hunting. That should give you an idea of how important the pheasant is to license sales in my home state.

The main problem with public lands, at least from the standpoint of the grouse hunter, is the state's interpretation of *management.* Here they're cutting down upland cover, even though the Fish and Wildlife Department's official excuse for abbreviating the grouse season a few years ago was the shrinking amount of cover statewide. We define things as *wild* based upon their ability to live without interference from man. A better definition would be those things that can prosper in spite of it.

What bothers me most is that they call the place a Wildlife Management Area. That's like a page out of Orwell's *1984.*

171

No wildlife is managed here—it's a put-and-take pheasant operation, and it's so heavily hunted that it's hard to find anything alive out there. On Saturday mornings it can be pretty grim: five hunters for every pheasant, and the equivalent of twenty-one-gun salutes can be regularly heard echoing in the hills. It plays out like an experiment a sociologist dreamed up to see how men would react in a noncompetitive sport when competition was suddenly required. I react to the sociologist's experiment with my feet—I stay away.

So I drive by. I don't love Poland Brook any longer.

There's a crazy zebra pattern of shadows on the fallen leaves, compliments of the late-afternoon sun through the leafless maples. Stella actively works scent among the shadows for a distance of several hundred yards all the way out of the little swamp we've been hunting. I've seen this act before; there's a bird running just in front of her. I have the gun at ready, but after we break out of the wet area she loses whatever scent she had been following. She hunts to the front, but sometimes a man's brain has to over-rule a dog's nose. I get her attention and we turn around. It's a safe assumption that the running bird has given her the slip and is now immediately behind us back in the swamp.

Once we return to the zebra stripes, Stella finds the lost scent and works back the way we came. After some false pointing she strikes a pose that says this is the real thing, and when I walk forward a hen pheasant jumps into the air off to the left. I was expecting a grouse, but this must be a fugitive from nearby Poland Brook. Hens are legal game in Massachusetts, a fact that speaks to the put-and-take status of pheasants here.

You can take rising birds by shooting right at them IF—and the if is always capitalized—you keep the gun moving. Sometimes the shot is so easy that you lift your head to see the bird fall or, more often, you shoot at a spot and fail to move the gun. Both are disastrous mistakes, usually done on easy shots.

This time, though, the shot isn't easy and I'm forced to concentrate enough to take the bird properly as it climbs through the swamp maples. The hen's fall knocks off a brittle dead branch, and both come down thirty yards away in a small extravaganza of swirling feathers and snapping branches.

Automatically I open the gun and turn back to Stella's point. I have the empty shell in my hand when the bird she has been pointing all along—a second hen pheasant—flushes and heads my way. I have the presence of mind to drop the empty and close the gun, but not enough of that fleeting commodity to change the barrel selector. Of course when I pull on the bird all there is is a *click* as the hammer falls on an empty chamber. I scramble and fumble with the selector, but there was only one *right moment* and now it has passed and all I can do is watch the hen make her way through the distant treetops.

When I opted for a modern lightweight over-and-under with a single trigger, I knew even then that this sort of thing would happen eventually. For the twenty-three years that I shot double-trigger guns it seemed at times my index finger could think faster than my brain. Occasionally, after a long shot, I'd chide myself for not pulling the back trigger only to open the gun and find out that I had.

But double-triggers are out of fashion. Modern shotgunners, for reasons unknown to me, reject that sort of gun as being too difficult to master. Instead, popularity has promoted the simpler (but internally much more complicated) single-trigger gun. When it comes to over-and-unders, that's all they sell.

A single, selective trigger seems like a wonderful idea, but selectors can only work in the future tense, never in the present. At least, for me they can't.

But things could be worse. We have one bird on the ground and a good line to follow on a second. Stella brings in the fallen hen, and after the few minutes it takes to field dress the bird we start after the escapee.

We break back out into the open fields. There is a way of directing the dog that I use: if I want her to work *over this way*, I start to walk *over this way* and, because I've trained her to stay in front of me, she ends up going where I want her to go. But when the dog is Stella's age and can't hear any longer, my method only works some of the time, and those times are when she happens to be looking at me. It's an adjustment I have to relearn each time out with Stella. Things slow down, and some time is spent waiting for her to check back. It takes patience, and things don't progress as rapidly as I'd like. But that's okay. Stella paid her dues long ago.

After several passes through the bordering woods and fields it becomes evident that the second hen has flown to Blinkville or someplace else where she's safe from us.

Twenty minutes later on the way out, we're passing through what's left of a ruined orchard overgrown with bittersweet vines and all but knocked down by a heavy snowfall a few years back. The breeze is coming uphill toward us. Out thirty yards in front of me Stella slows as she winds something, not yet sure of what information the breeze is bringing her.

When I happen to glance to the right, not twenty yards from me a rooster pheasant has flattened himself on the ground, trying to be invisible. He almost succeeded. The bird is like a multi-colored Persian rug, yet I wouldn't have spotted him save for the white ring around his neck. But it's not me that concerns him—his whole being is focused on Stella and the noise her beeper collar is making. She tiptoes in slow motion as she labors at un-raveling the scent trail.

With one eye on the rooster and the other on Stella, I click the selector to the upper barrel. It seems like a pretty good idea to stand right where I am. It'll be interesting.

Stella continues downhill, but then there is a signal moment when she obviously realizes that she's going the wrong way on a one-way scent trail. At that sign the rooster knows instantly that the jig is up and springs into the air, cackling profanities as he makes for the sky.

But we're in the woods, and pheasants are hardly aerial acrobats. The bird bumps into several tree branches over the fallen orchard, and can't seem to generate much forward speed. I wait until the cock has gone far enough for the pattern to open up, then shoot him with the tight barrel. There's a thud as the rooster hits the ground, then a single *cluck* that says he survived the fall and won't be there long.

Pheasants are notorious for favoring the infantry over the air force, so I have to get Stella into the tangles to find the still-alive bird before he runs off. She's still standing fifty yards away, wondering if she heard a shot.

"Miss Belle. Come on. We have a bird down in here." I call and wave frantically to her as I break into the tangles. To mark the spot, I hang my handkerchief on a branch where I estimate the bird fell. And here, on a little twig, is a bit of feather fluff, and there are several others on the ground. Stella appears, searching more for me than for the pheasant. I sit her down, then exaggerate the hand motions that accompany the command of "Find dead bird." She gets to her feet and walks away.

I begin moving some of the vines and blowdowns, hoping the rooster has crawled into the nearest hiding place. Stella seems lost, wandering aimlessly nearby. I bring her back to the handkerchief and go through the "Find dead bird" routine once more. She used to be good at this, but when I look up she has wandered off again. After another few minutes of poking around, I start out to collar Stella. She's not working scent as far as I can tell, and even though she's an old dog I'm in no mood for her shirking a job I've asked her to do. She wanders farther away at my approach.

I'm about to become angry when an incomplete thought crosses my mind. That thought begins with *Maybe. . .*

Stella wanders ahead. I hang back a hundred feet or so, letting her wander. At no time does it seem she's following scent, but after a while there's a direction to her wandering, and then, in her fashion, she points.

When Stella was young she pointed elegantly. She used to have so much style and intensity that she trembled on point. Her tail was high, her head strained forward, and her legs were rigor-mortis-stiff. Now she's old, and the panache is gone. Her tail is limply horizontal and nothing about her seems alert. It appears that she has simply stopped while walking. Ah, but she still trembles.

She's standing in front of a little lump in the ground. There's a small pine tree and a leafless bush growing out of a mound the size of a water heater buried on its side. With the gun at port arms I walk around the lump, looking hard. The forest floor is covered with freshly fallen leaves, but I can see that there's nothing there.

I go to Stella and push her rear end. "Go ahead," I say. She won't move.

Now I look even harder at the lump. There's nothing there but a couple of rocks and some sticks—and the tiny striped end of a tail feather sticking out from the leaves covering the bird's back. I make a grab for what I estimate to be the right spot and have my hand around the pheasant's neck.

The rooster is very much alive, and when I lift him out of the leaves Old Miss Belle pretends she's Young Stella once more and jumps in the air. Or at least her front end does.

I hadn't centered the bird, but it turns out that he was hit with at least eight pellets of copper-plated No. $7\frac{1}{2}$s, mostly in the belly and legs. His right leg is twice broken, and so is his right wing.

It's 181 paces back to the spot where I hung my handkerchief. Amazing. I couldn't run that far with a hangnail, let alone a broken leg, yet this is the sort of thing shot-up pheasants routinely do. They can be tough to kill, and it's not for nothing that real pheasant hunters favor tight chokes and heavy shot.

And what about Stella? Hunting birds with a dog is an elaborate rock-scissors-paper game: *Flight trumps dog; gun trumps flight; dog trumps gun.* Sure, as I said, there are times when a man's brain has to overrule a dog's nose. But the brain also has to be smart enough to recognize the occasions when *nose trumps brain.* For my particular brain, that can be quite a challenge.

As we drive home, a full moon is rising over the eastern hills beyond the Connecticut River. In the old days this November full moon was called the Hunter's Moon. Some people will argue and say that title belongs to October's full moon, but that only serves to show how far we've come from a time when that sort of thing was an important part of everyday life.

I wrote a dog book a few years ago and subtitled it *Things Bird Dogs Have Tried to Teach Me.* On days afield like this, I'm sure Stella wonders if I'm ever going to catch on. She's snoozing on the floor behind the seat, exhausted by a three-hour outing. Dogs grow old too soon. But on the plus side, at least I don't have to worry that she's chewing the seat belts like Hanna.

Driving home in the moonlight, I reflect on the idea that it's November 13. If there's a halfway mark in the season, it's way behind us. I can feel the autumn evaporating, and, like a kid with an ice cream cone on a hot day, it's easy to spend more time chasing after the part that's dripping away than enjoying what's left of it.

That may be equally true of old bird dogs. I reach behind the seat and scratch Stella's ears. She awakens for a moment, then resettles her position on the rug before drifting back off to sleep.

Interlude: Idle Sunday

> *"Negotiations and love songs*
> *Are often mistaken for one and the same."*
>
> Paul Simon
> "Train in the Distance"

DEER SEASON IS UNDER WAY in Vermont. For sixteen days in November—that is, all the time between three consecutive weekends—rifle hunters go after venison-on-the-hoof. Although it's completely legal to continue to hunt grouse with bird dogs, I'm not that crazy. I stay south of the border.

But it's Sunday, and though they changed the blue laws, there's still no Sunday hunting in Massachusetts. I'm not much for watching football on TV, so I head over to the skeet club.

Target shooting is usually something I do when it's not hunting season. Yet, whenever I do manage to get to the range during the season, my poor scores serve as a graphic reminder that I can't stay sharp without practice.

Today I have the 20 gauge with me. It was my mainline gun for years before I bought the Ultralight 12 gauge, but it's now been relegated to the role of spare gun. If I don't get it out and shoot with it once in a while, its status will soon degrade from spare to strange. When I find myself in a situation where I have to use a gun I'm not used to, I'm like a guy at a dinner party who can't quite get the hang of the ornate silverware. The unfamiliarity means that I have to concentrate on something that normally is second nature. Just to stay current, I'm going to put a few boxes of shells through the 20 gauge today.

Once at the club, I run into Russell. He owns a handsome English setter named Max. Russell likes to talk dogs with me, and has often referred to me as a "dog-training expert." Although I've always hastened to deny his assertion, once it became apparent what he'd done with his bird dog—or more accurately, what he HADN'T done—I realized that expertise is far more a matter of perspective than position.

He has Max with him today, and wants me to have a look. The dog is on the front seat of Russell's car, and I scratch Max's ears through the open window. You wouldn't have to mix any colors to paint Max's portrait: he's cleanly white and black with raw sienna eyebrows.

"You know, he's a good dog most of the time," Russell says over my shoulder. "But he just runs wild when I first let him out. He chases up birds and won't listen to me for an hour or so. He's been that way for two years now. What am I gonna do to make him stay with me?"

Oh, Max's troubles are no mystery—he's an untrained dog. That is, he's a dog that will not stop when told. Max is then put into the worst possible situation: a Saturday-morning pheasant hunt in an area stocked with birds and thick with other hunters and their dogs. In such a situation, an untrained dog behaves like an untrained dog. Why should that surprise anybody?

But, of course, I can't say that.

So instead I tell Russell, if not the truth, at least something true. "Max is a good dog with all the desire he needs. He'll get better. He has plenty of good qualities—just be patient with him."

There. Nothing that I've said is untrue. It's a remarkable phenomenon, but it is difficult to screw up a bird dog. Really. We're asking the dog to do something he wants to do anyway, so that part is easy. Thankfully the dog has a brain, and if the owner-operator can keep from doing certifiably stupid things, chances are the dog isn't going to be too far off the mark. Eventually they all come around.

But Russell is having none of that. "You told me the same thing last time. Max ain't no puppy no more. This is his third season and he's getting worse instead of better."

Okay, he wants the truth.

"Has Max been yard trained?" I ask.

"Oh sure; he'll sit and heel and fetch and—"

"Let me rephrase that, Russ. I only want to know if he'll stop when you tell him to? If he won't, he's not yard trained."

After a moment Russell looks away and mutters, "He's never been too good with that."

"Normally, Russ, my next question would be 'Is Max field trained?' but if he won't obey 'Whoa' in the backyard he's certainly not going to stop when you tell him to in the field."

"Well, he likes to hunt and I take him out a lot. . . ."

"Russ, you asked me what was wrong. Here it is: before you put any bird dog into a hunting situation, he has to be field trained—by that I mean he has to stay in range. Now, there's a lot of ways to teach that. Some people use ropes, and some use shock collars. But none of them are going to work unless the dog will stop when you tell him to. When it comes to obedience, you have to insist. Go after him and shake the living daylights out of him when he doesn't obey, and make sure you do it every time

he pulls that crap. Once you get him to stop on command you can teach him everything else he needs to know. But without the 'Whoa' command he's out of control, and you can yell all you want but you're not going to teach him anything."

Russ looks none too happy, but I have a head of steam now and might as well get it all out.

"Dog training is only about controlling the situation," I say. "With a dog that obeys 'Whoa' you never lose control as long as you don't lose your voice. I train puppies by *The Shotgun Method,* but Max is too old for that. You might get a handle on Max if you decide to get tough with him starting today, but not likely. He has been ignoring you for three years, and that running start has become a habit that'll take some doing to break."

Russell nods, but nobody likes being told he's done a lousy job. Russ is a nice guy, but he apparently doesn't have the stomach to physically discipline a dog and be consistent about it.

On the other hand, I can't believe I've said anything that Russell doesn't know already. It doesn't matter that Max will behave himself in the kitchen and will sit, stay, heel, fetch, and roll over. Hell, it wouldn't matter if he could open his own can of food and balance a checkbook. The only thing that DOES matter is the first thing, and in dog training the first thing is "Whoa." Without "Whoa," a dog is neither yard trained nor field trained, and that qualifies him as a Corvair Setter—a bird dog who is unsteady to wing, shot, voice, and icy pavement at any speed. In other words, a dog out of control.

And, in reality, no part of the fault lies with Max. It's his owner who needs a kick in the pants.

George Bird Evans wrote a classic bird-dog book titled *The Troubles with Bird Dogs.* Great title. In my own answer to the question implied by that title, I can tell you that the troubles with most bird dogs, Max included, have to do with their owners. The *train 'em with love* advocates coddle their dogs without ever really training them, others lock up their dogs without ever training them, still others exercise the hell out of their dogs, also without ever training them. I don't think I'm going too far out on a limb when I say that without exception EVERY troublesome bird dog could be a good and valuable hunting companion if he had an owner who put some time into the discipline that is training— even just a little. The trains only run where they've laid down railroad tracks.

Dog training is not difficult nor does it require any great amount of skill, but it is work in the dictionary definition of the word, and it has to be done. There is nothing that you can substitute for it. Despite the unfortunate title of my dog-training book *(Pointing Dogs Made Easy),* there is no "easy" way, no "shortcut," although books and magazines are full of easy ways and shortcuts. People like Russell think there's a trick to it, some insiders' secret that only men with good dogs are privy to.

There is no trick. It's just a matter of showing the dog what you want, then going over it and over it and insisting the dog do it.

But you have to insist.

Later, Russell outshoots me at five-stand and is seen smiling at his dog when he puts his shotgun back into his car.

Day Thirty-Five: Jack Fell Down and Broke His Crown

"Set the foot down with distrust on the crust of the world—it is thin."
Edna St. Vincent Millay

THE GHOST OF the waning phantom moon hangs transparently white in the clear morning sky. It's the first wool-shirt day of the season here in Massachusetts, and the air is cold enough so that the puddles are frozen. On the forest floor, all the leafy ferns and weeds have turned to crumpled bits of brown, and the concealed things I used to trip over earlier in the season are easily avoided now.

The witch hazel shrubs are blooming with their stringy, yellow-green flowers. Blossoms in November seem out of place and faintly absurd—the leaves have already fallen, yet this bizarre shrub is in bloom. And they're loaded this fall with their strange, exploding nut pods. Good. That's more food for the grouse in this apple-less year.

Hanna is back in action after her eye surgery. Loafing around the kennel for the past few days seems to have done her no harm. Up ahead she pauses where a woods road crosses and looks back to check my direction, then continues on.

"Good girl, Hannaberry," I hear myself say out loud. The fact that she didn't sprint off along the trail represents considerable progress. Puppies routinely do that sort of thing, and it can be distressing—any dog that runs an unencumbered straight line for even ten seconds is out of earshot. Puppies don't know where the birds are. (As proof, whenever they find one they're surprised.) They like to do things like sprint down a woods road, NOT because they think they'll find birds there, but because it seems like fun. That's where you, the trainer, come in. Keeping Sparkey on the playing field so he CAN find birds pretty much describes the critical path in puppy training.

Hanna passes through a sun-sprinkled grove of hemlocks without pausing. It was in this grove that Sophie pointed the final woodcock of last season. I remember that I had a clear glimpse of the bird, but it passed behind the screen of evergreens just as I fired. Sophie's habit of watching birds rather than running after them paid a dividend. She saw this bird fall and went to the very edge of the brook and picked the woodcock out from between some stones and brought it to me—a bird I was certain I had missed.

All coverts contain memories, some more than others: memories of birds taken and shots missed and wonderful points and retrieves. They accumulate like growth rings on a tree, and hunting a familiar covert is a bit like paging through a scrapbook. How many birds have I taken here over the years? How many have I missed? How many points have I had by thirty years' worth of bird dogs? And when I lose a covert to posting, along with a place to hunt I've lost all the memories that are bound up in that piece of topography, all of them pronounced extinct by a landowner with an armful of signs and a perverted sense of entitlement.

Like all souvenirs, this particular grove of hemlocks doesn't mean anything to any other soul in the world. But thankfully Sophie's last point is alive and well each time I pass this way.

The sudden rumble of a grouse flush grabs my attention. Twenty yards ahead of me the bird breaks from the pines, already in full flight, and passes to the rear beyond my right shoulder. I see him clearly, but my fastest response can't catch up and my shot is behind the target. The grouse dips and curves left and is gone, and the moment is quickly over.

As I stand staring at the spot where no grouse feathers float in the air, the tip of a dead tree branch that was struck by the bird's wing continues to vibrate. Opportunities like that are a challenge to my abilities, and too frequently I miss. There is no excuse. I'm simply not good enough to make fast crossing shots with consistency.

Hanna checks back, and I whistle her in, then stand for a moment with the gun open and again see the bird—definitely a gray-tailed cock—hurtling through the dappled sunlight in the clearing. Once more I feel the twinge of panic at not being able to catch up with him. What was spectacular was not the shot, but the chance. Grouse hunting is more than just skeet shooting with trees: The shots are often makable but always challenging, and they dare you to do something on the cusp of difficult. Even the easy shots aren't so easy.

My grimace fades into a smile, more of appreciation than amusement. I drop a fresh shell into the barrel and whistle Hanna ahead.

We pursue the grouse to the far side of the ridge. There is an open farm field below. Grouse won't cross open spaces unless they're pushed, so he must have flown into the scrub on the hillside. I tell myself that the bird is here. When we've hunted farther than I estimate he flew, we loop downward and work back closer to the edge of the field. We've already covered a lot of places where he's not, so each step brings us closer to the moment we'll find him. Some folks call that sort of thing *faith*. I like to think of it as a combination of applied experience and positive thinking.

Ahead of me the dog's bell goes silent and her beeper sounds. I can't see her, but she has the bird in the brushy oaks and laurel at the field margin. *Move into the open, or stay in the cover?* Every hunter has pondered that dilemma. I'll delay my answer until I can get a better look. I move toward the sound of Hanna's beeper and am still in the thick stuff when I hear the grouse flush. The gun comes up, but the grouse doesn't show himself until he enters the trees eighty yards away.

Part of that "applied experience" factor is the knowledge that there wasn't much I could have done. A single hunter can't surround a pointed bird—at least, not very often. This one skirted the edge of the cover rather than come back at me or cross the open field.

It's easy to agree with the prizefighting sentiment, "May the best man win." But when the "best man" ends up being a bird with a brain the size of a cashew, what does that say about me?

As I make my way down the rocky bank to the brook, the water bounces and foams around the boulders, softly singing the world's oldest lullaby. There is some rim ice around the edges of the quiet backwashes, but nothing really seems any different than it was when I crossed here on mild days earlier in the season. Right here is a place where I can step from one dry rock to another without getting my feet wet.

The engineer part of me has tried (seldom with any success) to explain to various seemingly interested people the basic thermodynamic phenomenon of *latent heat*. I'm not about to add you to that number. Let me just say that there is a property of water that delays total freezing when the temperature is thirty-two degrees: water and ice can and do coexist at that temperature.

Having said that, the rocks in the brook appear dry, but the unseen mist from the flowing water has turned into invisible black ice on the stepping-stones and made them as slick as any vaudeville banana peel. I step onto the first stone and go down hard as soon as I begin to shift my weight. In an automatic reaction, I try to break my fall with my right hand and the gun submerges in a foot of water. Somehow I manage not to land on my back, but my right shin takes the brunt of the impact on a rock. It all seems to be happening in slow motion. I find I'm thinking *Okay, that part still works,* as I regain my footing and get back up on the bank of the brook.

There's something about whacking your shin that causes the pain to stay with you—it hurts as much a minute later as it did the instant you rapped it. And rubbing doesn't change anything. My shirtsleeves are wet, my pants are soaked, and my right boot is full of water. I undo the laces and wring out the sock and innersole, then put them back on, intending to change into dry clothes at the truck. My shin continues to hurt. There aren't any little red stars coming out of it like in the cartoons, but there might as well be.

The pain has subsided just a bit by the time I lace up and prepare to get moving again. The gun has been underwater and has a shiny new ding on the side of the top barrel. I open and close the action a few times, then experimentally fire a pair of shells to make sure everything is in working order. Hanna stares at me, uncertain just what's going on but trusting that soon we'll get back to hunting.

And all the while, in the background, the brook continues its seductive murmuring.

Of course, I still have to get across.

A walk upstream—not more than a hundred yards—finds an easy spot to cross. This time I take nothing for granted and test the footing as I go, but the stepping-stones here are in quiet water and are ice-free, and in fifteen minutes the key is in the truck's ignition. I dig out the war bag for some dry clothes to change into. The shin still hurts a lot more than just a little.

Grouse hunting is an athletic event, and I wonder how many more years I can do it. I've already given up softball and everything else involving running (with the possible exception of occasional sprints after puppies-in-training).

But looking at myself at fifty-one, I seem to be holding up well. Although I joke about getting old, other than reading fine print and hearing whispers, there aren't too many things that I once could do that I can't do any longer. Oh, there are spider veins on my ankles, my hair is disappearing, and I can't easily turn to look out the truck's rear window while backing up, but all in all the kid with the gray mustache seems to be surviving the aging process in pretty good shape.

Then something like this happens. The bruise is already beginning to show on my shin as I change out of my boots, and will form an egg and turn purple before the day is out. Within a week my ankle will swell up as all the trapped fluid answers gravity's call.

Of course, I could have broken my leg, and would have had to crawl out of the woods. Yikes.

In the final analysis, good health is all that matters. A fancy car, a big salary, or, in my own case, time to hunt the entire season are all just a mockery if you're unable to enjoy them. Health is everything. There is always an inherent risk in going into the woods. That risk is compounded by being alone, as I usually am.

I dress to stay warm while moving, but if I had to spend the night in the woods in winter I'd freeze.

I'm not about to stop hunting, but the possibility of injury is something to consider each time I stumble while crossing a stone wall or trip on some long-forgotten barbed wire. Or fall on the rocks while crossing a brook.

It's not always the grouse that lose when you go grouse hunting.

CHAPTER FIVE

Next Stop, Canaan

Day Thirty-Eight: Patterns

*"This is man's environment, and
ours should be a way of life that
cherishes it."*

Hal Borland

THE DOGS BARK a greeting when I go to the kennel. Hanna, full
of puppy energy, springs in the air and looks me in the eye at the
apex of each leap. Stella is also at the gate, making groaning sounds
that pass for talking, eager to go and afraid she'll be left behind.

And in the background paces little all-white Amy.

After letting out the other two to race around the yard, I
spend a minute with Amy. There was a time not so long ago when
it didn't seem age would ever slow her down, but it's happened.
She's an old fifteen, deaf, blind in one eye, and with the stale smell
of a too-old dog. Winter is approaching—a tough time for old
dogs—and she probably should have been put down this past
summer. But one dog's death seemed more than enough.

When she was in her prime, Amy was a lulu. She didn't like
other dogs or riding in cars, didn't think she owned the yard or
the kennel, and, in truth, she wasn't even a very friendly pet. Her
single purpose in life was running, and I didn't think she'd ever
stop. Her hunting style revolved around covering ground with
the throttle wide open. She even retrieved at a dead run. She'd
come to me with a thorn in her foot, but wouldn't stop unless
I grabbed her.

Amy was a hardhead, and at times it seemed her life was one
long remedial lesson. Yet she was the only dog I've known that
would routinely circle and pin running birds. And if ever a dog
was an appliance, Amy was it. I could put her down anywhere
and she'd hunt at full voltage. She pointed a lot of birds for me,
but she'd regularly become so excited that she'd go crazy. I
couldn't calm her down at such times. It wasn't that she wouldn't
listen to me; I honestly believe she COULDN'T. The longer she
stood on point, the tighter she'd wind up. Although *normal Amy*

191

was a handful, she was within the realm of manageability. But when she'd get overexcited she became *Amy squared,* and that was more than I could handle.

I have hundreds of stories about Amy and her craziness. Retelling most of them causes my voice and my blood pressure to rise. I used to laugh and say that I'd spent more time angry with her than all my other dogs put together. Then I realized it wasn't a joke at all. It's probably very close to the truth.

I've owned good bird dogs that other men admired: Hazel and Stella and Sophie in the past twenty-five years, and two Brittanys back when I was a young man. All of them were work-manlike dogs that never gave me any trouble; dogs that trained easily and learned from their experiences and were a pleasure to hunt with. But when the memories unfold, it's like the story of the prodigal son where the bad boy gets all the attention: crazy Amy hogs the spotlight.

Last April, when the time came to pick Hanna out of her litter, there were four female puppies to choose from. Hanna and two of her sisters were perfectly ordinary seven-week-old pup-pies with a healthy blend of curiosity and a five-second attention span. They bit each other on the rear end and attacked my pant cuffs and my shoelaces. But the fourth sister was all high-speed motion. She scampered everywhere, investigated everything, left the room, climbed onto the table, ran up the walls. The human voice had no effect on her, and her feet didn't stop running even when she was picked up.

The breeder referred to her as *The Live Wire.* "She carries her tail well. That's important to some people," he said. After a pause, he looked sideways at me and added, "But she's going to be a handful for somebody."

I chose my words carefully. "No matter what anybody tells you, this dog is not *The Live Wire.* Her name is Amy. That's a fact because I've already owned Amy, and this is her all over again. And believe me, I don't want anything to do with another one."

At the kennel gate I scratch Old Amy's ears until she grows impatient and retreats into the doghouse. She knows she's not going hunting, and she's glad the puppy isn't there to harass her. After Stella is back in the kennel and the gate is closed, Amy's face continues to peer out at me from the doghouse.

I salute her with a wry smile. "Miss Amy, you were something else."

Hanna and I start in at the Muddy Road covert. They're deer hunting in Vermont, so we'll remain close to home until after Thanksgiving.

I'm still limping from the fall on the rocks a few days ago. It's surprising, because I continue to think of myself as a kid. Admittedly, I'm a kid with bifocals and a bald spot, but a kid nonetheless. Life keeps giving that kid previews of what it's like to be old. Bumps and twists and minor things I used to shake off now bother me for days. Or, as in this case, I fall while crossing a brook and limp around for weeks. The previews keep getting longer and more frequent. I suspect that when they begin to overlap, the kid will have arrived.

In front of me, Hanna crosses a little muddy watercourse and runs by a patch of thorny brush. A moment later, as I'm negotiating the same mire, a hen grouse that Hanna missed flushes out of the thorns. The bird wants to get somewhere behind me, and passes close over my right shoulder on her way there. I see her coming and try to pivot for a shot, but lose my footing in the mud and can only genuflect as the hen passes. Amen.

After we check to see if the grouse had a buddy, we start up the slope after the thorn-patch hen. We circle out and then back again on a curve that will take us at right angles through the zone where she most probably landed. Direct pursuit often pushes the bird up too far in front of you, but the loop method, when it works, results in crossing shots.

Of course, any pursuit technique is predicated on *The Maybe Factor*. Maybe the bird will hold still once she lands, but maybe she won't. Or maybe I miscalculated how far she flew in the first place. Or maybe we just missed her—the woods are a big place, after all. Whatever the reason, after several fruitless passes the mud has dried on the right knee of my pants, and it's time to admit we're not going to find this grouse again. At least, not today.

Off to the right I see Hanna running a straight line, but when I whistle, then yell "Hut," she never breaks stride. Now she's heading up the side of a steep hill at full gallop. She's heard me, but I know the signs. She's chasing turkeys again.

It happened twice last week. She ran off on one of her casts, and when I went to look for her she had gone over the next ridge. It had all the earmarks of turkey chasing, but the evidence was only circumstantial since I couldn't catch her in the act. I pulled her around by the ear and let her know I was unhappy about her running off, but even as it was happening I wasn't sure how effective punishment was going to be.

Today there's little doubt. The leaves on the forest floor have been turned over in lawn-sized patches—a sure sign of turkeys scratching for mast. I start out after her, and, as if to confirm my suspicions, a shadow passes across the sun, then another, and after following the line of movement I catch sight of several turkeys gliding off in the distance.

I've had a lot of luck keeping my dogs from chasing deer, and I'm eternally thankful for that. But then the subject of turkeys comes up and I have to take it all back. All of my dogs have been guilty of turkey chasing.

In the classic case, the dog runs off and stays gone until the turkeys have flown. I holler and tell the dog "No!" but they always act as if they can't help themselves. Turkeys must be something of a siren song to a bird dog. Since they're game birds, they probably smell pretty inviting. They don't try to hide, trusting to their running ability instead. And of course they're so big a dog can probably see them moving ahead. Compounding it all is the fact that it's never just one turkey—there's usually a bunch of them. Of course a dog is going to be interested.

Staying away from turkeys just isn't possible. You can't hunt where they're not. Turkeys are like rats and seem to be everywhere these past fifteen years. The folks in the Fish and Wildlife Department are excited about it. I have a different opinion.

Unless I'm willing to put up with Hanna running turkeys every chance she gets, it's imperative something be done right now. It's time we had a "discussion" on the subject. I'll intercept her while she's coming back from the scene of the crime, which will be any minute now since the turkeys have flown to Blinkville.

It's been a while since I've physically beaten a dog. It's one of those things I'm almost afraid to write about in these politically sensitive times. Some men use an electronic collar in these situations. It's a way of giving an instant kick in the pants when a dog is doing something it knows to be wrong but feels insulated from you by distance. I own a shock collar and I'm not above using it. But it's at home, so right now I'll have to revert to the way men trained dogs for the ten thousand years before the shock collar was invented. When I walk over the hill, sure enough, Hanna is on her way back and looking as pleased as Popeye when he discovered the spinach patch. I grab hold of her collar and smack her with my folded leather belt until her yips become continuous.

Training is demonstration and enforcement, and when the dog is deliberately breaking the law, you need to do some enforcing of the kind that'll make her wish she hadn't. If there's another way that works, I don't know it.

With the exception of Amy, each of my dogs has had a brief love affair with wild turkeys that abruptly ended with a whipping.

Corporal punishment laid on while the dog is in the act made certain that there wouldn't be a next time.

I say Amy was the exception because there wasn't much of anything that I could do to her that had a lasting effect, be it about turkey chasing or anything else. Miss Amy was a real piece of work.

Whenever Hanna might be tempted by turkeys in the future, she'll associate her temptation with today's painful thrashing. That is, unless she's more like Amy than I realize.

Along about the middle of November, I begin to feel a small panic that comes of seeing the season slipping away. The end can be seen looming just a couple of weeks ahead, and those places where birds were found earlier need to be revisited. Today I'm purposely hitting the coverts in Massachusetts's Berkshire hill towns for what might be the last time this year.

When I park outside the Four Corners covert the scene looks like a late-autumn landscape by the American impressionist Willard Metcalf, except that the brushwork is a good deal finer; there are hills and pastures and stone walls and birch trees artistically arranged beneath a cerulean sky. There were a bunch of woodcock in those birches when I hunted here in late October, but I don't expect much today. The woodcock season is the briefest of all—the birds aren't even gone yet and I miss them already. They migrate according to a bunch of factors, none of which have to do with the calendar. Nonetheless, once it gets to be double-digit November in New England, a bird hunter's time is more profitably spent looking for grouse.

Having said all that, as soon as we cross the stone wall at Four Corners Hanna works to a point. She's in a wet flat, and from her almost sitting posture it's likely that she has a woodcock. But as a creature of habit, I go first to the distant spot a grouse might have run to, then work my way back to the nearer places. With each step closer to the dog, the chances improve that the bird being pointed is a woodcock.

When I'm just a few paces from Hanna's point a pair of woodcock springs up. They're tiny birds that fly in opposite directions, one climbing toward the spindly treetops, while the other seems content to fly straightaway at eye level. The first shot drops the low bird, then I bring the gun up again and swing through the climber as he starts away, and he too falls.

Woodcock doubles take a lot of cooperation on the part of the birds. Although they're not tough targets individually, legitimate, makable double chances are few and far between. While Hanna is searching for the fallen birds I try to remember the last time I succeeded in taking a genuine double. *None last year, and was the pair that Stella pointed at Tripwire the year before? Or the year before that?* It's a good thing I have it written in my journals, because, like so many other "unforgettable moments," they all run together after a while.

The wind has been out of the west all day. There is some darkening in that part of the sky, and suddenly it's snowing. The flakes swirl on the wind, occasionally blowing horizontally, and then, ten minutes later, as quickly as it began, the snow squall is over and what accumulation there is looks like fallout from a spray-paint job.

Later, against the back hillside, Hanna is apparently working scent, then seems to lose interest. When I hack her back she picks up the scent again, but continues on, this time in a different direction. If there was a bird here, he's obviously given us the slip.

Every grouse in the wild has scenting predators after him on a full-time basis. Foxes, weasels, coyotes, bobcats—all of them hunt with their noses, just as a bird dog does. Yet grouse survive. A bird dog is at best only a part-time hunter no matter what his breeding or training. No wonder a grouse can give any dog the slip so easily. Whenever I begin to estimate the percentage of birds that never get pointed, no matter what number I care to use I always feel that it's too low.

During the next hour and a half we chase three separate grouse, none of them pointed and all of them flushed in the same areas where we found grouse the last time we were here. Are they the same birds? If so, we've given them an education. *Be well and multiply* is my parting wish for them as we make our way out.

When I break out onto the hard road, there are two kids playing back toward the houses at the other end. I check my watch, and sure enough, it's already after school. One kid has a bike, the other a skateboard, and like curious boys everywhere they come down to see what's going on.

"Is that a real gun?"

"Sure. It's a shotgun."

"Can I try it?"

I laugh. "Not today." The boys look the gun over with a healthy blend of fear and fascination.

"Why is your dog wearing a bell?"

"So I can keep track of her in the woods."

"Can she do any tricks?"

I smile, then take off my hat and scale it over the brushes that line the roadside. "Hannaberry, fetch dead bird." It's small potatoes for her, and when she brings in the hat and sits to deliver, I pause for effect before giving the "Thank you" release command.

"How's that for a trick, fellas?"

The boys are impressed. "Can I pet her?" one of them asks.

Hanna, normally shy around people, is nudging the kid's hand so the question answers itself. While they're occupied with the dog, I put the trigger lock on the gun and slip it back into its case behind the seat of the truck.

"Did you catch anything?"

I take the two woodcock from my vest and lay them on the tailgate for the kids to examine, but they seem disappointed that I don't have a pheasant. One boy runs his finger along the bird's beak.

"Are they good to eat?"

"They're okay, but not really terrific."

Then I ask them a loaded question, "Does your father take you hunting with him?"

One shakes his head and says, "My dad doesn't like guns."

The other boy says, "My father lives in Baltimore."

Too bad, fellas. This is a lot of fun, are my thoughts, but I only nod at them. The boys stand around while I load Hanna in the truck, then return my wave as I drive off.

Peter, my sometimes hunting partner, is part of the Big Brothers program, and he has a kid he takes out once in a while. These boys aren't so lucky. Kids are curious, and there's a whole world out there; not just woodcock and bird dogs, but skies and weather and songbirds and owls and animals that leave tracks in the snow, wildflowers and trees with names that you can look up and read about in field guides. And although every boy doesn't necessarily need to grow up to be a bird hunter, he at least ought to have someone there to introduce him to nature.

But in these politically correct times, this hunting thing that you and I do is socially unacceptable. We are, after all, not what we EAT, but what we LIKE, and those of us who like shooting game birds with shotguns are automatically suspect. License sales everywhere continue their forty-year decline, and not just in my home state of Massachusetts. Kids and young people just aren't going afield, and the world is poorer for it.

We're on our way out of Deep River, the last stop of the day. Hanna has pointed three of the four woodcock we've unexpectedly found on the far hillside, and now the late-afternoon sun is slanting low through the bare trees.

There are crows flocking ahead, calling to each other stridently. At this point in November just about all of the songbirds have migrated south, but the crows remain. In cooperative, tribe-like flocks they manage to prosper in a climate that most other birds abandon. They chase owls and hawks just for the hell of it and seem to spend a lot of time having fun. Outdoorsmen universally have a begrudging admiration for them.

The flock moves over the ridge, and their calls fade into the distance.

Along the sunny hillside Hanna slows to work scent. As I've been doing all year, I encourage her to "Go ahead" with a two-note whistle. When a dog is learning, I promote boldness: be daring, run ahead, point the bird if you can, bump him up if you must, but don't potter. Hanna is on the road to experience and she's developing a style along the way. I'm not going to expect a great percentage of points from any puppy, but I can at least encourage boldness.

Right now Hanna's boldness is a bit misplayed and she pushes up the grouse that had been slinking away in front of her. The gun comes up, but the shot is in the much-too-far category. I put the safety back on as the grouse sails low along the distant stone wall that leads down into a wet swamp. He appears to be a cock with a very brown tail.

There is open pasture to the right, so the bird won't turn that way. To the left the swamp opens to beaver floodings with no cover at all. It seems the bird has flown out onto a two-hundred-yard isthmus of swampy cover that connects to the wooded hillside beyond the pasture. Although I can't put my hat on the exact spot where the bird might be, we have him isolated in a fairly cramped area.

With Hanna at heel, I circle out into the pasture to the far hillside, then cut back in and work the isthmus from the opposite direction. Although it was breezy earlier, the wind has died this late in the day, and what little there is seems variable.

With the grouse immediately in front of us, each step forward increases the chances that the bird will flush RIGHT NOW, and I feel my grip tightening on the gun as Hanna works the cover bordering the open water.

She slows almost to a stop, then moves to her right and firms up before a downed tree that the beavers have stripped of its bark. There's a lyrical quality to her almost questioning look as she stands on point with all four feet on the ground.

When I walk forward the bird erupts from the deadfall, banking sharply to the left rather than flying across the beaver pond. Those finely detailed wildlife portraits with a game bird frozen in flight are popular, but what I usually see in the woods is blurred by motion, like a painting by Manfred Schatz. But not this time. During his burst of speed through the gloomy woodland shadows the grouse catches a skinny sunbeam, and the strobe effect seems to freeze-frame the bird for a moment in all his brown-tailed glory. The gun pushes ahead and the bird falls, but when it's over I can still see the illuminated grouse in my mind's eye.

Hanna retrieves the bird and prances around with it rather than bringing it directly back to me. We've had an even ten grouse flushes today, and although I've had the safety off on every one this is the first time I've pulled the trigger. That it should come over Hanna's only grouse point is fitting.

The shot was through some brush, but the bird was dead in the air—what I've come to think of as a *defining No. 8 shot hit*.

There seems to be a dichotomy of opinion on what to shoot at grouse. The *penetration* school of thought says that coarse shot—No. 5s and 6s—knocks birds down by punching holes them with a few big pellets: break any bone and the bird comes down, and if just one pellet strikes the bird's vitals, it's dead.

The *shock-effect* school says that a swarm of small pellets is a more reliable killer; that is, the synergistic impact of simultaneous hits is so great that the bird is killed instantly. You don't have to be lucky and hit a particular spot—all you have to do is hit the bird. This brown-tailed grouse is a textbook example of that effect. I hit him in the back and the wings at a less-than-fatal angle, but he was dead when he hit the ground.

I've been a practitioner of both approaches. Ducks and geese have a shock-absorbing layer of down feathers, and clean kills over decoys require the penetration of high-velocity loads of big shot. But on lightly feathered birds such as grouse I've come to prefer the consistent results of the shock-effect method. As such, patterns become very, very important.

High-quality No. 8 shot in the standard $1^{1}/8$-ounce, low-brass 12-gauge load will pattern as close to perfection as you're ever going to get. Once the leaves are down I use No. $7^{1}/2$s in the tight barrel, but my mainstay load for grouse and woodcock is No. 8 shot. The resultant swarm is dense enough and carries enough pellet energy to be reliably deadly on grouse out to thirty yards, which is a long shot in the grouse cover.

None of us are right on every grouse we shoot. Of course there are going to be down-but-not-out birds that are the result of fringing or of trees taking a bite out of your pattern no matter what shot load and choke combination you settle on. That's an accurate reflection of the way things happen in nearly every hunting situation.

But that's not the point.

The point is that a grouse properly covered by the pattern should be cleanly killed EVERY time. Adapting the shock-effect approach to grouse shooting pretty much guarantees it, and I think it's important to understand that.

Some of my hunting friends maintain that they kill grouse just fine with the same loads they use for pheasants. Shooting a few birds doesn't mean much from a statistical standpoint. You're going to get some clean kills no matter what you're shooting, so why adopt the shock-effect method?

I think I have a good answer: I'm looking for every chance I can get to make a clean kill rather than cripple a bird. The shock-effect method ensures that centered birds are dead every time.

Will it matter on your next shot? Of course not. But will it make a difference over a full season? If a hunter keeps track of that sort of thing, he'll know the answer to that one is "Absolutely."

Similarly, arguments that using light loads or small-gauge guns give the bird *a sporting chance* never made a lot of sense. At least not to me they didn't. Hunting was never intended to be *fair*. It's not ballplayer against ballplayer, it's man killing something.

The sporting chance idea is applaudable right up to the time the hunter mounts his gun. After that, fairness and good sportsmanship amount to doing a thorough job. To me, that means maximizing the pattern so that the bird is hit hard with a big load of shot from a big gun. A feathered grouse that flies off with a couple of pellets in its body hasn't been given a sporting chance. Rather, it has received a death sentence. Some wounded birds survive. Most don't.

Again, that's just my opinion. I could be wrong.

It takes a few minutes to field dress the bird while Hanna waits. The turkey-chasing incident apparently hasn't adversely affected her. The real proof will come the next time we run across a flock. She still has a fluffy grouse feather stuck to her nose when I tuck the bird in the game bag. I scratch her ears and tell her she's a good girl, and we start back.

And then, like a coda to the whole event, a pair of mallards that had been sitting against the shore of the beaver pond through all the commotion decides to finally take wing. They climb upward through the shadows until the low sun catches them, then they level off and make for some distant place only they know about.

Day Forty-Two: The Next Level

> *"I get by with a little help from my friends."*
>
> Lennon & McCartney

WHEN I PARK beyond the PASS AT YOUR OWN RISK sign, I remark to Peter how greatly different my expectations for the puppy are compared to those I had when I parked here on Massachusetts's opening day just a month ago. Hanna is progressing, I know. But this sort of point-to-point comparison can be a revelation as to just how far she's come in five weeks.

There are still some late woodcock around, but that season closed at sunset yesterday, so we won't be shooting them today. Instead, this will be an opportunity to address the idea that the puppy shouldn't chase the birds she points. That seems to be the critical path to the next level of Hanna's training. I'll use the electronic collar today. Hanna has worn it when I needed to stop her barking in the kennel, so she knows how it works.

The same no-chase lesson could be accomplished with a long check cord. I've used that low-tech method with other puppies, but Hanna hasn't worn a check cord these past several weeks. I used it as a handle when standing her up on point, but she doesn't need that lesson any longer. Also, I used the check cord as a leash to keep her close when looking for a dead bird, and Hanna has done a fine job and graduated in that area as well. I sometimes use a check cord to get hold of a dog that is trying to get away from me, but I've never needed that sort of control with this puppy.

Arguably, the toughest thing to teach any hunting dog is steadiness to wing and shot. Oh, you can teach it, but making it stick is another matter. The hunter, after all, is paying attention to the bird and doing some essential maneuvering with his shotgun at the very moment the dog is breaking. Most hunters consider steadiness a refinement necessary only to win field trials, so they don't even try to keep the dog from breaking. As such, hunting dogs routinely chase birds.

There are a bunch of reasons why that's bad news: a chasing dog often prevents you from shooting at low fliers; additional birds nearby are often flushed by the commotion; second opportunities at the same bird are minimized, since birds tend to fly out of the county when chased; a steady dog can do a better job of marking downed birds; dogs can and do injure themselves by running headlong into fences while chasing.

But having said all of that, I'll add that permitting the dog to chase is in and of itself not so bad—what chasing often leads to is the real problem. If the pointed bird can be seen to move, sooner or later Sparkey will begin to interpret that movement as *the flush.* And if *flush* has come to mean *chase,* then you no longer have a pointing dog.

There are varying degrees of staunchness. Rock steady really is something of a circus trick, but it's the ultimate demonstration that the dog will not chase a flushed bird. In truth, that amount of exactitude is hardly necessary in any hunting situation.

I don't need the ultimate—a step or two at the flush is okay. What I DON'T want is a dog out of control. To me, that's a dog sprinting after a flushed bird, or breaking at the sound of the gun, or not stopping when I yell "Hut."

Amy, the now-retired little white setter, needed to be steady, but she never bought into that idea. She wasn't a chaser per se, but when the gun would go off, so would Amy. She came unhinged like the mainspring of one of the watches I was going to fix as a kid. By the time I'd round her up and calm her down, as often as not what started as a routine retrieve had turned into something much more difficult. The truth is that I lost more birds with Amy than with any other two of my dogs combined, and all because she couldn't contain her excitement at the sound of the gun.

The surest way to get any dog into that same state of high

excitation is to let Sparkey chase birds. Requiring the dog to remain steady encourages him to stay calm.

Hanna likes to charge forward *à la* Amy, particularly on low-flying birds. She's on the way to making a habit of it. Today, with the application of a little electricity, we're going to speak to that habit. Peter has agreed to help me, and his dog Kelly has remained at home.

"All I'd like you to do is fire into the air if she's pointing a woodcock," is what I tell him.

"Okay. What if she's got a grouse?"

"Throw your hat over it and hang on tight until I holler 'Pull.'"

The day is overcast and mild, but like so many sunless November days there is no threat of rain in the lemon-gray sky. When I glance uphill the gray birches stand out against the dull purple background of the leafless forest.

We work our way up through the scrub and bittersweet tangles in the Pass At Your Own Risk cover's abandoned pasture, and I find I'm humming "San Antonio Rose" all over again. There were mushrooms here earlier in the year, but no signs of them now. Along the rusted fence that delineates the state-owned land, Hanna points. She has her rear end down, so I suspect a woodcock and wave Peter ahead.

Like the deliberate hunter he is, Peter circles Hanna's point and approaches her head-on. My thumb hovers over the electronic transmitter's zap button. The bird flushes, and Peter fires a shot into the air, but Hanna simply stands there, watching, and there's nothing to do but say, "Good girl."

Peter is reloading as I talk to him. "I think I have a handle on the problem now. She only chases when the bird is away from her. Next time, come up from behind the point."

Twenty minutes later we get another chance. We're at the edge of some alders along the top where Hanna nearly pointed a woodcock on opening day. She strikes a classic pose, and Peter comes up behind her. In the moment I have to survey the scene, it could easily be one of those old-time Peters Cartridge Company calendar pictures from the turn of the last century. To be completely accurate, of course, Peter would have to tuck his pants into his boot tops and swap his over-and-under for a side-by-side, but hunting scenes have changed little in the one hundred years since Arthur Frost and Lassell Ripley showed America what sportsmen and their bird dogs looked like.

Compared to the flight speeds of other game birds, woodcock are supposed to be slow. And I'll admit, they are. But if you lined them all up on a starting line and had a race, one woodcock would be faster than all the others. And, of course, one would be declared the world's slowest woodcock. That seems to be the bird Hanna has found here. He labors up through the bare branches and floats away, almost as if he knows the season has closed. I've seen faster butterflies.

Peter fires a shot in the air at the same time I holler for Hanna to "Hut," but neither does any good. When I touch the zap button Hanna yelps and, after a moment, pretends she was just about to turn and run back to me. I stand her up back where she was pointing and have Peter fire another shot. She's hardly intense, but she doesn't move, either.

I step away and give a thumbs-up signal to Peter.

"Patience," he says quietly.

Off to my left there is a rumble of wings and Peter's cry of "Bird." A grouse is carving a low arc away, staying below eye level as it dodges between evergreens. I can see over Peter's shoulder as he puts in a virtuoso performance on a very difficult shot requiring a compound lead. The bird is cleanly hit, but forward momentum carries it out of our sight. It all happens almost instantaneously.

I call Hanna in and put her at heel, then walk to where the bird fell. The grouse is dead on the ground, and the retrieve is simple, but I have Hanna carry the bird back to Peter.

It's no accident that Peter does well. Whenever I catch sight of him in the woods, his gun is at high port arms. Always. He's ready, and he's a good shot, and when he's in one of my coverts I know he's going to shoot some of my birds. Other people who can't hit anything aren't a concern, but hunters like Peter will diminish the grouse population. When I take him out, I'd better be prepared to absorb the cost—and the currency of the realm is birds.

People hunt differently, and expect different things of their dogs according to the way they hunt. I don't presume that everyone hunts in the same manner that Peter and I do, but, at the same time, I have to resist buying into their expectations.

When I was a young man I once hunted at Maple Spread just after an overnight snow. It wasn't terribly cold at 10 AM on that late-November day, and the fluffy snow was only a few inches deep—the sort that would be gone in a day or two.

I parked on a back road where I always do. While I was getting the dog out an older fellow came walking down the road. (In retrospect, he was probably the same age as I am right now. "Older fellow" indeed.) He had an Irish setter with him and a shotgun under his arm.

When I asked if he had had any luck, he said he had been out since dawn and had hunted the entire area and not seen a feather. Of course, he was talking about pheasants, because the state regularly puts out birds in the open cornfields below. From my earlier experiences in this covert I knew the woods had a pretty fair population of grouse, and I told the Irish setter's owner that I'd have a look for them myself. In so many words he let me know I'd be wasting my time.

As I hunted the area I came across the other fellow's footprints each time I passed beneath the high-tension wires or intersected any of the several tote roads that crisscrossed the cover. Apparently, he had never left the beaten path, and if the tracks in the snow were to be believed, neither had his dog. His idea of what constituted hunting was obviously different from mine.

Like him, I didn't find any birds on the road. But I chased around
a bunch of grouse and shot a pair of renegade pheasants that had
leaked into the grouse cover, and could have taken three others
had I wanted to stretch the limit.

Quite often other hunters in your coverts are road walkers,
snoopers, rabbit hunters, or targets-of-opportunity shooters. They
aren't a big threat to your birds. On the other hand, finding someone else's boot prints in the snow can be disquieting when they
indicate the other guy was hunting the cover in the same way
that you are.

The athletic event that is following a dog in grouse cover
is never more obvious than when I take nonhunters hunting.
They poke along, stop frequently, never manage to catch up, and
as a result of my own politeness I hack the dog rather than hack-
ing my guest. It is not a good experience for any of the parties
involved.

You and I both know the *social hunter*. He has Ogden Pleiss-
ner prints on the walls of his office, and wears a little grouse as
a tie tack. He belongs to Ducks Unlimited and to the Ruffed
Grouse Society, and his magazine rack is filled with catalogs from
Orvis and L.L. Bean. He likes other hunters, tailgate lunches, shotguns, and all the paraphernalia that goes along with hunting. He
likes shooting and he really likes bird dogs. He even likes the *going
out* and the *coming home* parts of a day afield. What he doesn't seem
to like at all is the huge amount of effort that goes along with actual hunting, and he manages to minimize it at every opportunity.

Most of us know one or two men who found hunting too
demanding of excellence and too strenuous, and gave it up. Then,
later, perched on the arm of an overstuffed chair with a drink in
one hand, that same fellow expounds to those listening how he
had tried hunting but had turned away from the idea of killing
for his own pleasure.

I've never been one to pretend that there is a hunter inside
all of us, any more than each of us has a need to till the soil or
work with wood. But how about a little honesty?

Between covers I drive by a side road that leads to Southampton Hillside. I haven't been in there in years, but it still must look good because it always has. The cover is extensive and should hold birds, but on a half-dozen outings over three previous seasons I never found anything except a couple of very wild grouse and, once, somebody else's cripple. I couldn't figure out why.

Then one day I ran into another fellow in the woods. The man said he hunted there two or three times each week. Two or three times a week! I must have looked incredulous, because the fellow repeated what he had told me. That explained a lot. Unlike migrating woodcock and stocked pheasants, there aren't any replacements for the birds a hunter takes out of a covert during the season. Grouse can handle a certain amount of pressure, but places can and do get hunted out. Southampton Hillside is a case study in how.

There's another nearby place that I haven't hunted in several years. I abandoned the cover when it became evident that kids ride motorbikes through the woods. There were several tortured trails with dirt banked up on the turns. The grouse left the covert, and I won't go back, either. I'm aware of what happens to grouse when invasive things go on in the woods, but I wonder how many other animals are similarly displaced by that sort of activity.

We're in Maple Spread when Peter quietly says, "Do you think that's a screech owl?"

A chukar-sized bird sits close to the trunk of a pine. It's a nondescript gray-brown owl. He's not hiding, but in the gloom we can't see the color of his eyes or even if he has ear tufts.

"I don't know, Pete. I'd guess yes, but I can't say for sure."

Every hunter I know is a bird-watcher. Not the kind with a life list and a SAVE OUR WILDLIFE bumper sticker, but someone with a genuine interest in birds in particular and wildlife in general.

As we turn away, Peter says, "There were turkey scratchings back there. Did you see them?"

I wink. "Don't tell Hanna."

210

I've told Peter about Hanna's escapade earlier in the week. *What does Peter think of that?*

In writing, characters are identified by the things they say, so as often as not writers try to express friendship between hunting partners by having them discuss immediate issues and respect each other's opinions. In truth, one of the reasons that two opinionated, bullheaded people can remain friends for twenty-five years is that we don't discuss immediate issues. Peter and I talk about golf and restaurants and national politics, but we steer clear of discussions that run to Browning shotguns versus Berettas or, in this case, how heavy a hand you should use in training a bird dog.

The Shotgun Method professes that you should never permit your dog to do anything you will later have to teach him not to do. A pragmatic approach recognizes that while you can hunt and train a dog at the same time, you can't do both at the same INSTANT. That's why professional trainers employ gunners— someone to do the shooting while the trainer handles the dog. With previous puppies I've had to put off staunchness training until the March woodcock migration. Hanna, too, will need some finishing work in the spring. But today, having Peter along to play the role of gunner will permit me to give Hanna a leg up on the next level of her progress.

We encounter four more woodcock. There is a pair in the birches that develop into the kind of shot that, on another day, I'd give a twenty-dollar bill to have a chance at. Then she points another, unexpectedly, along the dry edge of a pasture. It seems for a moment that Hanna is going to hold on the single, but the woodcock is a short flier. When the bird sits back down just in front of us, Hanna charges ahead and gets an electrical reminder that she shouldn't.

"You should've listened when I said 'Hut.'" I repeat "Hut" each time I stand the puppy up.

Anyone who puts an electronic collar on a dog has to be aware of its limitations. The greatest of those is that the dog must know what it is you're trying to enforce. That is, does Hanna KNOW I don't want her to run ahead when the bird flushes?

The collar can be a cure for disobedience, but it cannot teach a dog anything positive. A dog must know what is right and wrong before you ever put electricity to him, and that implies judgment on the part of the trainer.

Wonderful things can be accomplished with the electronic collar. It can be both an immediate and long-distance tool in dog training. The immediate effect is significant, because at the heart of all obedience training is the doggy equation that says, "If I do this I get that." The collar can eliminate the time lapse between *this* and *that*.

The long-distance part is the other key. Dog training, and all its inherent ramifications, boils down to *controlling the situation*. Getting Sparkey to do what he should when you're not right there to physically make him do it is a control problem. The collar can be a long-distance control solution.

But it takes judgment. There can be alternate endings. We all have seen dogs ruined permanently by the injudicious use of a shock collar. Like anything potent, it can be abused.

The short-flying woodcock has a partner not fifty paces away. Hanna points, the bird flies up and Peter fires a shot, but Hanna just stands and watches as the bird flies off. She doesn't move until I whistle her ahead.

This time Peter gives me a thumbs–up.

Ah, progress.

As is recently the case with so many other coverts in western Massachusetts, there are ticks here. During a break I pinch a half-dozen off my pants and take a similar number off Hanna's head.

In the unlikely event that you're unfamiliar with the little bloodsuckers, I can tell you that in tick country they will get onto you and your dog no matter what you do. They'll get inside your shirt and fall down to your waist. I always find them on my love handles. Ticks have the ability to suppress your immune defenses, increase your blood flow to the area where they're sucking, suppress clotting, and shut off your itch sensation so that you won't even know you've been bitten. That's the bad news.

The good news is that they are slow, they don't jump, and they don't fly. They take twelve hours or so to attach themselves to you and another twenty-four hours to begin exchanging fluids, so you have time to find them before they do you or your dog any harm.

God must have been having a bad day when He made ticks. They've been around for a long time, of course, but until recently were never a widespread problem in New England. But they are now. Lyme disease, as well as several other equally insidious but less newsworthy ailments, is spread through tick spit.

Some hunters have told me they don't have a problem with ticks. They just put their dogs back in the kennel and never check them. No problem, my foot. If they took the time to go over their dogs after a day afield they'd find they have a lot to be concerned about. There isn't much any dog by himself can do in the way of a defense against ticks. Dogs depend on their owners for that, and you shouldn't let Sparkey down.

Ticks are so small that they're easily mistaken for bits of dirt in your dog's coat. When you do find them, they seem to be armor plated and defy crushing with a fingernail. Oh, they'll die if you put them on an anvil and hit them with a ball-peen hammer, but few things short of that will do the trick.

And if you don't find them, they burrow in and hang on tight, and after a few days they become swollen with the blood they've sucked out. They seem to have an affinity for the vascular parts of a dog's body, as well as the places where he can't scratch. Look for ticks between Sparkey's toes and under his tail as well as in the more obvious spots around his collar and the back of his neck, on his ears, and near his eyes.

Some people think that tick repellent makes them jump off like a cat thrown onto a hot stove, but it just can't work that way, even though we all wish it would. That's because ticks are like cockleburs, and similarly attach themselves to your dog by a passive mechanical action. In the wild, a tick will position itself at the tip of a blade of grass with its hooked forelegs elevated so that they might catch on a passerby. The tick doesn't care if that passerby is a deer, a mouse, your bird dog, or you. In cold weather, they depend on the host's body heat to bring them out of dormancy.

There are sprays that work, and the stuff that you spread along the dog's spine will kill ticks after a day or so. Since bird dogs are in and out of every brook and pond they come to, these products need to be applied often, and a wise use of tick-killing spray finds it being applied AFTER the hunt.

Since loosing Sophie to cancer, I've become gun shy about any and all chemicals where my dogs are concerned. As such, I consider a thorough combing out after every hunt the primary defense against ticks. I use everything else sparingly. Sometimes I'll find a tick that I've missed, usually in the doghouse after it has done its work and fallen off the dog. They're the size of a raisin, blue-black and swollen hard and round, and it's the kind of evidence that always strikes me with a sense of failure.

Hanna is visibly working scent as we follow a brushy stream bank, but then, just as she slows, a grouse flushes in front of her.

As I said earlier, some grouse cannot be pointed, but I suspect that it is much more difficult to get a point at a not-so-secret place like Maple Spread, where the birds are no stranger to dogs and hunters, than at a remote covert where I might be the only human the bird encounters all year.

We're in pursuit of the bird when, from my vantage point, it appears Peter has shot straight upward. The grouse apparently flushed from an overhead tree, but I neither heard nor saw the bird.

"Well?" I ask.

Peter just shakes his head.

Five minutes later, as we're passing through a low swampy area, I notice Hanna sprinting into some hemlocks, then she turns and heads directly back to me. It takes a moment to digest what I'm seeing. She's carrying a live grouse.

I yell to Peter to hold up for a moment, and walk to him with Hanna immediately behind me.

"What's up?" he asks.

"Miss Hannaberry has a present for you."

Even as it's happening I know this will be a savored memory. Lost birds found are always good stories.

Peter tries to take the grouse from Hanna, but she's playing favorites and backs away and circles to me once again.

When I take a souvenir photo of Peter posed with his arm around the puppy, Hanna smiles her openmouthed dog's smile back at the camera. I remark that she's ready to move up to the next level.

Peter scratches Hanna's ears for a moment, then offers, "I think you're mistaken. She's already there."

Day Forty-Three: Bright November Days

> "...for no matter how keen a sportsman one may be, he has missed a great deal if he has never known the intimate companionship of a good dog."
>
> Burton Spiller

TODAY IS ALL that November has to offer to a New England bird hunter: a cold breeze, frozen ground, and a clear cobalt-blue sky that goes all the way to the horizon.

The leaves are all down now—at least, those that are coming down are already there. Illogically, there are a few oaks and beeches that hang on to some of their leaves right through the winter.

Neither tree makes use of the old leaves, and they represent a liability when winter storms load snow and ice on a tree's branches. Yet, in mocking testimony against the obvious, the dried leaves remain on the trees. I've never figured out why, yet I take a small comfort from the paradox.

For reasons equally unexplained, a little woodland tree called opposite-leaved dogwood hangs on to its leaves as well. The tree never gets very big, and it has a posture very much like a small apple tree. For some reason its leaves remain, limp but still green, well into December.

A few weeks ago the world was brimming with October beauty. It was breathtaking and distracting, sometimes to a degree where paying attention to hunting took an effort akin to acting normal around a woman so beautiful that you can't keep your eyes off her. It took that sort of effort.

But it's all gone now. What was autumn's beauty is just a washed-out crispness underfoot. Still, in late November you can appreciate the more subtle beauties of the scene: the translucent bark of a yellow birch tree, the aqua-green lichen on weathered granite, the delicate play of lacy shadows. Like the ancient ground pine that now shows vibrantly green on the forest floor, all would be so much devalued currency in the circus of color that was taking place just a month ago.

Hanna and I are hunting the Horseshoe Swamp, with its impressive stand of black cherry trees. Each time I admire the tall, straight boles, I wonder why some lumberman hasn't found the stand. There must be a hundred trees of harvestable size in this grove not far from the hard road.

Hanna is off on the right as I'm weaving my way uphill beyond the cherry grove. A cock grouse flushes from underfoot and curves away below eye level in a whirlwind of sound and motion and is gone that quickly. I manage a single shot, and even as I pull the trigger I know that I'm behind the bird.

There's a lot of space around every grouse, and it's easy to miss them. And, to further my excuse, I'm out of breath and walking uphill, and the bird was below eye level.

But this shot was easy.

Oh, I can hit targets. I routinely score well at sporting clays, so I know how to make the shots, particularly the easy ones. Nevertheless, I manage my share of groaners while bird hunting. Afterward I'm thoroughly disgusted with myself because I can't seem to shoot as well as I know how in the moment an un-expected grouse takes off. There are times when I'm elated at having made a good shot, but they're more than offset by the dark feeling of having blown an easy chance like this one. It's not the sort of thing I can take very much of.

I whistle Hanna in and push her nose on the spot where the grouse flushed.

"If I wanted to flush my own birds I'd have bought a Chi-huahua. He'd be a lot better company than you." I'm still huffing and puffing when I add, "Now stay 'In front.'"

I wave her ahead and we start off in pursuit of the bird. She doesn't exactly give me the okay sign, but I think I see a hint of perception in her expression.

Hanna might have found that grouse before I stepped on it if she had been covering the ground like she's been trained to do. It would be easy to take out my anger and blame her, but it wasn't the dog that missed that easy uphill shot, and that's really what I'm fuming about.

But she should be in front of me nonetheless. I curve to the left after the grouse, and Hanna sprints in that direction once she sees where I'm heading. Some men want their dogs to hunt like windshield wipers, back and forth as the handler walks along. It's a pattern that some dogs fall into naturally, and a few of those evolve into absolutely mechanical automatons.

Some of my dogs started out that way, but eventually devel-oped a more productive style than the windshield-wiper strategy. Hazel and Stella each learned to recognize good cover and to use the wind. In their prime, I was privileged to watch them cruise the downwind side of likely corners and good-looking runs with their heads back, sampling the breeze at a fast trot. They were doing something more than just running and hoping to bump into a bird. They were *hunting;* thus, they were creating opportunities. It's the equivalent to what sports teams' coaches are talking about when they speak of moving without the ball.

Hanna has to make an arrival before she can make such a Hazel/Stella-style departure, and that arrival consists of learning to stay in front of me. She hunts like Hazel some of the time, but she still gets sidetracked much too often. If I had a nickel for every time I hollered "In front" to her during the past three months, I could roll them up and trade them in for a bunch of one-hundred-dollar bills. She should have it down by now. "In front" means *do it all correctly*—hunt to the front, stay in range, check back.

Now she's lingering off on the right again. When I whistle to her it's as if she mentally snaps her fingers. She doesn't look my way, but scampers to the front. *Good girl.* She's done so much already that it's difficult to believe she's a couple of weeks shy of being ten months old.

Now, where has the grouse gone? I ask myself. Along the sidehill are tangles of rosebushes and laurel, hiding places all, but they seem too close to the point of flush. It's more likely that the bird has flown into the hemlock clumps beyond the overgrown field.

Hanna casts into the evergreen thickets, and for a moment it seems we've guessed right because she catches the bird's scent and I stop to see where it will lead her. Then there is an indefinite rumble of wings that says yes, the grouse was here, but now we must start our search all over again. Hanna sprints a buttonhook pattern at the sound of the bird's flush, a doggy equivalent to my own muttered curse through clenched teeth.

Knowing grouse habits can pay dividends when all you have to go on is that you heard a bird flush *over that way.* Nevertheless, it's going to take some luck to find a grouse we only heard.

Uphill from the hemlocks the bird we're chasing flushes wild, but he can be seen in the distance long enough to read his line of flight. He's going to be up on the hilltop along the cut where the high-tension wires run—he'll be right on the edge, because he won't voluntarily cross the opening.

Ten minutes later we're working the brushy margin when the bird goes out. The distance is right on the cusp of too far, and although I have the safety off, I pass. Deer hunters like to say that if a deer had the rifle, he'd be enough of a sportsman not to shoot you in the ass while you were running away. I feel the same way about chancy shots at grouse.

The bird soars high and over the treetops on the far side of the high-wire clearing, and might just as well have flown to Honolulu for all our chances of finding him again. Forced across an opening, grouse must fear that an aerial predator has seen them. They will fly long and stay put. Also, there's the fact that this bird is now out of his home range, and further pursuit might drive him so far that he would be unable to find his way back. There's nothing to do but turn around and work a different route on the trip back toward the cherry grove.

In late November the sun is low in the southern sky even now, at noon. At this time of year that blinding glare is always a factor on a clear day. Any bird that flushes to the south stands a good chance of escaping unsaluted. Sunglasses won't help, and they're counterproductive in every other situation.

Of all the statistics I've extrapolated from my hunting journals, most told me things I knew or suspected already. Chief among them was the suspicion that regardless of range, regardless of flight path, regardless of whether the bird is pointed or flushes unexpectedly, *the better I see the bird the more likely the chances are that I'll hit him.* Toward that end, on most days I won't wear sunglasses in the woods.

There's white birch here; big, sleek, clean trees that break the gray-violet of the now-naked forest. In the branches overhead are cedar waxwings. They have a subtle beauty, something you have to look closely to appreciate. They're always in flocks, and chatter constantly so that I used to hear them before I'd catch sight of them. The field guide describes their call as a "high, thin lisp." It's evidently in an auditory range that I can no longer hear, because it seems the waxwings are a lot quieter these days.

Out of some thin alders along a beaver pond Hanna flushes another grouse. This one hugs the ground and sails back toward where the truck is parked. There's a little graveyard and some overgrown sandy fields in that direction, but nothing to hold a fleeing grouse. After a fast pass, I try to direct Hanna to work farther into the cover, but she seems intent on hunting beyond the cemetery. A month ago I would have overruled her, but as a measure of just how far she's developed as a hunter, I follow her lead.

Hanna has her head high and is working the breeze as we pass into some thin scrub beyond the graveyard. At the rim of a sandy washout she switches back once, retraces her steps along the edge, then comes to a point—and for a moment it seems that I'm watching Hazel again. The bird is below her in some cedar. As I'm wondering how I'm going to get down into the scrub he flushes, hugging the ground as he flies down the washout. Below-eye-level shots are normally an anathema for me, but I lean forward from the waist and manage to hit this one. When the bird falls, Hanna creates a minor landslide in the sandy gravel as she makes her way down into the washout, then another as she brings the bird back up to me.

"Miss Hannaberry, you are one mighty fine bird dog," I tell her as she sits to deliver the grouse. I scratch her under the chin and look into her eyes. "Or are you Hazel having come back to me?"

For weeks I've been telling Susan that the puppy hunts and behaves and points her woodcock just like Hazel used to. We have old photos of Hazel, and since Hanna's ticking came in the puppy looks enough like her to be, if not her twin, at least her litter-mate. But my wife unfortunately only remembers the old dog that was Hazel in the years before she died. Susan couldn't have known the wonderful hunter that was Tekoa Mountain Hazel.

George Bird Evans wrote of a bond he had with certain of his bird dogs, saying they lived in each other's souls. It always seemed a bit melodramatic to me, but then Hazel came along and I had an inkling of what he was talking about. She was the first crackerjack bird dog I owned, and was the answer to any hunter's prayer. When I think back to Hazel, the singular term that describes her best is *steady*. Like Hanna, she was low key and a bit shy around people, and also like Hanna she was a precocious puppy, doing everything well from the very outset.

I used to think Hazel was inimitable. Lately I've unconsciously started calling the puppy *Hannaberry,* which is a variation on the nickname I had for Hazel. All of her life, that dog was *Hazelberry,* and when I was being formal she was *Miss Berry.*

When Hanna and I start off again, I hear myself say it out loud. I give the puppy an underhand wave and say, "Let's go, Miss Berry."

In November, without greenery or the softening effect of snow, the true shape of the land is visible. In the distance, the outline of hills can be traced beneath their hairlike covering of trees. Underfoot, boulders and rocks seem to poke up through the soil. A drive along the interstate belies that impression. The dynamited cuts in the hills reveal that the earth is made of rock, not dirt, and in New England the mantle of topsoil is frighteningly thin.

Hal Borland wrote of the comfort found in living with the land and constantly rediscovering the great assurances of nature. The forest stands silent and naked, and it can seem that life has stopped. But there are certainties in the rhythms of the seasons, and you need only look at the branch tip to witness the faith of the trees expressed in each bud to realize that the year is a continuity, like some Möbius strip made of calendar pages.

Human measurements of time are invariably more convenient than conclusive. One who thinks of autumn in terms of death should take some measure of comfort from that observation. Although it seems that life is suspended in November, time flows by as surely as it does in May. The fallen leaves have already begun to break down and return to the soil. Life hasn't quit, it only waits for the spring that it knows is coming. It's a time for waiting and for patience. Only the wind hurries.

I have Harry Chapin on the truck stereo as we drive down the road a half-mile to hunt the Poor Farm covert. Even though we don't move a bird in there, I manage to remember all the words to Harry's "Corey's Coming" as we hunt the overgrown fields. There are thickets of gray dogwood growing like waves on the ocean. Earlier this year the ends of the branches were loaded with pale gray-green berries that some people call doll's eyes, although there are several other berries that might lay claim to the nickname. It's all gone now. Autumn's bounty is a thing of the past by the time the middle of November rolls around.

To say that the dog AND I are hunting is a bit of stretch. I'm following Hanna while she hunts. Oh, I know where the birds are; that's why I drove here in the first place. But finding them is a different story. That's where the dog comes in. She sees to the scouting, plays the wind, handles the tactical maneuvers, and when she points, it's as if I planned it that way. In life there are few other thrills in the same category as having lost track of your dog, then discovering her on point, standing with eyes bulging, waiting for your appearance on the scene.

I was duck hunting this morning, and as always was struck by the juxtaposition that is grouse hunting and waterfowling. In the latter, you wait for the bird to happen to you. If the ducks aren't flying, and they weren't this morning, you can't improve your luck by waiting faster or harder. But in grouse hunting you go to the bird, and success—at least opportunities for success—is a matter of how hard you hunt. I have seldom come to the end of a day of grouse hunting without having had enough opportunities to have taken a few birds. If the game bag was empty I had nothing other than poor shooting to blame for my lack of success.

It would be easy to say that if this bright November day turns out to be perfect, it'll have very little to do with shots and limits, and that birds and bird dogs are only a part of the whole picture. Only a part, yes, but it's the part you underline, the part that gives meaning to everything else. As much as I stand in awe of nature, it's a lot easier to enjoy the beauties of a day afield when the dog is pointing birds and you're shooting well. At the end of such a day you're tired in a good sort of way, and you feel like kissing somebody.

There just aren't enough of these days.

It's 3 PM when I park outside the Get Lost covert. I named it that because I did just that when I first hunted here a few years ago. I navigated around all four corners of a triangular field, then wondered why my sense of direction had betrayed me. Of course, I had been hunting rather than paying attention to details. Like so many other mysteries in life, once the solution became apparent I was left wondering how I could have been puzzled by something so simple. I mention it only because anyone who's spent time out-of-doors has done things just as silly.

We're down to the last hour and a half of daylight. From a grouse-hunting standpoint, the most productive single hour of the day is the last one. The birds may or may not feed during any other time period, but universally every grouse is trying to stuff his crop just before he goes to roost at sunset. You'll tick off some bow hunters, but that's the hour to be in the grouse covers.

We're hurrying along a stone wall that separates two overgrown pastures when a doe gets up ahead of us, then another, then a buck with thick antlers and wonderful posture. He has six, or maybe eight, points—it's hard to tell as he's running—and the rack is very beamy, the sort you could rest your shotgun across. Massachusetts deer hunters will be looking for him in another week, and I wish him good luck as he bounds into the woods with the two does. They seem intent on graphically demonstrating just why they are called whitetails.

Beyond the triangular field we cross in and out of the seeps along the hillside, and spend too much time searching for a gray-tailed cock bird we had chased around on an earlier visit. He must have called in sick for work today because he's not in any of the obvious corners beyond the wet hillside.

When I start back to the truck, sunset is approaching fast. The day has been a success, and I've mentally begun phrasing the report that I'll put into the tape recorder in a few minutes: *Moved the same bird three times at Horseshoe Swamp—No, wait a minute, it was four times. . . .*

Then, off to the right, Hanna turns at the end of one of her casts and strikes a pointing posture. She still regularly plays her this-is-how-I'm-going-to-point-'em puppy game, so I don't pay much attention even when her beeper collar announces a point. It's happened before, and I whistle to her and wave her ahead. But she remains standing, not quite on point.

When I go to investigate, a shadowy hen grouse flushes from a tree immediately in front of the puppy. My shot is at a glimpsed target that passes behind some spruce tops just as pattern and bird were about to intersect. I'm not such a good shot that I never miss, but when I do I usually know why. And that shot felt like a hit. I get Hanna back among the spruce trees, sit her down, then tell her to "Find dead bird."

She searches for a minute but turns up nothing. *Did I hit the bird? Should we keep searching for a possible cripple, or take a chance that we can reflush the unhit bird before dark?* Hanna decides for me when she moves ahead uphill through the dark spruces.

We haven't gone a hundred yards when she strikes scent and works to a point. When I walk past her I find I'm gripping the gun so tightly my hands hurt. The moment of anticipation lengthens until it becomes obvious that there's nothing there. Hanna softens and moves ahead fifty yards, and the scene is repeated with similar nonresults at the edge of a tiny clearing in the spruce grove. Still working scent, she leads me to the steep face of a little hill where she points again, this one with a third-time finality about it. I work the twenty feet up the little bluff, expecting the grouse to thunder out every time I take a step. I arrive at the top and straighten upright and wait a long moment before I hear Hanna's bell behind me. When I turn to her she's bringing the dead hen grouse up to me.

I'm fond of saying that we seldom know how happy we are in even the best of times until later when those times are over. But then there are moments like this that can make a liar out my pessimism. I kneel and take the bird from Hanna, then wish for a moment she were bigger so that I could hug her more tightly.

What happened? The inconclusive conclusion is that the grouse was hit in the lungs by however much of the pattern made it through the screen of spruce branches. The bird had enough life left to fly a short way, then run from the dog before the fatal hit did its damage. I've seen enough ducks lung-hit to know the symptoms.

I slip the hen into the game bag. The sun has already dipped below the horizon and a thin silver sickle of moon shows low in the western sky. When I start out there is a moment when I feel like the little boy I used to be. That kid celebrated successes, both major and minor, by throwing his hat in the air.

Unfortunately, that little boy isn't around any longer to pay for the consequences of his actions. The balding guy that is me has to spend a few minutes in the gathering twilight finding a stick long enough to get the little boy's hat back down from the tree where it has gotten lodged.

Day Forty-Five: Dream at Evening

> *"My dog, by the way, thinks I have much*
> *to learn about partridges, and, being a profes-*
> *sional naturalist, I agree. He persists in tutor-*
> *ing me, with the calm patience of a professor*
> *of logic, in the art of drawing deductions from*
> *an educated nose. I delight in seeing him*
> *deduce a conclusion, in the form of a point,*
> *from data that are obvious to him, but specu-*
> *lative to my unaided eye. Perhaps he hopes*
> *his dull pupil will one day learn to smell."*
>
> Aldo Leopold
> *Red Lanterns*

FROM MY VIEWPOINT in the gloom of the woods, Stella can be
seen off to the right. She's at the edge of a field, and the open sunlight illuminates everything out there like some glowing amber
blanket. She seems to be unsure of where I am and is apparently
looking for me, so I make a big production of waving my hat to
signal her.

Ah, now she's seen me, and she starts in my direction. But
after coming a hundred feet she turns to the right and takes the
long way around a deadfall before continuing.

What's she doing?

It takes a moment to recall that I walked around that same
deadfall two minutes ago to get to where I'm now standing. Stella
is following my scent trail.

When she's fifty feet away she finally looks up and for the
first time, actually sees me. Her ears drop in recognition, and she
casts out in front and begins hunting again.

Stella has begun to employ the deaf dog's trick when she
gets lost—she cuts my trail and follows it back to me. Dogs don't
use their eyes much. That doesn't mean they don't see, because
obviously they do. But dogs use their vision mostly to orient

themselves and to keep from bumping into things. They don't actively look for much of anything. For that they use their nose.

For nonscenting humans, it's hard to imagine any world unlike our own, especially a dog's world that's made up primarily of smells and scents. Colors and shapes, if they can identify them at all, must have no more importance to a dog than scents and smells have for us.

The stories of people going blind and then discovering their senses of touch and hearing illustrate the point. We all have those abilities, but because we rely so heavily on our eyesight we never fully develop our other senses until our vision leaves us. Similarly, dogs have sight, but they've never invested enough to trust wholly in what they see. If I walk into the yard and don't utter a word, my dogs will bark and raise a fuss until I either speak to them or they can wind me and identify who I am. Oh, they see me—they might even recognize me—but until they can smell who I am or hear my voice they don't completely trust their eyes.

Stella has always had a style that I call *double pointing*. She would go on point on her first encounter with scent, then stand and wait for me to come abreast of her. Her point might soften, and when I'd whistle her on she'd relocate quickly, moving like a shadow as she slinked through the cover to come up on a much firmer second point. On good days, the bird would be right where she said it was on that follow-up point. November 30, 1992, was one such good day: she pointed thirteen grouse during a hunt in Vermont. Hazel had eleven one day, but that's as close as any of my other dogs have ever come to equaling Stella's feat.

But her style lost her covey finds when we hunted quail in Kansas. She'd point initially and I'd call my hunting partner over. Stella would go soft, and by the time I'd whistle her ahead my partner's dog would have figured out where the birds were. Never the aggressive warrior, Stella seldom won the race to the covey she'd found.

We work through the broken November sunlight beneath the aspens. Every cover has a sweet spot—one perfect location where the birds are most likely to be—and right now I'm trying to maneuver so that we can come into it with the wind in Stella's face.

Because I hunt so many different coverts, I sometimes wonder if the dogs recognize a place. Does Stella know this is the Gallery? We've hunted this cover every year of her life, but does she remember things that happened here? I've got plenty of evidence both for and against, so it's nothing I'd want to argue about.

The sweet spot is just ahead. It's a little stony hollow where the poplar woods thin out and give way to juniper and barberries. Evergreens shelter the little depression along the north side, and make for a grouse spot so perfect that you might be tempted to just hang around and pass shoot.

As we approach, Stella comes to a stop in the sunlight, not quite on point. Her tail is waving slowly, and the almost-point says, "Hey, come on over here for a minute." It's not exactly Lassie signaling Timmy's mom, but it's good enough for me.

And, as I've come to expect, once I get to her she moves ahead cautiously. There's a bird in front of her, and she knows that the bird knows what's up. Maybe she'll point it, and maybe she won't, but she wants to make sure we get a chance one way or the other.

The key word in that last statement is WE. Stella's mature style demonstrates the sort of cooperation that can take place between an experienced bird dog and a hunter. It doesn't seem that a young dog is capable of fully buying into such two-party cooperation since the whole thing evolves once the dog realizes that you, the human hunter, cannot scent a bird. Most bird dogs come to that realization sooner or later. Until they do, dogs can't appreciate the extent that you depend on them for information.

Now Stella works into a trembling old dog's point. Up ahead, just in front of a blown-down oak with the leaves still on it, is an obvious tangle of juniper where the bird must have run and is now hiding. The windblown dry leaves are thick here, and rustle noisily as I walk forward. It takes a moment, but I see how I can step from one moss-covered rock to another and come up on the left side of the juniper clump without making a sound. After a mixed handful of long strides and baby steps, I quietly arrive at the far side of the tangle. I step off the last rock and think *Here's the payoff pitch with the runners going. . . .*

With a roar of wings the grouse comes boring out of the thicket in a whirlwind of dried leaves, staying low as it cuts beyond the leafy deadfall. In the moment that I have to make the shot I manage to keep the muzzles moving and dump the bird cleanly.

Stella has seen the bird fall, and goes to the far side of the fallen oak to make the retrieve. I've got the camera out and move up to take a photo of her, but once she has the grouse she starts directly back to where I was when the shot was made, then wanders back even farther, searching for me. My calls do no good, of course, and I have to run to catch up with her. Finally we get together, and I sit her down and take a photo.

Although I can't know it at the time, it turns out to be the four hundredth grouse point of Stella's life and, by the most capricious of coincidences, her four hundredth grouse retrieve as well. She's a week shy of her twelfth birthday. She sits and poses with the grouse as if she realizes all that.

Stella's orange and white markings are such that she has been mistaken for a Brittany with a tail. Her mother was a Grouse Ridge dog out of that kennel's famous champion, Billyboy, and her father was a son of the Grand National Champion, Mr. Motion. One of Stella's male littermates won some sort of national title as a derby dog.

But in spite of her noble breeding, she's led a jinxed life. Her troubles started in her fourth year. I was in Maine in early October, hunting with my nephew around the college he was

attending in Farmington. After we came out of the woods, he
announced to me that Stella had cut her foot and was bleeding.

Annoyed, I lifted her onto the truck's tailgate and took a
minute to dig out the first-aid kit. When I got back to her, she
was standing in what had to be a cup of her own blood. A cup!
This was no ordinary cut-pad injury. She had stepped on a broken bottle and had severed the tendons at the hock of her right
rear leg. I got the bleeding stopped, then rushed her into town
to the local vet. He surgically repaired the damage, but because
tendons don't heal quickly she should have stayed in the cast for
several months and remained out of action for a year. But like the
greedy fool I can be, I rushed her back into service before the
season was out, and that foot was never right again.

Two years later, equally early in the season, Stella blew out the cruciate ligaments in her left knee while we were hunting some downed timberland in Vermont. I'm not unconvinced that the favoring of one leg didn't lead to the damage to the other. This time I listened to the vet's advice and she stayed out of action for a full year, and healed properly.

But the long and the short of it is that she missed two seasons during the height of her career. Like Ted Williams and the years that major-league baseball lost him to military service, I'll always wonder how many more great things she might have done had she been completely healthy all through her prime.

When she was firing on all cylinders she was a top-notch, athletic bird dog, but those days weren't as plentiful as they might have been. Now, late in her life, she operates courtesy of an aspirin before and after each outing. I suspect that the lasting effect of her injuries impacts her performance even now.

Back at the truck, Stella tries to hop in when I open the driver's side door, but she stumbles and falls clumsily back to the ground. I put a hand under her belly and another on her collar and lift her in.

She settles herself in the back, then stares out at me. Much of the orange on her face has faded to white. She's an old dog, and I wonder if this will be her last season.

"Stella, where does the time go?" I rub her chin for a moment, and she makes groaning noises that, if she were a cat, would be purring. "It's going to be okay, Miss Belle."

She smiles her dog's smile back at me, and at least one of us seems to believe that I'm telling the truth.

CHAPTER SIX

Bleak in the Morning Early

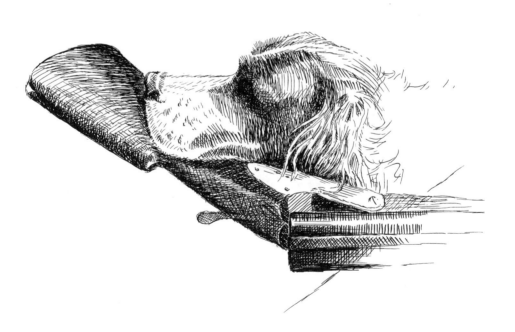

Day Forty-Six: Thanksgiving

> *"It is those who attempt to make a moral issue of lawful hunting who make fools of themselves, even if their foolishness is currently fashionable."*
>
> Ed Zern

As WE WAIT in the dark, the dogs whine and mutter behind the seat of the truck, for once impatient. Or perhaps they sense my own impatience at waiting. Outside, the leaden sky does not seem to have lightened at all. The day threatens to dump something on us before the morning is out—the weathermen are in disagreement as to whether that something will be rain or snow or worse, or even if it'll come down at all.

I'm pheasant hunting today. It's a family tradition, although I'm the only member out on this Thanksgiving. My dad is eighty-one and hasn't hunted in years. One of my brothers no longer owns a gun, and the other is halfway around the world. Of my three nephews, only one is a hunter and he's after ducks on Cape Cod this morning. That leaves me as a party-of-one to hunt the pheasants the state puts out. The weather is against the idea, but I've spent too many Thanksgivings at sea where even radio waves couldn't find me. I'm here.

All along the farm road the cars of pheasant hunters are pulled into the edges of the fields, and their randomness makes them seem abandoned rather than parked.

I check my watch again for the third time in the last five minutes: 6:20 AM becomes 6:21, then 6:22. Legal shooting time comes and goes, but I can't start pheasant hunting in the dark.

Then, from the indefinite distance, a couple of shots sound. I get out and breathe the cold air for a few minutes while the dogs go about their morning business. Ultimately, I decide against the folly of hunting without adequate light and get back in the truck.

Some states establish a definite time for starting—9 AM, for example. Here in Massachusetts it's a nebulous *half-hour before sunrise.* That translates to a different time every day, of course, and even that changes according to geography; official sunrise in Boston is considerably earlier than official sunrise in the Berkshire Hills. Under the thick overcast sky it hardly matters. I'm not going anywhere until I can see something more than just the distant outlines of the landscape.

Finally, at 6:50, I can make out some colors and conclude there's enough light to get started. A pair of blaze-orange vests has already crossed the field where I intend to work. I hold out hope, though—the previous hunters didn't have a dog. On mornings like this the pheasants ought to be tucked in and will hold tight, which works against the stomp-'em-up-yourself strategy that dogless hunters employ.

Hanna casts out into the weeds ahead of me, chasing up sparrows and running off pent-up energy. A few shots in the distance announce that others hunters have started as well. My plan is to use the puppy alone for the first run of the day, then hunt both dogs as a team for the balance of the morning. Stella watches us from the rear window of the truck. She didn't vote in favor of my plan.

We used to hunt the Northampton Flats on Thanksgiving, but lately that three-mile stretch along the Connecticut River has been given over to "modern" farming practices. The scattered asparagus beds and roadside swales are gone, and the Northampton Flats is now one continuous cornfield recently cut to three-inch stubble by a dangerous-looking monster harvester. So I'm here, across the river, to try the farms in the Hatfield meadows.

I've still got the 12-gauge Beretta Ultralight, but since I'm after pheasants today I've changed the chokes from the skeet and improved cylinder combination that I use for grouse to the more serious improved cylinder and modified. And I've got copper-plated No. 6s in both barrels.

After an unproductive forty-five minutes I'm back at the truck. Stella does all but hand me her beeper collar when I let her out, and we start in on the other side of the farm road.

There are rows of nursery stock here, although it appears that most of the plants have been dug up, leaving only craters and a few misshapen rejects behind. The field is overgrown with several years' worth of weeds. Sumac has sprung up along the fence line, and cedar has sprouted among the forgotten Japanese maples and flowering crab apples. Cedars often appear in wasteland here in New England, much the same way that cactus springs up in the deserts of the Southwest—self-spacing, taking hold where no other trees seem interested in growing.

We're still not far from the road when Stella points abruptly, looking down into a crater on her left. Hanna had been out in front of our little parade, and now she comes in and passes on a chance to back her kennel mate. She stops when I shout "Hut," but she's hardly on point.

When I walk abreast of Stella I can see a rooster huddled in the crater. As magnificent and defiant as the bird seems in flight, when caught on the ground beneath the point of a hunting dog there is nothing he quite so resembles as a frightened chicken. The bird flushes, and after missing cleanly on the first shot I catch up to him with the tight barrel and he falls among the nursery stock, just a few feet from Hanna.

The puppy has somehow managed to hunt the entire autumn without encountering a pheasant. Now she's unsure if she should retrieve the rooster even though I holler, "Find dead bird." Stella has no such reservations, and snatches up the ringneck and brings it directly to me.

This is the first time I've had both dogs on the ground together. Up until now, even for something as innocuous as preseason exercise runs, I've wanted to be alone with the puppy. She needed to learn to keep track of me and adjust her range to my pace. It's something the puppy had to figure out for herself, and not the sort of thing accomplished while running with older dogs.

There have often been times the whole kennel needed exercise, and out of necessity I would sometimes run all the dogs as a pack. But I won't put an untrained puppy in that situation again. I've made that mistake in the past, then had problems because the pup hadn't developed the skills to stay with me in the woods.

In the same vein, people sometimes ask if a puppy learns from an older dog. I once wrote that all one dog ever learns from another are bad habits, but that was based on my experience with my first few dogs. Since then, I've revised my judgment—during a puppy's first year I don't want another dog along when the youngster is being field trained. In that situation, the presence of another dog, no matter how well trained, is always counter-productive.

On the other hand, when it comes to obedience training, it's handy to have other well-trained dogs around both for example and for demonstration. (Notice I said "well-trained." A problem dog is best kept away from your puppy no matter what the situation.) In my backyard, each puppy in turn watched the older resident dogs and learned what to do in response to "In the kennel," or "On the floor," or "In your house," or "Outside," or "Be quiet." I haven't had to teach those commands in years.

Here, hopefully, Hanna has just learned from Stella that downed pheasants are to be retrieved.

In the next field two distant hunters abruptly reverse their direction and descend out of sight into the tall woods along the river. It takes a moment to understand what they're doing: a game warden's vehicle is parked out on the farm road, and he's checking licenses of a father-and-son duo at their car.

There was a time (and I don't believe my memory is clouded by sentimentality) when I remember my dad enthusiastically talking to game wardens. He traded stories with them, and they in turn spread the news about where other guys had been taking birds or catching fish. Oh, they checked our licenses, but that's not the point. Mostly, it seemed, they were "appointed pals," friendly not just to my father, but to everyone I knew. If there was an us-against-them aspect to their work, it wasn't evident to the kid I used to be.

In Massachusetts they're not game wardens any longer, but Environmental Police. And it's not just their title that has changed. Their comportment as they check licenses is uncomfortably similar to that of a state cop approaching a speeder caught in a radar trap. They are hardly *pals*.

But I guess I'm a fool because I still follow my father's example and offer my hand to wardens whenever I meet them. Universally, they're suspicious of me. The fact that they're wearing street shoes with a shine on them says a great deal about law enforcement people who are supposed to be out in the open doing their work.

The game laws were once written so that a hunter motivated by a sense of fair play would have nothing to worry about. My dad used to say that he could go the entire season without breaking a game law, but lately it's tough to back out of your driveway without giving a warden cause to ticket you. The laws have become so convoluted that it is difficult to know where you stand, and that often leads to an in-for-a-dime, in-for-a-dollar mind-set. When we had the waterfowl point system, that sort of thinking got a lot of duck hunters into trouble when they discovered they were accidentally over the limit.

In Massachusetts, if you get a ticket you lose your Firearms Identification Card—FOREVER. Without that, you can't own a firearm. A restraining order, driving while intoxicated, or just about any game violation is enough for them to confiscate your FID card. I know guys who used to pop squirrels at their bird feeder from their back window, but they don't dare nowadays. If a neighbor doesn't like what you're doing, suddenly the Gestapo show up and take away your guns. No wonder hunters slink away at the sight of a warden's car. Too bad. The way popular sentiment has been going these days, the sportsman could use a friend on the other side of the badge.

It begins to sprinkle, then turns to light sleet.

I put the dogs in a field of standing corn and spend some time discovering that there are no birds in it. I had hoped I could get the dogs to hunt on opposite sides of me, but they fall into a natural near-and-far pattern. Old Stella does the thorough search work in close, while Hanna makes end runs that keep her out farther.

Back at the truck I linger over a cup of thermos coffee, wondering if I should be content with the single rooster I've taken. With the family venue for Thanksgiving dinner at our house this year, I've promised Susan I'd be home in time to help out. I haven't heard a gunshot in the last hour. The roads might be icy. Most of the other Thanksgiving-morning hunters have conceded to the weather and have started for home. Are they smarter than me?

One more hour, I decide.

There's a twenty-acre asparagus bed along the river where a few years back Amy rousted out a rooster that was my dad's last pheasant. I move the truck a mile or so down the farm road and set out.

Asparagus, in case you know it only as the topping for veal Oscar, is cultivated in permanent plantings. Asparagus growers cut the familiar thick shoots as they emerge from the ground in the spring. When they stop cutting, the remaining shoots develop into lacy, fernlike plants that grow four to five feet high. A bed of asparagus makes a great hiding place for pheasants because they can run unseen on the bare ground beneath the thick growth.

Of course, asparagus beds and other birdy cover appeal to pheasants that are acclimated to their surroundings. Birds like that can be fun to hunt, since they can be counted on to try to outfox a hunter. But most of these Thanksgiving birds were stocked last night. They haven't had time to get smart, so they're unpredictable. Sometimes they'll act like game birds, but just as often it seems they're intent on committing suicide.

The weather has proven out the predictions of the most pessimistic forecasters, and driven sleet as sharp as stair tacks stings my face. I pause and pull up the hood of the anorak. It's a definite handicap—I've never been able to shoot with a hood over my head, and the nylon creates enough noise next to my ears so that I can't hear much of anything.

There is a row of pine trees edging the asparagus bed, and when we break through both dogs quickly disappear in the sea of still-green foliage. I keep whistling and pausing to listen for their bells, but depend on the occasional glimpse of each dog to gauge their progress.

Two hundred yards later I come to the farm road that defines the far edge of the bed. I had both dogs in front of me a minute ago, but now I can neither see nor hear them. In desperation I push the hood back off my head. Ah, now I can hear Stella's beeper behind me. I own only one beeper collar, and I spend an extra few moments listening for Hanna's bell, but hear nothing.

When I get to Stella she's standing at the very edge of the asparagus, pointing at the bordering row of pines just a few yards away. I pat her flanks, then step forward with the gun at ready and discover Hanna on the far side of the tree line. She's pointing in her four-footed style into a thicket of dried-out goldenrod.

"That's a good girl." I pat her back as I walk by.

A quick dozen steps into the matted undergrowth produces nothing. I pause for a long moment, listening intently, but hear only the sleet on the dried weeds and Stella's beeper behind me. As I'm about to whistle Hanna ahead, a slender weed stalk off to the right does a brief hula. A step in that direction brings a hen and a rooster into the air together. It's a wonderful moment, and I might even have let the cock get out a bit too far before putting the gun up, but he falls heavily at my shot. The sound of the gun brings another rooster blasting straight up, this one closer to me and cackling ludicrously as he spews a white stream in his wake.

The limit is two, so I watch the second cock sail down the line of pines following the hen in front of him. They turn together and glide over the asparagus, dropping lower and lower until it seems they're about to set in. The hen backs her wings

and drops, but the rooster gives a last
effort and glides across the road to finally
turn and set into a swale on the other side. *That one's a real pheasant.*

When I turn back, Hanna is sitting at my feet holding the downed rooster in her mouth.

I put the dogs at heel, pull the anorak's hood tightly around my head and tuck my hands into what are euphemistically called the vest's "handwarmer" pockets, and start back. The sleet has turned into pelletized stuff I'm not even sure they have a name for. Mine is the last remaining vehicle on the Hatfield meadows.

The cock that flew on was a handsome rooster with a classic tail, but the two I've taken are obviously stocked birds—the combined length of their tail feathers is zero.

What will the dogs tell Amy when they get back to the kennel? Did they know there were three pheasants in front of them? Did Hanna steal Stella's point? Or did Hanna find the birds alone, and Stella just came up and backed her? I wish I could have seen it develop, but it's enough to have enjoyed the results.

After a raw morning spent in the worst of weather, now I'll have to creep home on slippery roads. I've got near-frozen hands, icicles forming on my mustache, and a waterlogged gun in desperate need of WD-40. All that for a couple of pounds of poultry that I'll have to clean. I'd guess that pretty much defines the term *disproportionate pleasure.* But hunting is rife with intangibles, most as thin as wood smoke.

On the news the other night, protesters at a sportsman's show were giving voice to the idea that hunting is violence. Violence—the real kind—is a huge problem in our society. But to associate it with hunting shifts attention from the true violence that exists today.

Don't let anyone kid you; those people are not interested in protecting wildlife from violence. They're not in favor of anything. They are anti-hunters, and they've seen fit to make us the object of their hate. Hating back doesn't make it in this case. As much as I might applaud the bumper sticker that says BUY A GUN: PISS OFF A LIBERAL, I don't think that's how we should be defending ourselves.

But these days the anti's regularly get a say in environmental issues, and their ideas seem to have taken hold of public opinion. They've managed to equate *hunter* with *gun,* and *gun* has become one of the words that you're almost afraid to utter in public. I sometimes read the morning paper and feel again the same vague chill I felt when I found the bear-killed deer in Vermont.

In just a few years, this period will be remembered as *The Twilight of the American Hunter*—the way things have been progressing, that eventuality seems certain. But hunting means so much more to me than my discontinuance of hunting could ever mean to the anti's. I *live* for it.

I recall hearing a famous circus aerialist state that life for him was nothing more than a series of waits between performances. At the time, I thought to myself, *How shallow.* Yet I find I've begun to think of my own life in terms of autumns, and the empty months spent waiting for the next one.

Others may think of that as being superficial, but I know better.

Day Fifty: . . . And the Days Dwindle Down

"What can you do
When your dreams come true
And it's not quite what you planned?"

Don Henley/Glenn Frey
"After the Thrill Is Gone"

IN VERMONT, the black spruces poke up through the forest canopy and seem like so many church steeples when seen from a distance. The early winter so far has been of the rarest kind—no snow. Here and there a snowshoe rabbit shows up like a white beacon in an otherwise drab gray landscape. Another name for them is varying hare. They've already changed into their winter white camouflage. Without snow cover, the predators must be having a field day.

I saw one such hare along this same power-line clearing when I hunted here last season, and that's what I'm thinking about when the puppy crosses the clearing and points just beyond the thick growth that crowds the edges of the opening.

It's a mistake to assume she's pointing a bunny, I tell myself even as I'm assuming it. When I walk in there's a part of my consciousness that's on the lookout for a patch of white, and my attention is divided when a grouse flushes. Underneath the overcast sky it's a gray-bird-against-a-gray-background problem, and I lose focus for just an instant. That's all it takes, and I know in just the briefest of moments that I've blown an opportunity.

A half-hour later I still feel like a numbskull.

It's that time of the year when every pickup truck in Vermont has a snowplow on the front and a chain saw behind the seat. Winter is approaching fast, and the remaining days of the season are dwindling down to the proverbial precious few.

I'm hunting in Vermont because the grouse season is finished in Massachusetts. A few years back we started on October 10 and hunted until the day after New Year's, with a week off in early December for deer season. But the folks in the Fish and Wildlife Department cut the season in half a few years ago, and now no U.S. state or Canadian province has a shorter grouse season than Massachusetts. This in the same state that gave us William Harden Foster, Frank Woolner, Tap Tapply, and Thornton W. Burgess. This year the grouse season ran from October 14 to November 25. We can't hunt on Sundays, so that amounted to just thirty-seven days of open season. A brief autumn's passage, indeed.

And in its place, the deer-hunting season has grown exponentially.

There are no two ways about it; Massachusetts has too many deer. They live in the suburbs without natural enemies, and homeowners' rhododendrons are eaten as fast as they're planted. Lyme disease, spread by deer ticks, is a genuine public health concern. Forests are being denuded as a result of too many deer and not enough forage.

In response to deer overpopulation, the Fish and Wildlife Department issues doe permits by the thousands, and the former six-day gun season has been lengthened to include the entire month of December.

But I don't like it at all. December bird hunting at home used to be a lot of fun, and my resentment of the ever-lengthening deer season is a result of having something important taken away from me and given to somebody else.

On top of all that, the department's solution to the deer problem isn't working. The herd continues to grow larger, and the troubles that come of overpopulation won't go away. Suburban deer can't be hunted, of course, but the larger problem is tied to the posted-land issue. The state has five million acres of forested land, and more than half of it is behind NO TRESPASSING signs. Hunters can kill all the deer on Wildlife Management Areas and state forests, but that won't affect deer that live in the de facto refuge that is the 2.5 million acres of posted land. How can hunting affect the population of anything when hunters are locked out of half the land in the state?

We're three days short of December, but here's a flock of bluebirds along the brook at Vermont Electric. On a sunny day, the males are vibrant, seemingly painted with manganese blue right out of the tube, but under the overcast sky their reflective plumage makes them appear dull. They're supposed to be insectivores, but a few hardy individuals somehow make adjustments to their diet and manage to hang around all winter.

Similarly, the coverts are full of robins that do the same thing. Well, maybe not full, but there are enough of them in the woods so that winter robins aren't something rare.

I haven't seen any snow buntings yet, but the juncos have been around for the past few weeks. Both species are called snowbirds, and they are sure signs of winter. They changed the junco's first name a while back from slate-colored to dark-eyed. Who has the final say-so on this sort of thing? Old squaws became long-tailed ducks, and Baltimore orioles are now northern orioles. If they're changing names, how about a new name for the titmouse, which is a perfectly fine bird with a perfectly ridiculous name. And how about resolving the confusion that results from two completely different trees being called hornbeam.

Stella points what ends up being the last woodcock of the year. We're not far from the pine edge where she pointed the first pair in September. The bird's normally perfect camouflage is too dark for the pale beech leaves matted on the forest floor. I can see him clearly on the ground ten feet in front of Stella's point. These last few malingers of the migration—they're always adult males—can be counted on to ignore traditional woodcock cover. They sit in the middle of unlikely places, and I'm always left wondering if they aren't carrying a pellet or have something else wrong with them. This one flies okay when I walk in front of Stella's point, and I can only wish him well as he squeaks off through the bare treetops.

We've been in a grouse-only hunting mode for the past couple of weeks. The woods—perhaps it's just my expectations—are different now that the woodcock are gone. Not worse, and certainly not better. Just different.

Farther along, Stella finds and follows a running grouse, but after seventy-five yards on walking point the bird blasts out of a hemlock just to my right. I've got the gun up and the safety off, but the thick evergreens shield the bird's departure.

Grouse are ground birds. Given their druthers, they seem to prefer to run from danger rather than fly. Flight exposes them to any variety of winged hunters, and they apparently fear goshawks and owls far more than anything with four feet. A running bird will sometimes hop up into a tree as this one just did, but I believe that's more to break the bird's trail and allow what's following him to pass by. Certainly, once in a tree, flight is the only remaining getaway option left to a grouse, but it seems they go to trees chiefly so they can get back on the ground once the danger has passed.

That's just a grouse hunter's opinion. Again, I could be wrong.

Here's a perfect place to take five on a fallen log. In an attempt to keep my butt warm, I put my gloves and hat on the deadfall and then sit on the seat I've made. Stella comes in and visits. She doesn't complain to me about running grouse that won't hold still for a point, and I don't grumble to her about being unable to get shots through opaque hemlock trees. It's part of a deal we made years ago.

Today is Stella's twelfth birthday. As a November dog, she worked out well, but in the field-trial world she'd be something of a pariah. Breeders try to arrange that puppies be born between the first of the year and the Fourth of July. That's because every puppy is officially pronounced "one year old" on New Year's Day, regardless of when its actual birthday might be. Of course, if you're not interested in entering a puppy in a futurity stake, then who cares? It certainly doesn't matter to me.

A fall-born puppy will be old enough to go out and learn a few things during the spring woodcock migration, and be ready for bird season before its first birthday. That was the case with Stella. The downside of an autumn puppy is that you have to put up with all the pain-in-the-neck stuff that a puppy in the house during the winter brings with it.

Puppies aren't ready to do much in the field before they're six months old, so springtime is a little late for a dog to be born that's supposed to hunt during the upcoming fall.

Lately, I've favored February pups. Hanna is one. They're old enough to hunt usefully in their first season, but it's convenient that the weather turns nice right around the time a February-born puppy is picked up from the breeder. The amount of in-house time is kept to a minimum.

But it's Stella's birthday nonetheless, and rather than a birthday cake or a half-pound of raw hamburger, I've taken her hunting as a gift. It seems that's what she'd prefer anyway.

We stop at the Culvert. It's a little in-and-out, fifteen-minute covert, so small it's almost claustrophobic. Little places like this are not the sort of thing that are worth going out of your way to hunt. Instead, they're stops that can make the trip between coverts a little more worthwhile.

In this case, the whole reason for parking the truck is an isolated half-acre of bittersweet tangles along a little brook that passes under the road through—you guessed it—a culvert. Sometimes a grouse or two will come out of the bordering hemlocks to feed on the abundant bittersweet berries. With an evergreen woods on one side and a cow pasture on the other, the little bittersweet patch is all there is to the cover.

After a short walk I approach the target. Hanna cruises right by the tangles without slowing. I'm about to whistle her back for a second pass when I notice that I have to look hard to find a red berry anywhere. The vines were loaded earlier in the year, but this late in the season all the berries have either fallen or been eaten. I might even have known that, but through force of habit here I am in the bittersweet as if a grouse will automatically appear even though there's no longer any attraction for them.

The Chief Inquisitor has a sarcastic remark for me. At times like these, his voice sounds a lot like my father's: *You know, Steven, you're supposed to be a smart kid. . . .* He leaves the rest of the sentence incomplete. I've heard him say that before.

When I pull into the farmyard below the Isaac Newton covert, there's a new Lexus sport utility vehicle parked at the house. There isn't a native soul in all of rural Vermont who would own such a vehicle, so I know even before I look at the out-of-state license plate that the people who actually live here have rented their place. Renting your home is a new source of income up here. Suburbanites who live in the megalopolis seem to have an idyllic dream of getting away from it all by spending a week in the North Country. And to tie it all together, when I talk to the renter at the farmhouse, he has a cell phone clamped to his ear.

Asking permission is out of the question. I tell him I'll be hunting the cover above the farm, and wave as I drive off.

These picturesque rural farmhouses, the ones with working shutters on the windows, are part of everyone's image of pastoral New England.

They're seldom what they seem.

When you get up close you discover you wouldn't want to live there. These old, old houses are cantankerous, as anything that's been around for a century and a half has a right to be. The doors are warped, the sills are dry-rotted, and umpteen coats of chalky white paint hold everything together. Floors sag and creak, and the rooms run small to tiny with ceilings and doorways that hardly welcome a six-footer. They're universally drafty. Everything leaks cold air. The quaint, distorted panes in the windows might as well be absent. The massive weight of the slate roof is sometimes the only thing keeping the house from blowing away. The wraparound porch, so characteristic of farmhouses, serves only to shut out the daylight and darken the house's interior.

People will buy one of these relics with the good intentions of fixing it up. But it's not just a matter of adding a little insulation and sticking in some replacement windows. Those well-intended people, of course, have never worked with structures made from hand-hewn timbers where nothing is plumb or even close to it. If the bathroom seems like an afterthought, that's because it was. Electricity and plumbing were retrofitted into the house long after it was built. And you can bet licensed electricians and plumbers didn't do it. The very wood itself dates back to the Civil War, and it's dying of old age no matter how well it has been cared for.

Those old houses make occasional guest appearances in my landscape paintings, usually in the background. They never look as good up close as they do from a distance.

Moving through the cover, there are places where you can shoot and others where a shot just wouldn't be possible. You hurry through the tough spots, but they're unavoidable. It's the nature of the cover. Some days, even though you flush a dozen grouse, it seems you're always bending over to get under a dead-fall or struggling in some thick stuff or blowing your nose at the wrong time, and the day becomes a frustration trip.

Today Stella and I flush three grouse: one while I'm bending over to get under a deadfall, a second while I'm struggling in some thick stuff, and a third while I'm blowing my nose. I know we're at Isaac Newton and not on the lone prairie, because a lot of discouraging words were heard.

All I bring out with me are a couple of empty shotshells left by some other hunter. I know I don't have exclusive rights to any of my coverts, but this sort of evidence always gives me pause.

We're in the last stop of the day, hunting along a hillside stone wall made out of marble chunks. The rocks are weathered and moss grown, and certainly not of the quality they make building fronts out of, but they're marble nonetheless. I guess it's comparable to the seashore, where they sometimes pave roads with clamshells. Here in Vermont they use what's available.

Grouse feed heavily before oncoming storms, and there's a doozie coming according to the forecast. Up ahead is a scattering of hawthorns, and the grouse I took here earlier this year had a crop stuffed with haws. If you didn't know better, you'd think those haws were tiny apples. There are enough variations in haw-thorns—subspecies and hybrids—to make a botany student change his major to physical education. The long nail-like thorns on some varieties can do serious damage to bird dogs as well as hunters.

There's a lot written about what grouse eat, some of it by me. They have preferences—favorite foods—although I've always found a sticking point in the idea that the birds swallow just about everything whole. How can they taste anything?

I've maniacally examined and recorded crop contents of every grouse I've taken since 1973, and here's what I've learned. When there's an abundance of apples, nearly every grouse crop will have some. The same can be said for bittersweet and grapes. Thornberries and barberries are bona fide staples in the grouse diet—fruits that never seem to have an off-year. It's a rare crop that doesn't contain at least some ground greens—cinquefoil, barrens strawberry, false violet, checker-berry—all weedy growth that creeps along the forest floor. Grouse seem to need greens and feed heavily on them, particularly before a snowstorm.

In checking grouse crops all year long I still haven't seen again that mystery seed that the Kangaroo Ranch bird was feeding on. Sometimes grouse will visit a backyard garden or a farmer's field. It's unusual, but I've found corn in crops and, on one occasion, seeds that could only have come from dried string beans. At times it seems they will eat anything that moves or grows as long as it can fit down their maw, so nothing that I find in grouse crops surprises me anymore.

But crops only provide information in the past tense, not always the sort you might use to find more grouse in the future. Just because a grouse stuffed himself with beechnuts or winged ash seeds today, there's no evidence that he'll be back for more of the same tomorrow.

Now, having said that, I'll add that two years back I accom-plished something that has been heavily overworked in hunting stories—I actually used information gained from the crop con-tents of one bird to take another.

Here's how: I shot a hen out of some alders at Deep River. An examination of her crop that evening revealed she had been feeding on apples. There was nothing unusual about it except there were no apple trees in Deep River.

For days I puzzled on the mystery, going over the covert in my mind trying to recall a little, out-of-the-way abandoned orchard or even a single tree that I might have forgotten. Finally I remembered a dead-end finger of cover sticking out into a pasture. It was just a skinny brush line overgrown with blackberry canes. I didn't bother with it because you walked out of it in the same tracks you made going in. Ah, but there were three or four old tumbledown apple trees out there, the sort that have fallen over and resprouted. When I closed my eyes I could see all the grouse at Deep River having a party under those trees in honor of Johnny Appleseed.

When I next visited the cover it was late in the afternoon. Sophie was in her prime then, and she was with me that day. With the wind out of the north, we had to cross the open pasture in order to put the breeze in the dog's face. As we approached the dead-end finger, I felt like a master strategist—Hannibal, maybe, only without the elephants.

Sophie pointed while we were still out in the grass, and a steel-gray cock grouse came out of the brush line when I walked in front of her. The bird offered a right-to-left quartering shot with nothing between him and me but air, and was as close to "easy" as grouse shots ever get. At the sound of the gun a second bird got up, this one farther down the brush line but still in range. I threw the tight barrel after that one to no avail, and at the sound of that shot the grouse Sophie had been pointing got up, virtually at my feet, and imitated low-house seven as he flew back into the cover. The gun only shoots twice, of course, but I didn't curse. Or, if I did, I was smiling at the time.

Sophie retrieved the apple-fed cock bird with the gray tail, and all was right with the world. I had just outsmarted a bird with the IQ of a barnyard chicken. I felt so smug.

That's all. End of story. What's significant is not that I took a grouse based on what was in the crop of another, but that it's the ONLY time I ever did.

It's breezy along the marble wall. I've been having trouble hearing the dog's bell and beeper collar all day, and now I've lost track of Hanna. I continue on, listening intently. Then the breeze shifts momentarily and brings a distant beep from behind me. She's somewhere in the hawthorns.

When a dog points a grouse, it's important to remember that it's not a woodcock—you don't have all day to assemble the troops for Pickett's charge. You've got to get to the point in a hurry. Havilah Babcock was talking about quail when he said, "Dogs just show you where the birds are. They don't hypnotize them." Babcock's statement applies equally to the professionally nervous ruffed grouse.

Hanna is on point among some rocks on the hillside when I locate her. It's got to be a forty-five-degree grade, and I'm hanging on to one tree trunk after another just to remain upright as I make my way into shooting position. The bird is suddenly in the air and I pay the price for not having both hands on the gun. I take a handful of branches with me when I grab for the stock, and although I get the safety off, I never can completely bring the gun into action in the brief moment that's given to me. Grabbing an occasional branch wouldn't be so detrimental except that in this case the branch is still attached to the tree it grew on.

The grouse is a dark-tailed hen, and I watch her curving flight until she disappears into the indefinite depths of the leafless woods.

When I look back at Hanna, she's still standing where she pointed.

It's nearly dark when I come out of the covert at quarter past four. Sunset is going on somewhere to the west, but there's not much daylight left under the overcast sky. When I empty out my game bag into the back of the truck, all I've accumulated is a discarded Pepsi bottle and two empty shells that aren't even mine.

I dig out the feed pans and measure out a half-ration for each of the dogs, and reflect that there have been other frustrating days like this—days when a bunch of birds are moved but I finish with the same two shells that I loaded in the gun that morning. It's not so much the putting the safety off and not getting a shot that frustrates me, it's the putting it back on again.

Just below the surface is the feeling you get at the end of the day when you know all you did was spin your wheels. Was it a profitless day? There are certainly too few left to be wasting them.

But then Stella nudges my arm.

With bird dogs along on the hunt, even a nonproductive day can be fulfilling. Obviously, with the puppy, progress is being made even if birds are not being shot. Hanna hunted perfectly, had two grouse points, and showed signs that the work Peter and I did a week back is paying dividends. And old-friend Stella continues to be what she's been all of her life—she's a joy.

Still, I'd like that chance above the hawthorns over again.

Day Fifty-Three: Vibram Conditions

> *"When one tugs at a single thing*
> *in nature he finds it attached to the*
> *rest of the world."*
>
> John Muir

BEHIND THE COUNTER, a girl dressed in Dunkin' Donuts pink asks me what I'll have.

"The standard bird hunter's breakfast."

"And that is?"

"A large black decaf and a couple of those lemon-filled doughnuts."

She keeps her expression blank. Obviously, she doesn't think that's funny or cute or clever. She's too young.

Lately, I've noticed that I've become invisible to all women under forty. Too bad. All my life flirting has been fun. I still consider myself a young man, at least in that department. Unfortunately, I seem to be a minority of one on that opinion.

We had to stay home for the nine days of Vermont's black-powder deer season, but Hanna and I are back at it again in mid-December. We're on the second day of an overnight Vermont hunting trip. Once the leaf-peeping season is over the motel rates return to normal. Forty dollars is back in my price range.

I drive up and park on the skinny shoulder outside what I call the State Forest cover. The first snow of the year fell overnight between midnight and dawn. It's just a few inches of dry powder, and now with the slanting morning sunlight and everything coated in white, it's a day that seems like the opening scene of a novel.

The blue-shadowed imprint of the truck tires in the new snow is so exact that it seems to ache. The parallel tracks branch away from the few others on the road, almost like a railroad spur that the truck has ridden to the end of rather than created.

I stand for a moment, leaning on the open door, watching the vapor clouds of my breath dissipate in the morning air. The next few hours that I'll spend here loom before me. *When I return to the truck, will I be elated? Or will I be disappointed with the way I've hunted? What memories will I gain here this morning?*

With Hanna at heel I start across the open area that serves as a cut-timber landing. When I whistle her ahead she races past me, kicking up a white rooster tail that glistens in the sunlight.

My ears are assaulted by the quiet. The powdery snow acts as a sound absorber, and the effect is eerily like being in a small room. Even Hanna's bell is quiet. I should have spray painted her blaze orange—in the white landscape my nearly all-white setter is a fast-moving shadow that my eyes refuse to remain focused upon.

The windless snowfall has left an inch-high ridge on every exposed twig and blade of grass, and the white expanse of the forest floor is filigreed with blue shadows in the morning sunlight. Snow, it seems, is nature's form of apology for the necessity of a bleak landscape through the winter months. A rabbit bounces away at the head of a lengthening series of tracks on the unblemished surface.

The temperature is in the upper teens, and I'm cold for the first fifteen minutes, or at least my hands are. My dad used to say that you had to move around and get your blood flowing. It seems to be true because after the predictable first ten to fifteen minutes of cold, I'll be okay for the rest of the day. I have four insulating layers under the anorak. There is a small joy that comes of being dressed for the weather and staying warm when it's cold outside.

Although I call this place the State Forest cover, it's not state forest at all, but posted private land where I have permission to hunt. Years back, when I first stopped here, a fellow was operating a tractor to haul out cut logs that had been piled in the landing.

"Who do I see about hunting here?" I hollered over the noise of the tractor.

The guy on the tractor yelled back, "Call Dave Morris."

What I heard was, "It's all state forest." I thanked him and went hunting. On the way out, with the tractor shut down and the operator having lunch, I showed him the grouse I had taken and thanked him for pointing out that it was public land.

"Yeah, Dave's a nice guy," he said.

"Dave who?"

"Dave Morris."

I phoned Mr. Morris. The tractor operator had been right, because he was (and still is) a nice guy. I've never actually met the man, but have a phone conversation with him each year.

We follow the stream to the confluence of two brooks. My ears track Hanna's progress as she skirts the far side of a stand of hemlocks, and from the end of that grove a white bird is suddenly in the air, flying low and silently. Part of me recognizes it as a grouse in flight, but another part of me says *Something's wrong with this picture.* In the moment's hesitation while both parts hold a meeting, the bird is gone.

The powder snow muffled the grouse's normal thunder, and the bright reflection from the bird's belly as it flew low over the snow threw me off. English sparrows skimming over the surface of a hotel swimming pool have similarly fooled me into thinking they were indigo buntings.

I turn to see where the bird has flown, but it disappeared, and is gone so quickly that I'm left wondering if it was ever there in the first place. I look around and nothing is different. Hanna is looking back at me, wondering why I've stopped. *Did I imagine the bird?* The continued calm only serves to heighten the feeling.

I'm not a mystic. Things from my imagination do not rule my conscious perception of the world. But just to be on the safe side, I investigate the ground beneath the hemlocks. My passing creates a continuous cascade of powder from the thick evergreens and some of it finds its way inside my collar. But I'm relieved to find grouse tracks, and just beyond the last tree in the grove are wing prints that mark where the grouse took off.

Most of the changes that take place in nature are gradual. The two exceptions are the autumn leaf fall and the first snowfall of the year. Both changes are anything but gradual in their drama and completeness.

When last I hunted this valley the trees seemed aflame. Stella and I located a family of grouse that acted nearly as naive as the group at the Corn Patch. But things change. Today the only color is an occasional sprig of princess pine that peeks through the snow, and grouse everywhere have grown wilder and smarter.

Right after the leaf fall, birds-of-the-year that had never known a defoliated world can make for some interesting shooting. But the young grouse soon learn what they must to survive in a leafless woodland, and by early winter a bird hunter finds that a box of shells lasts a lot longer than it did just a few weeks before.

We work the rest of the length of the brook course without moving another bird, and emerge below the little dam that forms a pond back in the hills. In the past we've found grouse in the swampy area along the outlet, but Hanna reports that they are feeding elsewhere this morning.

Honeysuckle has nearly taken over the timbered hillside around the pond's edge. As usual, the hillside is littered with deer sign, but today there are grouse footprints mixed among the deer tracks.

Below me, at the very edge of the frozen pond, the puppy's beeper sounds. A grouse flushes ahead of her point as soon as I

start downhill. He sails a hundred and fifty yards, just above the snow-covered ice, paired with his blue shadow immediately below, and the illusion is of two birds in flight. From my elevated vantage point I'm able to watch the bird climb over the treetops on the far shore, then fly another hundred and fifty yards before dropping down into the woods. Grouse, of course, never fly more than two hundred yards when flushed. I wrote that in an article once.

Most coverts seem to run to what I like to term a "logical conclusion," and the pond is it for the State Forest. We take a look for the far-flushing grouse, but the land above the pond is recently timbered, and after fifteen minutes it becomes obvious that we're wasting our time.

If the day has warmed, I haven't noticed it. A wisp of breeze begins blowing powder off the trees, and the effect is lovely. The Finns, I think it is, have no single word in their language for the general term *snow*. Instead, living as they do in a world of sleighs and skis, they have a multitude of nouns for the various types and conditions of snow. Today's powdery stuff is certainly a far cry from the heavy wet snow associated with suburban driveways and heart attacks, but both are inexactly called the same thing in English.

We hunt our way back along the little valley, and recross the stream where the two feeder brooks join. I find my own boot prints, still looking as fresh as when I made them. I see where I was when the grouse sailed by, and my detour to investigate where the grouse flushed from the hemlocks. A little farther along a squirrel has left his tracks along the top of a fallen tree, and there are several tiny prints made by songbirds. And just beyond the shadow cast by an old wall, several lines of grouse tracks cross over my own.

Daniel Boone, tracker of the untamed wilderness, crouches low to examine the animal spoor. Tracks are fun to look at, but I've never had much luck following them. More often than not they only confuse me as a feeding bird crosses and recrosses its own path. Or, worse, the tracks end in a set of lacy wing imprints in the snow.

But there seems to have been three separate birds, and since the tracks pass over my own, the birds must have walked by sometime since I was here an hour and a half ago. I follow them just far enough to conclude that the meandering lines of grouse footprints lead into a little side valley off the brook.

Charge ahead? Wisdom is caution: I'd only push the birds out well in front of me. I'm better off putting my trust in Hanna's nose. We set a course that will permit us to loop around and come into the head of the little valley up at the top of the ridge where it originates. It's only several hundred yards, and she'll have the slight breeze in her face.

The valley is really just a washout that has grown to juniper. I'm still in my Daniel Boone mode and keep looking for the birds' tracks, but the snow is undisturbed. Then, ahead of me, Hanna turns abruptly in midstride and points into a tangle hard up against the eroded bank. Her head and tail are high and her eyes bulge in a look that announces, "Your bird is right here!"

As I'm walking toward her I keep glancing at the ground, still looking for tracks on the blank surface. There's a moment when the bird should flush, and because nothing happens I'm tempted to send Hanna ahead. But as I step in front of her a grouse comes out in a flurry of motion, heading back up the valley. My shot catches the bird as it passes behind a small pine sapling, and it tumbles. A moment later two more grouse boil up in a shower of snow from the juniper blanket, and the nearest one falls at my shot.

Someone's voice is saying, "I got two. Boy oh boy, I got two."
The voice is mine.
This wasn't a legitimate double, but who cares?

261

The surface of the snow is littered with bits of gray fluff. Every other hit must draw a like amount of feathers, but they normally go unnoticed in the fallen leaves on the forest floor.

Hanna brings in the first bird, and I send her to find the one that fell in the junipers.

These might be the last grouse of the season for me. I've read that Indians used to say a prayer over their fallen game, asking the animal's spirit to forgive the hunter. Cro-Magnon hunters must have felt the same need when they painted animals on the walls of their caves. The power behind that sentiment becomes obvious as I hold a grouse in my hand as the last of its life evaporates. I love grouse, yet, in the strange manifestation of that emotional attachment, I kill them. Maybe a prayer is in order after all.

When it comes to outdoor ethics, by its very nature hunting creates a constipated body of literature. We're lately obsessed with defending a sport that should require no defense. Catch-and-release may be an option when using a fishing rod, but not when you go afield with a shotgun. "Kill with principles," we're told. "Hunt, but don't be too successful." We can't make up our minds just how we should behave in this deadly game we pursue. Worse, in these politically correct times, we don't know how we ourselves should perceive what we're doing, and are forever attempting to justify it not so much to others, but to ourselves.

I previously mentioned my view of bird hunting as a medieval altarpiece triptych, with new importance given to the bird and the dog. But who's on the middle panel? I'm not sure any longer. Maybe the whole arrangement has been redesigned, with the gunner still in the center but now dwarfed by the importance of the bird dog and the bird.

I do know that man-the-hunter is still part of the picture; not a spectator, not an intruder, and certainly not just a consumer. In the grand scheme that is nature, we're participants.

As I approach the truck I notice, next to the driver's door, my footprints from two hours before. I think back to my ponderings at the time, and reflect that if it was good memories I was hoping for, I've brought back a limit. Hanna had never hunted in the snow, but she had two points and handled well. Somehow, the birds in the valley held still while we circled behind them. Were we lucky? Certainly. But as wonderful a piece of luck as that might be, it has very little to do with the actual essence of hunting. That essence is—for me, anyway—having something turn out exactly as you had planned it. That's reason enough. Today the plan was fruitful, but when everything goes right it hardly matters whether or not the shot is made.

Hanna gets behind the seat and peers out the rear window, ready to get going to the next covert. Her look is the stuff dreams are made of.

Day Fifty-Seven: Empty Days

> *"Chill December brings the sleet,*
> *Blazing fire and Christmas treat."*
> Old Nursery Rhyme

HANNA AND I quit early today.

Ahead the overcast has broken and turned into a watercolor sky: the overlapping series of blue-violet clouds are fringed with peach by the low sun, and their torn-Kleenex ragged bottoms indicate that snow is falling from them. *Virga,* I think it's properly called.

Autumn is gone. It doesn't last long enough. Long before the calendar pronounces the arrival of astronomical winter, the reality of that season descends and autumn is over for another year. There's been a definite winter slant to the light for the past several weeks, with the sun hanging low in the southern sky. The sunset has more south than west in it, and the greenish tint that shows along the rim of the twilight sky is a promise of an icy morning tomorrow. We're just a few days shy of the solstice.

Even the twilight is noticeably briefer, and darkness swiftly follows the setting sun.

The moon will rise late, in its last quarter tomorrow. After sunset, in the brilliant winter-brittle night sky, the handle of the Big Dipper nearly touches the horizon and even a casual stargazer can identify Orion and Cassiopeia. One of the great disappointments of my boyhood was learning that the constellations were not celestial dot-to-dot puzzles. Connecting the dots only produces a confusing jumble that no more resembles a walking bear or a queen sitting on a throne than I do. In artistic terms, the connected dots are a gesture rather than a contour drawing.

Winter: It's not always the crystal clearness of a blue-sky-over-fresh-snow day that makes for evocative Christmas card photos. Mostly, it's lemon-gray overcast days, damp and cold, like today has been. And, of course, it's the sort of icy turquoise sunset I'm seeing through the truck windshield on the drive home.

In a need for silence, I shut off the truck's radio. There's nothing on but Christmas music, and I'm afraid that one of those songs will get stuck in my head and drive me crazy. It happened to the composer Robert Schumann. I'd bet the one that did him in was "Have a Holly Jolly Christmas."

There was a snowstorm at the beginning of the week. When we went back to the Corn Patch to look in on the family of grouse there, the heavy snow was still fresh on the tree branches and bushes. The second time I checked the gun and found snow in the barrels, I quit and drove back home. You can't hunt if you're afraid to pull the trigger.

But today the snow had blown off the trees and we went back, this time to Pierre's Switzerland.

Almost as soon as we started, three grouse flew out from under a pair of thick hemlocks at the turn of the high pasture. The tracks and accumulations of grouse turds under the trees indicated that they had been holed up there for days, venturing out just a short way to visit nearby barberry bushes. In heavy snow like this, sometimes grouse find a fortress and stay put.

That was five hours ago. I couldn't know it then, but I was going to move only four grouse today, and 75 percent of them had just flown off. We pursued them to the bottom of the hill and might have moved one of them again in the spruce woods. With my ears, I couldn't be sure that I heard the bird go.

There were no grouse tracks to be found. That fact doesn't mean the birds have abandoned the cover. Instead, it means they're in the trees rather than walking around.

An hour later a grouse blasted out of a spruce. That sort of thing is often as fleeting as a lightning flash—it either hits you or it doesn't, but it's so quick you don't have time to do anything about it. In this case the lightning missed me, and by the time I reacted to the flush the bird was too far out for a reasonable shot.

The only good thing that happened all day came when I was trudging uphill through the pines. The surface of the snow was littered with fallen pine needles and bits of bark the weather had knocked from the trees. And in one open area, mixed with the detritus and a scattering of what appeared to be birch leaves were pale tan, papery things that I had seen before. On closer examination, they proved to be the same mystery seeds that were in the grouse's crop at the Kangaroo Ranch.

They had apparently fallen from one of the overhead trees, but I saw only bare branches everywhere I looked. Yet here was one of the seeds still attached to a stem. It took a long moment, but then I recognized it as what was left of a "hop" from a hop hornbeam tree. Hops are really overlapping, flowerlike seed clusters. Obviously, they're a sometimes grouse food. Mystery solved.

There was ten inches of snow on the ground. Bird dogs can't hunt in snow that deep, and neither can I. At least, not for very long.

I knew that before I started. I spent the day reminding myself that hunting should never be work, but I just couldn't quit.

Habit is the surest way to repeat mistakes, and for some bone-headed reason I continue to go out as long as the season remains open. Hunting in these conditions is half challenge, half faith, and not always a lot of fun. Just when the exact closing date of the grouse season might happen to fall on the calendar is often irrelevant, because snow effectively ends all hunting once it gets deep enough.

And, as I reluctantly concluded at 2:45 this afternoon, the snow is "deep enough." The season is done.

Hanna is still a few days short of being ten months old. It has been a year when grouse numbers were markedly down. Yet, at the end of the season, when I total things up, she'll finish with forty-seven grouse points, a number that even from this distance seems amazing.

She started out as a well-bred puppy. Her father was a two-time grouse champion named Wrongway, and her mother was a Grouse Ridge dog named Rebecca, a daughter of their great champion LeRoy. What *good breeding* means is that Hanna started with the potential to take all the training I gave her, and that's saying a lot.

Did I push her?

Of course I did. That's what *The Shotgun Method* is all about. Progression in training is compressible, both in space and time. If you're following *The Shotgun Method,* as soon as the pup is capable of absorbing instruction, start instructing. If it takes one hundred grouse to make a grouse dog, or one hundred hours in the field to get the dog to hunt properly, then the more quickly the pup can be shown those grouse or can put in those hours, the better off you'll both be. But you have to get the puppy out. He isn't going to become a bird dog in the backyard.

Dogs are hugely receptive to training in the first eighteen months of their life, and the adage that you can't teach old dogs new tricks has its basis in fact. A dog that hasn't learned how to hunt by his second birthday represents an opportunity lost.

Hanna has been a precocious puppy, and she learned quickly, but I don't believe a dog must be anything out of the ordinary to prosper under *The Shotgun Method.* You don't have to be an expert trainer, but you do have to know what you want and be willing to insist the dog do it. Good dogs are made up of yard training, field training, and experience. More than anything else, those three commodities take time—yours as well as the dog's.

But that time can all be compressed into a few months. That's *The Shotgun Method.*

Driving home, I revisit the fallacy of spending the season looking forward to the next step—the leaves coming down, the first killer frost, or even just the end of the week. Things keep slipping away and at the end of so many weeks you're all out of time.

Hanna sleeps behind the seat of the truck. The deep snow has worn her out. A warm spell might melt some of the snow and make it possible for us to get out again this year, but not likely. Ahead of us is a January trip to Kansas for quail, and Hanna will prove on every day of that trip that she's still a puppy. Then the woodcock will be back shortly after Saint Patrick's Day, and we'll use them to do some serious field work on the staunchness idea.

I put the truck's lights on.

Time moves quickly. Beyond the purple Berkshire Hills the wintry sun sets and the year keeps flowing, but it's been an awfully brief autumn's passage.